The Price Waterhouse Book of Personal Financial Planning

The Price Waterhouse Book of

PERSONAL FINANCIAL PLANNING

REVISED EDITION

by Stanley H. Breitbard
& Donna Sammons Carpenter

AN OWL BOOK
HENRY HOLT AND COMPANY · NEW YORK

Copyright © 1987, 1988, 1990 by Price Waterhouse
and Donna Sammons Carpenter
All rights reserved, including the right to reproduce
this book or portions thereof in any form.
Published by Henry Holt and Company, Inc.,
115 West 18th Street, New York, New York 10011.
Published in Canada by Fitzhenry & Whiteside Limited,
195 Allstate Parkway, Markham, Ontario L3R 4T8.

Library of Congress Cataloging-in-Publication Data
Breitbard, Stanley H.
The Price Waterhouse book of personal financial planning /
by Stanley H. Breitbard & Donna Sammons Carpenter.—Rev. ed.
     p. cm.
"An Owl book."
ISBN 0-8050-1419-5 (alk. paper) (pbk.)
1. Finance, Personal.   2. Investments.   I. Carpenter, Donna Sammons.
II. Price Waterhouse (Firm)   III. Title.
HG179.B727   1990
332.024—dc20   90-4489
                                                        CIP

First published in hardcover by
Henry Holt and Company, Inc., in 1988.

Revised Edition

Designed by Liney Li

Printed in the United States of America
Recognizing the importance of preserving the written word,
Henry Holt and Company, Inc., by policy, prints all of its first editions
on acid-free paper.∞

10 9 8 7 6 5 4 3 2 1

This publication is intended to offer guidance on personal
financial planning subjects. It is sold with the understanding
that the authors and publisher are not herein engaged in
interpreting laws or in rendering legal, tax, investment, or
other professional services. This book should not be used as
a substitute for professional advice. Expert assistance in
developing and implementing financial planning programs
should be sought from competent advisers.

Contents

v

_437_ **INDEX**

_449_ **ABOUT THE AUTHORS**

Acknowledgments

*T*his book could not have been written without the expert assistance of Deborah Rothschild. Nor could it have been written without the editorial guidance of Abby Solomon. Both have been with the project since its inception. The manuscript profited as well from the untiring efforts of Roger Hindman and Tom Richman. Thanks are also due to Rob Cowley, Helen Rees, and Dom Tarantino for their guidance and support.

We owe our gratitude to the following Price Waterhouse professionals for their contributions: Sam Berger, Dave Blesy, Stephen Caflisch, Carol Caruthers, and Elaine Church.

Also: Jim Coffin, Tim Farrell, Dan Feheley, Barbara Glazier, Dave Grevengoed, Pat Hamel, Faith Horowitz, Ron Humenny, Dick Johnson, Pat Kearney, Rick Mackessy, Jeannine McCrady, Dan Noakes, Bob Odmark, David Rogers, Dave Satcher, Joanne Stack, Richard Stanger, Pat Trapp, Gary Tillman, Mike van den Akker, Bob Wagman, Becky Whitmore, Ed Wojeski, and Eric Ziegler.

Thanks, too, to these Price Waterhouse professionals: George Barbee, Bill Bawden, Dick Behrens, Jack Buelt, Gayle Butler, Luther Campbell, Ken Doyle, Allen Goldstein, Andy Harwood, Paul Kiffner, Sheldon Laube, Jay Levine, Daniel Phillips, Barbara Pope, Mike Redemske, Kevin Roach, John Stine, Fred Werblow, Keith Wilson, and Allen Young.

Finally, we are grateful to Ben Baldwin for his contributions to the insurance chapters and letters, Arnold Rudoff for his assistance with the real estate chapters, and Stuart Tobisman, Esq., for his help with the estate planning chapters.

PART ONE

The Price Waterhouse Approach to Personal Financial Planning

1 *The Good Life*

Building a Firm Foundation

Why, you may ask, do you need a financial plan at all?

The answer is quite simple.

There is only one sure way to achieve financial security: You must identify your goals, then adopt strategies to meet them.

True, if you're like most people—the vast majority of Americans, in fact—you seem to get by from year to year without a financial plan. You collect your salary, pay your bills, and keep yourself and your family housed, clothed, and fed.

But what happens if a financial crisis occurs? You may find yourself lacking the funds or insurance to cover mounting bills.

And what about those luxuries you've always longed for—an ocean-going sailboat, perhaps, or a mountain hideaway? Do they seem always to dangle just beyond your financial grasp? And how will you pay for your child's education? Or support yourself adequately in your retirement?

If you talk with the people who are most comfortable in their lives—the people who have achieved true financial security—you'll find they took an organized approach to financial management early on. Some did the work themselves. Others hired competent advisers to help them. But, somehow, they made sure the job was done.

The bottom line to financial security: You can get what you want only with an organized financial plan and the discipline to make it work.

And the best time to start planning is now.

The Importance of Organization

Why do most people fail to achieve lifetime financial security? Lack of financial goals is one reason. Ignorance of the tax law, poor investment strategies, and failure to take full advantage of company benefit programs are others. But the chief culprit is lack of organization.

Organization is critical to sound financial planning.

Organizing your finances provides an exceptional measure of security. It protects you from surprise, and it also places your finances—both current and future—under a "master control" program that gives you a system of checks and balances. The system provides security when the unexpected occurs. And it even allows you to indulge yourself occasionally.

Then, too, an organized plan can save you and your family from financial disaster. It helps you establish a pattern of spending, saving, and investing that ensures financial stability now and growth for the future.

Above all, though, an organized plan builds financial independence. And financial independence equals financial peace of mind.

Our Approach

If you learn only one lesson from this book, make it this one: Financial planning is, in actuality, life planning. That thought underlies our entire approach to the financial planning process. It explains why our system is not only a way to manage money but a way to think about money—and a way to think about yourself.

The wrong way to begin the financial planning process is by making investments. It is far more valuable first to develop a financial profile of yourself, then to match appropriate strategies to your specific needs.

So our approach to financial planning is built on answers to three deceptively simple questions:

- What do you have?
- What do you want?
- How do you get what you want?

Answer these questions in as much detail as possible, and you'll create a flexible, workable, and successful financial plan. Repeat the exercise in a year or two or when your circumstances change, and you'll update your plan.

The job is not as easy as it sounds. To answer these questions in a way that is truly helpful to you requires considerable effort. But the results are worth it.

In the following chapters, we provide you with the information you need to answer these key questions. First, though, let's look a little more closely at the questions themselves.

What Do You Have?

Step one in the financial planning process is to determine what you have. And that involves developing your personal financial profile.

Your profile is a composite of your stage of life, life-style, tolerance for risk, responsibilities, and financial resources.

We'll provide you with the tools you need to construct your personal profile in Chapter 2. For example, you'll learn that stage of life is the sum of your age and circumstances—married, single, supporting children, not supporting children, and so on.

And you'll see that life-style is about choices—your career choice, say, and how you choose to spend and save.

You'll also learn how to evaluate your responsibilities—elderly parents, perhaps, or other relatives who require financial assistance—and weigh your tolerance for risk. Can you afford to take risks with your money? And, if you can, what risks are you willing to take?

Your financial resources are simply what you have in dollars and cents. How much do you have in your checking and savings accounts? What is your cash flow—the amount that comes in and goes out each month? How much is tied up in retirement funds? Do you own a car? A boat? A plane? Is your house furnished with antiques? What about art on your walls? Do you have stamps or other collectibles?

The fact is, you can't make informed financial decisions without first evaluating your fiscal health. In Chapter 2, you'll learn how.

What Do You Want?

"If you don't know where you are going," says business writer Laurence J. Peter, "you will probably end up somewhere else."

Nowhere is Peter's observation more true than in the area of personal finance. Perhaps the most valuable aspect of a personal financial plan is that it forces you to state your financial objectives in dollars and milestones. What do you want and when can you get it?

In Chapter 3, you'll learn in detail how to set financial goals that take into account your unique circumstances and aspirations.

How Do You Get What You Want?

Once you know what you have and what you want, you're ready to develop comprehensive strategies for every aspect of your financial life. These strategies must be flexible enough to respond to changes in your personal and financial fortunes.

Your financial plan also must include a blueprint for implementing these strategies—a blueprint that lets you know when and how to act.

Chapter 4 helps you develop flexible strategies for getting what you want. And it shows you how to direct your financial resources to reach your goals.

Next!

In the pages that follow, we show you how to build a financial plan that protects you from surprises, accommodates your needs, and makes room for your dreams.

But be prepared. Personal financial planning does take effort. In the last analysis, no book can do the work for you. What we can do, however, is give you the means for developing your own plan or working more efficiently with a professional financial planner.

If you want to put your financial house in order—if you want to assure yourself of financial security—this book provides the requisite tools.

2 *What Do You Have?*

Constructing Your Financial Profile

When you sit down with a professional financial planner, the first thing he or she does is construct your personal financial profile.

You should begin there, too.

A financial profile is a snapshot of your life as you live it day by day. And it is the cornerstone of your personal financial plan.

Your financial profile is more than just your income and net worth—although income and net worth are certainly part of the picture. Rather, your profile is a composite of your stage of life, life-style, tolerance for risk, responsibilities, and financial resources.

In this chapter, we'll run through each of these five interrelated parts and describe how they affect your financial planning.

Your Stage of Life

Evaluating your stage of life is the first step in building your financial profile. What we mean by "stage of life" is simply your age and circumstances—a general sense of where you are today.

Why is this information so important? Knowing where you stand helps you set your financial priorities.

Say you are thirty years old, single, and with bright career prospects. You obviously have different goals and needs than a retired person of seventy.

7

Here's one simple way of looking at your stage of life: Are you accumulating assets or disposing of them?

If you are in the accumulation stage, you are building wealth. But if you are in the disposition stage, you are consuming your assets. Typically, you remain in the accumulation stage until retirement, then shift to the disposition stage.

Another way of categorizing stage of life is by decade. In our twenties, most of us begin a career and, possibly, a family. By our thirties, we may be advancing in our careers and raising young children. In our forties, we're probably earning—and spending—more money and beginning to pay for college educations for our children.

During our fifties, most of us cease contemplating career changes, and our earnings peak. We think seriously about retirement. And, if we have children, they are becoming more self-sufficient.

What about the sixties? This is typically the bridge to retirement. Estate planning becomes more important to us, and our grandchildren may be a priority. By our seventies, the majority of us are retired, and one focus of our financial planning may be making gifts to our families.

Naturally, these patterns don't apply to everyone. Far from it. You may, for example, be a late bloomer—someone who did not start a career until your thirties. Or you may have retired very early—in your middle forties, say.

Moreover, the circumstances of people's lives today are almost infinitely varied. Here are some typical categories into which you may fall:

- Single
- Married with no children
- Married with children
- Single with children
- Living with a significant other—with or without children
- Divorced with children
- Divorced without children
- Divorced and remarried with stepchildren
- Divorced and remarried without children
- Widowed

As you see, the list can go on and on. And each of these categories requires different approaches to financial planning. What is important:

assessing your own stage of life and circumstances and tailoring your financial plan to meet them.

Your Life-style

Stage of life identifies general characteristics. By contrast, your life-style, the next element of your financial profile, is more specific to you.

One significant aspect of your life-style: your career choice. When you select a career, you lock in, to some extent, your earnings potential.

For instance, if you opt for a career as a librarian or teacher, you're unlikely ever to earn a six-figure income. By contrast, if you work in investment banking, say, or sales, chances are good that you'll become a high earner.

Or maybe you are one of those people who is willing to make less money in exchange for more leisure time. This decision, also, is a life-style choice.

Your spending and saving habits are another aspect of your life-style that will significantly affect your financial planning decisions. Are you, for instance, oriented toward immediate or deferred gratification? Are you more concerned about living for today or planning for the future?

We all differ on how we view finances. And frequently these differences crop up within a family. In fact, surveys have consistently shown that money is number one on the list of items married couples argue about.

Usually, our disagreements focus on trade-offs. With a limited amount of resources, do we save or spend—and what do we spend our money on?

Our decisions usually boil down to personal preferences. What's more important? A nicer car or a better home? A vacation house or an exotic vacation?

These decisions also involve confidence—or lack of confidence—in the future. Can you spend more than you earn today because you know that at some later point you will earn more than you spend?

Life-style decisions by their very nature are personal. There are no absolute rights and wrongs. Whether you choose to spend your money on entertainment or clothes is your business. Again, the important point: You should know yourself and not try to fit into someone else's mold.

Your Tolerance for Risk

You must ask yourself two questions when it comes to assessing your tolerance for risk: Do you *have* any money to risk? If you do, what promised rate of return would it take for you to risk it? The first is a question of resources; the second a question of attitude.

To some extent, of course, it really doesn't matter if you're the type to stake all on a spin of the roulette wheel—or inclined to tuck your money under the mattress. What is vital: accurately assessing how much you can gamble—the resource side of the risk coin.

If you can afford to lose all or part of the amount you invest without undue hardship, the odds that your investment will pay off are vitally important.

If you can't afford to lose your investment, the odds are irrelevant, because you can't make the investment no matter how great the potential payoff.

Let's say you have the opportunity to invest $1,000. And you stand a chance of making $10,000 or losing the entire amount you invested. You go ahead with the deal: You like the possibility of earning $10,000, and you can afford to lose your $1,000 stake.

But suppose the same opportunity required a minimum investment of $100,000. And you could make $1 million or lose your entire investment. Although the odds are identical and you would like the chance to earn $1 million, you pass. The reason is simple: You can't afford to lose the $100,000.

Once you analyze your resources and figure out what you can afford to lose, your attitude comes into play. And be advised: If you think you are a risk taker, you could be in for a surprise.

Researchers have found that the risks people take with their money differ from the chances they take in other areas of their lives. We know a skydiving enthusiast, for instance, who invests only in the bluest of blue-chip stocks and a staid kindergarten teacher who regularly trades commodity futures.

When Frank Farley, a University of Wisconsin psychologist, studied one hundred people who consistently invest in risky ventures, he found that people who are willing to take risks with their money differ significantly in their psychological makeup from those who are risk averse.

When asked about their long-term goals, for instance, high-risk takers singled out success, risk-averse people happiness.

Risk takers say they wouldn't hesitate to put money into a new business that could fail—as long as the possible return was high. The same people steer clear of investing in "safe" stocks—those with steady returns but little potential for appreciation.

Furthermore, Farley found, those who risk the most are obsessed with their investments. Money is at the center of their lives.

Here are some other differences Farley discovered between high-risk takers and the risk averse:

- Risk takers are better money managers.
- Risk takers spend more time reading about money and investments.
- Risk takers have confidence in their money-making schemes.
- Risk takers have leadership abilities.
- Risk takers are good salespeople.

The Farley study also revealed that, when it comes to risk taking, some stereotypes don't hold water. Women, for instance, are no more risk averse than men.

But people are less likely to take risks with their money as they grow older. The reason is simple: Their fear of loss is greater than their hope of gain. Or, as Will Rogers once put it: "It's not a return on my money I want. It's a return *of* my money."

Like life-style choices, there are no absolute rights and wrongs when it comes to attitudes about risk. The important point to remember: Know your own tolerance, and make financial decisions accordingly.

Your Responsibilities

If you're like most people, you have responsibilities—children, perhaps, who look to you for support, or elderly parents who require financial help.

But everyone defines responsibilities differently. For example, do you consider it your responsibility to supplement your parents' retirement income? Do you think you owe it to your children to help them buy their first house?

When it comes time to develop your financial profile, you must take your responsibilities—as you define them—into account. They influence how you spend, save, and invest.

Here's an example. Say you are married, the father of two teenagers, and, in your view, it is your responsibility to foot the entire bill for your children's educations. Say, too, that a friend approaches you to invest in his small business. The price tag: $50,000.

You don't bite, because you can't afford to invest in anything that's less than 100 percent secure. Why? You want to use the $50,000 to pay for your children's college educations. And if you lose any part of that money, you're in trouble.

To assess how best to meet your responsibilities, you must examine your financial resources—both present and future.

Your Financial Resources

Your financial resources come down to three broad categories: your net worth, your cash flow, and your other resources, such as fringe benefits, Social Security, and anticipated inheritances.

Adding up your net worth is a vital element in creating a solid financial plan. You must know what all your resources are before you can manage them properly.

Figuring your net worth also serves another purpose. It shows you how you've allocated your assets. For example, you may have invested most of your resources in various types of bank accounts or personal property—or you may have put the bulk of your assets in the stock market.

Unfortunately, many people who, twenty years after the fact, can recite their college admissions test scores don't have the slightest notion of how much they're worth. You'll find a net worth work sheet in Appendix II so you can add up your assets and liabilities and calculate your bottom line.

You can't grow financially—no matter how high your income—unless you take in more than you spend. So your next step in evaluating your current financial situation is to look at your cash flow to get a notion of where your money is going.

This information is vital to your financial plan. The idea is to see what flows in and what flows out over an entire year and determine how much money is available to achieve your financial goals.

One easy way to get a picture of your cash flow is to flip through your check register. You may find that you're running on empty just before each paycheck. Or you may discover that a balance is building in your account.

Another way to get a fix on your finances is to construct a cash-flow forecast. You'll find a cash-flow work sheet in Appendix III.

Tip: Get a handle on cash outlays by keeping a journal or diary of your expenditures for a week or—better yet—a month. You'll see how daily expenses, such as lunches, taxi fares, and dry cleaning costs, drain your pocketbook.

The final step in determining your financial resources is nailing down all those "other resources." This task may involve the cooperation of others— your company personnel department, for example, may help you get a handle on your retirement benefits.

Many people have no idea of the value of their "hidden assets." Social Security is only one example. You must know how much you will receive. Otherwise, planning is impossible.

Your Goals and Objectives

Now you've sketched a portrait of how you live today. You know what you're worth, and you know what cash comes in and what goes out.

But what about your goals and objectives? In the next two chapters, you'll find out how to go about setting and achieving them.

3 *What Do You Want?*

Winning by Objective

Now that you have a handle on the present, it's time to decide what you want for the future. In other words, you must outline your goals and objectives.

What's the difference between goals and objectives?

Goals are broad forecasts of what you want to achieve. An example: "I want a comfortable retirement." *Objectives* are more specific and tied to a time frame. "I want to retire on December 31, 1999, with income of $50,000 a year," for instance.

Goals and objectives are at the heart of your financial plan. This chapter tells you what you need to know about setting both.

The Big Picture

Not surprisingly, it's easier to figure out what you really want in life if you take one step at a time. So you should paint the big picture—your goals—first. Then you can worry about filling in the detail—your objectives—later.

As with every other part of the financial planning process, it's important to commit your information and ideas to paper. So get out a pad of paper and pencil or pen, and write "Goals" across the top of the page. Then jot down your list.

We recommend that you keep this page and all the other elements of your financial plan in a loose-leaf notebook. When it comes time to review your plan in six months or a year, you can easily update the individual parts.

Maybe you have only one goal—to save for retirement. Or maybe you have twenty. You are unique, so the details of what you want are unique as well. But we have found that five general goals apply to just about everyone. Here they are.

GOAL 1: Protection Against Risk

What you want:

- Establish an emergency fund
- Purchase adequate insurance

GOAL 2: Financial Security for Your Family

What you want:

- Meet all family financial obligations without straining resources
- Provide for the care of all dependents
- Fund family tuition needs
- Aid children in their careers or home purchases
- Provide for special needs, such as the care of an elderly parent

GOAL 3: A Comfortable Standard of Living

What you want:

- Travel frequently
- Purchase a new home or make improvements to your existing one
- Buy a vacation house
- Join your local country club
- Help finance special celebrations, such as weddings
- Entertain your family and friends
- Enjoy cultural events

GOAL 4: A Secure and Comfortable Retirement

What you want:

- Keep the same standard of living you had during your working years

- Maintain financial independence during retirement
- Achieve financial security so that you may retire early
- Shield yourself from financial disaster in case of medical emergency

GOAL 5: A Well-Planned Estate

What you want:

- Provide for your spouse
- Provide for dependents
- Arrange for the continued management of your assets
- Minimize estate taxes and estate management fees
- Make charitable bequests

Two points to keep in mind: The importance of each of these goals will change as you change and grow. For example, if you're twenty-five years old, your priority is more likely "a comfortable standard of living" than "a well-planned estate."

And sometimes unanticipated changes can make a big difference in your financial plans. For instance, a divorce might necessitate a change in your tax and employee benefits strategies. A new marriage might prompt you to change your will. The birth of a child might cause you to take a hard second look at your insurance and estate planning objectives.

Or you might receive an unexpected windfall. In this case, you might want to rethink your goals and objectives.

Also, the goals we've listed form the core of most financial plans—but they are not the only ones you should include. Your goals are uniquely yours. For instance, one of your goals might involve the lifelong care of a disabled child. In the final analysis, you—and you alone—must decide what you want.

What Next?

You've set your goals. Now it's time to establish your objectives. Go back to your original list of goals, and construct a chart that looks something like this.

GOAL: Protection Against Risk
Objective: Establish an emergency cash fund
When: Three years from now
Cost: $5,000

GOAL: A Comfortable Standard of Living
Objective: Purchase a second home
When: Five years from now
Cost: $20,000 (down payment)

Your list, of course, will be much longer, more detailed, and more specific. Be sure you schedule short-term objectives as well as long-term goals.

Once you set your goals and objectives, you must measure your progress. With short-term objectives, it's easy and obvious. For example, you can readily see if you've met your objective of accumulating $5,000 in an emergency cash fund.

It is not so simple to know if you're on the right path to achieving your long-term goals—planning adequately for a comfortable retirement, say. So you must set bench marks along the way.

Here's an example: "To meet my retirement savings goal, I plan to put $5,000 a year in my company's 401(k) plan. Last year, I was able to contribute only $3,000. So I will contribute $7,000 next year to help put myself back on track."

Remember, too, that you should review your list of goals and objectives at regular intervals—at least once a year—and update it as your circumstances change.

4 *How Do You Get What You Want?*

Finding the Right Strategies

*Y*ou've now dealt with two of the most arduous parts of the financial planning process. You've learned how to develop your personal financial profile. And you've figured out how to set your personal financial goals.

The rest of the book describes and explains different strategies that you can use to achieve the aims you've set for yourself. We start, in this chapter, by showing you how to adopt strategies that match your financial profile and your goals and objectives.

Strategic Planning

When you set your objectives, chances are you found yourself focusing on eight key areas. Your objectives related to:

- Investments
- Debt management
- Insurance
- Tax planning
- Children's education and other family matters
- Company benefits
- Retirement
- Estate planning

As you'll see, we've divided this book into parts that mirror these key areas.

Dollars and Sense

To see how to get what you want, transform the list you made in the last chapter into a series of specific goals and objectives with price tags, time-tables, and broad strategies attached to them.

You'll find tools to help you out in the appendix. The table in Appendix IV shows how much $1 invested at certain interest rates can grow over a specified number of years. Appendix V is a table that shows how $1 invested each year can grow at various interest rates.

Now, here's what your goal/strategy outline might look like. Remember, the following is only an illustration. It is not meant as a model.

GOAL 1: Protection Against Risk
Objective: Establish an emergency cash fund
When: Three years from now
Cost: $5,000
How: Invest $130 a month for thirty-six months at 5 percent (after-tax rate of return)

GOAL 2: Financial Security for Your Family
Objective: Provide for my daughter's college education
When: Twelve years from now
Cost: $58,000 (estimated future dollars)
How: Supplement my child's existing college fund by investing $2,000 per year in Series EE U.S. savings bonds in my child's name

GOAL 3: A Comfortable Standard of Living
Objective: Purchase a second home
When: Five years from now
Cost: $20,000 (down payment)
How: Invest $295 a month for five years at 5 percent (after-tax rate of return)

GOAL 4: A Secure and Comfortable Retirement

Objective: Maintain my present standard of living after retirement
When: Thirty years from now
Cost: $70,000 a year in current dollars
How: Supplement my company pension plan by investing $2,000 per year in an IRA and $7,000 a year in my company's 401(k) plan

GOAL 5: A Well-Planned Estate

Objective: Minimize estate taxes
When: After my death
Cost: None except legal fees
How: Change my will to take advantage of various tax planning opportunities

Let's summarize the steps you should take in order to get what you want. First, set your goals. Next, set your objectives. Finally, determine your strategy. And if you discover that the strategy you choose does not work? Go back to the drawing board and sketch out a new one.

After you develop your goal/strategy outline, you must implement and follow through on your plan. And you must update it as your life and circumstances change.

Keep in mind, too, that you can ask financial planners for help, periodically consult with other professionals, and turn to magazines and newsletters—but you are the only one qualified to define and refine your plan.

Getting It

Of course, the examples of goals and objectives we have just given are fairly straightforward. So let's work through two more difficult examples.

As we do, remember: You can solve any financial problem by asking the three basic questions—What do I have? What do I want? How do I get what I want?—in ever-increasing detail.

Let's take a look.

PROBLEM: *What Happens If I Die in My Prime?*

What do I want?	To provide for my family after my death
What do I specifically want?	To provide my family with $50,000 annually, an amount that equals 60 percent of my current salary
When do I want to be protected?	As soon as possible
What do I have?	Company benefits and my personal assets

From my company: Death benefit from my pension plan of $20,000 a year; income from my group term insurance proceeds, invested at 6 percent, or $9,600 annually; stock-savings plan worth $2,000 a year

Total from company: $31,600 a year

From my personal assets: Life insurance proceeds invested at 6 percent, or $6,000 annually; and income from personal investments of $4,000 annually

Total from personal assets: $10,000

Grand total: $41,600

What do I need?	An additional $8,400 a year to reach $50,000 a year
How do I get what I want?	
Short-term solution:	Buy additional term insurance that pays $140,000 at my death (invested at 6 percent equals $8,400 annually)
Long-term solution:	Boost personal assets to reduce insurance needs
How do I reach my short-term solution?	Contact an insurance professional
How do I reach my long-term solution?	Look at an investment plan that allows me to accumulate additional assets

PROBLEM: *Can I Afford to Retire?*

What do I want?	To enjoy my retirement in the life-style to which I've become accustomed
What do I specifically want?	$65,000 a year in current dollars, an amount that equals 80 percent of my last year's salary
When do I want to retire?	In fifteen years
What do I have?	Company benefits and my personal assets

From my company: Pension plan worth $32,000 a year; stock-savings plan worth $5,000 a year; 401(k) plan worth $4,000 a year
Total from company: $41,000 a year

From my personal assets: Social Security benefits paying $10,800 a year; annual IRA withdrawal of $1,500 a year; income from personal investments of $4,000 a year
Total from personal assets: $16,300

Grand total: $57,300

What do I need?	An additional $7,700 a year to reach my objective of retirement income of $65,000 a year
How do I get what I want? Solution:	Accumulate an additional $128,300 in assets for my retirement. This amount—invested at 6 percent—will yield interest income of $7,700 annually. To accumulate these assets, I must set aside $440 a month for the next fifteen years in an investment earning 6 percent annually.

What's important here: that you learn the key to getting what you want. And that key is simply asking the big questions first, then gradually focusing in on narrower and more specific questions until you identify your strategy.

Following Through

As we've seen, once you develop your plan, you must faithfully implement it. And you should follow through by regularly checking to see if your actions are bringing the results you want.

Occasionally, you may have to modify your strategies to adjust to shifting circumstances—a change in the inflation rate, for instance, or a lower rate of return on your investments.

Pay special attention to the "when" category in our financial plan illustration. You should always have in mind a detailed timetable for every aspect of your financial plan. In the retirement example, we allowed fifteen years to reach our goal. You may decide that you should reach your goal in twenty years—or ten.

What's critical is writing down a time goal for meeting all your objectives. And, since the same principles apply to every aspect of a financial plan, you should target times for reaching even the shortest-term objectives—buying a piano or a new set of golf clubs, for example. Finally, at the end of every year, you should challenge and evaluate your priorities.

Don't be afraid to modify, expand, contract, and change your plans. Update your plan at least every few months for your short-term objectives and every year or so for your long-term objectives. (We recommend keeping your old plans behind your new ones in your loose-leaf notebook so you can see how your goals and objectives change over the years.)

If you follow these simple rules and concentrate on breaking down the three key financial planning questions—What do I have? What do I want? How do I get what I want?—into logical, manageable bits, you can achieve your goals.

PART TWO

Your Investment Strategies

5 *Making the Right Investment Choices*

What You Need to Know About Asset Allocation

*T*o many people, investing means giving a broker the green light to buy a certain stock. But buying stock—or any other specific investment vehicle—is really one of the last steps in investing. And—believe it or not—it is among the least important ones.

Before you invest—and long before you think about which product you want to buy—you must decide how to allocate your resources among the different categories of investments.

Why Allocate?

Why is allocation so important? Here's the reason. More than 94 percent of the total return on your investment dollars is a result of the way you allocate your resources. Only 6 percent depends on the specific assets you buy.

You can see why asset allocation is the single most important aspect of a successful investment strategy. And asset allocation is really a simple concept. It just refers to the way you divide your investment dollars among different types of investment vehicles—cash, bonds, stock, real estate, and so on.

Before we show you how asset allocation can work for you, we're going to spend some time explaining the issues involved in asset allocation. We guarantee it will be time well spent.

Where Does the Money Go?

Let's assume that you've managed to accumulate $40,000 in savings. Naturally, you want to invest it to your best advantage.

So you do your homework. You quiz your friends, your co-workers, your sister-in-law, even the guy you meet on an airplane.

They all have advice, and it comes down to these choices:

- Leave the money in the bank
- Buy stock in a small high-technology company
- Buy stock in a well-known, diversified multinational corporation
- Buy a corporate bond
- Buy a municipal bond
- Invest in a real-estate limited partnership
- Buy shares in a mutual fund

So what do you do? One of them? All of them? Some combination? Which combination? If you hesitate before answering, you're on the right track.

The fact is, you can't make a sensible choice without more information. And you need lots more information—not about the specific options on your list but about the factors that should guide your investment strategy. You need to evaluate and consider

- The relationship of risk and return
- The forms of return
- The relationship of the form of return to risk
- The types of risk
- The need for diversification

Let's run through each of these issues.

Risk and Return

The higher the return you expect on an investment, the higher the risk you must be prepared to take. It is an inescapable investment axiom, as Table 1 illustrates.

TABLE 1

ASSET	AVERAGE RETURN
Small company stocks	12.3%
Common stocks	10.0
Long-term corporate bonds	5.0
Long-term government bonds	4.8
U.S. Treasury bills	3.5
Inflation	3.1

SOURCE: *Ibbotson Associates, based on actual returns from 1926 to 1988.*

Of course, greater risk does not guarantee greater return. If it did, you would always choose high-risk investments. "After all," you might say, "the higher-return investments carry more risk, but I'm certain to be well rewarded—just look at the table."

The returns shown on the table, though, are *average* returns of assets in those categories. The table really illustrates the fact that, as the expected average return from an investment rises, the range of possible returns also expands.

As Table 2 shows, while the average return increases as you take on more risk, the possibility of lower returns also becomes greater. Small company stocks, for example, may bring you a handsome return of nearly

48 percent, but they also have a chance of rewarding you with a 23 percent loss.

TABLE 2

ASSET	AVERAGE RETURN	AVERAGE ANNUAL FLUCTUATION (+ or −)*
Small company stocks	12.3%	35.6%
Common stocks	10.0	20.9
Long-term corporate bonds	5.0	8.4
Long-term government bonds	4.8	8.5
U.S. Treasury bills	3.5	3.3
Inflation	3.1	4.8

Two-thirds of the returns varied from the average by plus or minus the percentage shown.
SOURCE: *Ibbotson Associates, based on actual returns from 1926 to 1988.*

Now that we've seen how risk and return relate to one another, let's look at the different kinds of returns.

Forms of Return

You can expect two types of return from any investment: current income and appreciation.

Current income is the amount of cash an investment generates on a regular basis. Various kinds of investments provide current income.

So-called debt instruments—Treasury bills, savings accounts, bonds, and similar investments, in which you're really loaning money to the government or to a financial institution—pay interest at regular intervals. This is current income.

Stocks generate current income in the form of dividends. And real-estate investments can produce current income in the form of rent.

Appreciation, on the other hand, refers to the increase in the price of an investment from the time you buy it until you sell it. Of course, the price doesn't have to rise; it can fall as well. This unfortunate event is known as *depreciation* (not to be confused with *depreciation* as the word is used in accounting and taxes).

An investment's form of return—current income and appreciation (or depreciation)—is, as we shall now see, closely related to its degree of risk.

The Relationship of the Form of Return to Risk

Generally, the more an investment depends on current income to generate a return—and the less it depends on appreciation—the less risky it is. In other words, betting on future growth is riskier than collecting dividends and interest as you go.

The reason: You know an investment that pays current income will usually return, at the very least, a specific sum at regular intervals (barring unforeseen circumstances, of course).

So a dividend-paying blue-chip stock is less risky than a nondividend-paying growth stock. A certificate of deposit carries less risk than a zero-coupon corporate bond.

But what, exactly, do we mean by risk? In fact, there are several different kinds.

Types of Risk

Investment risk falls into a number of categories. But bear in mind that any one investment can be subject to more than one type of risk.

Inflation Risk
Inflation risk refers to the loss of value in your investment caused by increasing depreciation of the currency. A constant rate of inflation, even

if it is high, is not risky. When you purchase a long-term bond, for instance, the price of the bond, and therefore its yield, already reflects the current inflation rate.

Rather, it is a *rise* in the inflation rate that is the source of risk. For example, you buy a long-term bond when inflation is low. If the inflation rate rises, both your bond's resale value and the value of the interest you receive will decline. After all, the same dollar is worth less when inflation is high than when it is low.

Deflation Risk

Deflation risk is, not surprisingly, just the opposite of inflation risk. It is the risk that the value of your asset will decline when general price levels fall during periods of severe recession or depression. Land that you buy during boom times, for instance, may lose value during a serious recession.

Business Risk

Business risk refers to the chance that some event might occur that reduces or destroys a particular investment's return. For example, you might buy stock in a company that has perfected a pill to cure the common cold. Then a competitor develops a vaccine that prevents colds entirely. Your company's product becomes obsolete.

Business risk can be more widespread—and more difficult to control. For example, changes in government policy, war, or erratic weather could suddenly wipe out the profits of the cruise ship company whose stock you just bought.

Interest Rate Risk

Interest rate risk is the decline in market value that occurs when the interest rate on new, similar investments rises. For example, you buy a five-year corporate bond paying 8 percent interest. The next year rates rise, and the same five-year bond fetches 10 percent interest. The value of your bond declines.

Market Risk

Market risk refers to the chance that an entire financial market may suffer a decline. Say you buy stock in a prosperous company, but the entire stock market falls sharply in value as it did on October 19, 1987. Your company is still doing well, but investors are wary of stocks in general, so the price of the stock you bought drops.

Illiquidity Risk

Illiquidity risk refers to the loss you might have if you're forced to sell an investment before you had planned. Perhaps you have an unexpected medical expense and must sell some real estate in a hurry to raise the cash. You'll have to take what the market will give you for your property, because you can't wait for a better price.

The question, now that you know what the different risks are, is what can you do about them. The answer, in a word: diversify.

Diversification—Balancing Return and Risk

No one, alas, can eliminate all risk in investing. But by diversifying, you can at least minimize it. There are two ways to diversify.

First, you can partially or completely offset your risk by investing in a number of different areas. Let's say, for example, that you use some of your investment dollars to purchase a small apartment building. At the same time, you buy a high-grade corporate bond.

Your real-estate investment provides a hedge against inflation. As prices rise, the value of your building rises, too. But its value could fall considerably during a prolonged deflationary period.

The value of your bond, however, would respond in exactly the opposite way to either inflation or deflation. Inflation would lower the value of the principal you invested in the bond as well as the value of the interest the bond issuer promises to pay you. The effect of deflation, on the other hand, would be to raise both the price you could get for the bond and the value of the interest payments.

What's important to note is that any change in the value of your apartment building brought on by inflation or deflation probably will be offset by an opposite change in the value of your bond.

So, neither inflation nor deflation would prove disastrous. And, if neither of these economic conditions becomes a serious threat, both your building and your bond will still generate healthy returns. You're braced against the harsh winds of economic change but positioned to profit in the calm of stability.

The second way of diversifying: spreading your holdings in any one investment area—especially when buying real estate and common stocks. When you diversify by buying shares in a number of companies, say, or several parcels of real estate, your return is more likely to approach the average for that investment category rather than the return on any single investment.

Now that we've covered the basics of asset allocation—risk, return, diversification—it's time to see how to balance these elements within an intelligent investment strategy.

Allocation Basics

We're going to break this discussion of asset allocation into two parts. First, we'll address the general principles of asset allocation. Then we'll show you how you can apply these principles to your specific situation.

In thinking about asset allocation in general, two questions pop up. First, among what kinds of investments should I be allocating my resources?

Well, if you read the ads or the mail solicitations that you probably get, you'd think there were hundreds of kinds of investment vehicles—all of them tailored "just for you." The fact is, you can easily boil down all investments into only six categories:

- Cash and cash equivalents, such as money-market funds, checking accounts, and short-term certificates of deposit
- Fixed-income vehicles, a group that includes tax-exempt bonds, corporate bonds, mortgages, and long-term certificates of deposit
- Equities, including both domestic and international stocks
- Real estate
- Natural resources, including oil and gas
- Tangibles, such as gold and silver

Obviously, there is a wide variation within these categories. Utility stocks, for instance, may behave at times like fixed-income vehicles, because they yield such a steady rate of return. And some short-term, fixed-income vehicles may behave like cash. You must take these variations into account when you are ready to adopt specific investment strategies.

What to Allocate

The second question that pops up: What resources should I be allocating among these six investment categories? There are some assets that you definitely want to exclude from your investment portfolio—your personal assets—and some that you definitely want to include—your investment assets.

The exclusions? A cash reserve is one. You should set aside some funds for emergencies in a secure, very liquid investment vehicle that does not fluctuate in market value. Examples include checking and savings accounts and money-market funds.

How much should you set aside? That depends. Many financial advisers suggest two to six months' living expenses. But that advice does not apply to everyone.

You may, for example, be employed by a start-up venture in a volatile industry. If that's the case, you're more likely to face an extended period of unemployment than your neighbor who works for an established company in a secure industry. Or access to short-term credit may reduce your need for cash on hand.

However much you eventually decide belongs in your emergency fund, exclude that cash from your allocation calculations later on.

What about home equity? Your home may be an investment asset to you—and then again, it may not. It depends.

If you plan to keep your home indefinitely or use all the sales proceeds to buy a new home that's just as expensive or more so, then your home is not an investment asset. It could double in value or fall 50 percent in value, and your standard and cost of living would remain exactly the same.

So, unless you deliberately intend your home to be an investment asset, keep it, too, out of your allocation calculations.

A subtlety: Even though your home may not be listed among your investment assets, you should consider it in your allocation plan if the value of your equity is substantial. For example, if the suburban home that you bought for $50,000 is now worth $350,000, you may decide—depending on the total amount of your investable assets—that you have enough real estate in your portfolio.

What about the inclusions? You may want to consider as investment assets some items that you don't ordinarily think of in this way. Among them:

- Insurance policy cash values
- IRAs or Keoghs
- Company-sponsored 401(k) or other savings plans
- Company defined-benefit plans

You should include these assets in your diversification plan because they are resources on which you'll rely in the future and because they may be affected by market forces between now and the time you're ready to use them.

Diversification: The Base Case

Now you know which assets to include in your allocation or diversification plan and which to exclude. And you know the six different categories of investment assets you can choose from in diversifying your resources. So, how do you diversify?

Let's ignore your personal circumstances for a moment, and build an allocation model that assumes a moderate, stable level of inflation.

You might divide your assets equally among the six investment categories on the theory that equal investment provides equal protection against all kinds of risk—and particularly guards you against the ravages of inflation and deflation.

But since real estate, natural resources, and tangible assets usually move up or down in value together, it makes more sense to lump them into one category. We'll call that category *hard assets*.

However, keep this point in mind: Putting your money in real estate is usually less risky than putting your money in either natural resources or tangibles. The exceptions: if you have some special knowledge or experience dealing with natural resources or tangible assets or have advice from a trusted expert.

Now an equal division looks like this:

Cash and cash equivalents 25%

Fixed-income vehicles 25

Equities 25

Hard assets 25
                                                                    _____
                                                                       100%

But you really shouldn't give cash equal treatment when it comes to allocating your resources. In most cases, an investment in cash is short term. Dollars you have "parked" in cash or cash-equivalent investment vehicles are dollars waiting to be invested more profitably.

So your cash investment actually represents your noncommitment to some other investment category. It's what's left over after you've made your investment selection.

Reducing the percentage of assets you keep in cash results in this more realistic model for moderate inflation:

Cash and cash equivalents 10%

Fixed-income vehicles 30

Equities 30

Hard assets 30
                                                                    _____
                                                                       100%

Now you've neutralized the potential impact of inflation. Cash is relatively unaffected by changes in inflation rates.

But equities—investments, such as stocks, that represent an ownership interest—are a mixed bag. For example, whether or not a particular stock moves in the direction of inflation depends on a variety of factors. Among them: the industry in which the company operates and the company itself.

Fixed-income securities are a hedge against deflation. And hard assets are a hedge against inflation. (Remember, to make sure your hedges are truly effective, you must also diversify investments *within* your asset-allocation categories.)

Now suppose your crystal ball tells you that inflation will be very low—or, conversely, very high. Here's how our model might look in each of these situations:

	MODERATE INFLATION	LOW INFLATION	HIGH INFLATION
Cash	10%	10%	10%
Fixed-income vehicles	30	45	15
Equities	30	30	30
Hard assets	30	15	45
	100%	100%	100%

Diversification: The Personal Case

By now you should feel comfortable with the general principles of diversification. So let's turn to the second part of our asset-allocation discussion: building a model that takes into account your own unique circumstances—the financial profile, goals, and objectives that you developed in Chapters 2 through 4.

To see how you might diversify your own resources, take a look at these sample asset allocations. There are six of them, so find the one that most closely matches your circumstances.

Remember, there are no hard-and-fast allocation rules. But these models should give you a good idea of how to create your own diversified portfolio.

Young Professional

Characteristics

Age: Thirties
Income: $50,000
Net worth: $100,000
Risk tolerance: High
Goals: Upgrade residence and personal property, and begin planning for children's education

Asset Allocation

Cash and cash equivalents . . . . 5 to 10%
Fixed-income vehicles . . . . 20 to 30%
Equities . . . . 40 to 50%
Hard assets . . . . 15 to 30%

Financial Profile

You're feeling optimistic about your life and career prospects. And you have a high tolerance for risk. After all, you reason, you can replace any principal you may lose, because your earnings are bound to spiral upward.

And, since you have plenty of time for your investments to pay off, you can ride out any fluctuations in value common to growth stocks.

Moreover, you have little need for income other than your earnings, since your salary amply covers your living expenses.

You do, however, want to protect yourself against inflation over the long haul. So you invest in vehicles with a solid performance record over time.

And you plan to make a down payment on a larger house in the near future. So you want to keep a good portion of your holdings liquid.

Investment Strategies

Your portfolio is tilted quite heavily toward common stocks and real estate. The reasons: Although they fluctuate considerably in value, common stocks are, historically, impressive performers over the long term. And they are very liquid.

Meanwhile, your hard assets—specifically your real-estate holdings—are an excellent hedge against inflation.

Rising Executive

Characteristics

Age: Forties
Income: $100,000
Net worth: $500,000
Risk tolerance: Medium to high
Goals: Educate children, buy a boat, purchase a second home, begin planning for retirement, and travel

Asset Allocation

Cash and cash equivalents . . . . 5 to 10%
Fixed-income vehicles . . . . 25 to 35%
Equities . . . . 35 to 45%
Hard assets . . . . 15 to 30%

Compared with the young professional's, the fixed-income portion of your portfolio increases slightly while the percentage of common stocks decreases.

Financial Profile

You still have a long time for investments to pay off, but since you are beginning to consider retirement, you take a slightly more conservative posture than you did when you were younger. You still may replace any principal you lose with future earnings, but your time frame is shorter.

You are also less confident of your ability to stash money away, since your expenses are now higher than they were.

You have slightly less need for protection against inflation, because your investment planning period is shorter. But you may need additional income because of high living expenses.

And you still need to keep some holdings liquid. You want money for a sailboat and cash for a down payment on a second home.

Investment Strategies

By allocating less of your portfolio to common stocks and more to fixed-income vehicles, you reduce your overall risk and gain current income. Because you want ready access to your resources, you change the mix of your hard assets from natural resources, say, to real estate.

Manager

Characteristics

Age: Forties
Income: $70,000
Net worth: $300,000
Risk tolerance: Low to medium
Goals: Educate children and begin planning for retirement

Asset Allocation

Cash and cash equivalents . . . . 10 to 15%
Fixed-income vehicles . . . . 30 to 40%
Equities . . . . 35 to 45%
Hard assets . . . . 5 to 20%

Financial Profile

Your allocation is more conservative and liquid than that of the rising executive. Granted, you're the same age. And your concerns are also very similar. But you don't expect your future earnings to be nearly as great. And you would be much worse off if you lost part of your principal.

Your focus is also more on such critical goals as retirement and your children's educations. You're less concerned with discretionary goals, such as a second home or a deluxe vacation. So you may need less of an inflation hedge. The reason: You expect inflation for basic goods and services to lag behind the inflation you anticipate in the cost of discretionary, or luxury, items.

Investment Strategies

To increase liquidity and boost your income, you allocate more to fixed-income vehicles and less to hard assets. Reducing your investment in hard assets also reflects your lesser need for an inflation hedge.

Senior Executive

Characteristics

Age: Fifties
Income: $150,000
Net worth: $1 million
Risk tolerance: Medium
Goals: Make gifts to children, grandchildren, and charities; and plan for a comfortable retirement

Asset Allocation

Cash and cash equivalents . . . . 0 to 5%
Fixed-income vehicles . . . . 30 to 40%
Equities . . . . 35 to 45%
Hard assets . . . . 15 to 30%

Financial Profile

Your cash flow is now quite healthy. Your earnings have increased considerably, and your expenses have decreased, since the children have all finished their costly college educations. Besides, you have now bought just about everything you want and need.

But you do want to plan gifts for your children and grandchildren. And you'd like to make a generous bequest to your alma mater.

Most important: You need to feel secure that your retirement years will be comfortable.

Investment Strategies

Since you don't need much ready cash, you transfer some of your funds from cash equivalents to fixed-income instruments. You can get a higher return from longer-term fixed-income instruments than from cash and cash equivalents. You still have a way to go until you retire, so you keep your inflation hedges—the hard assets—constant. Right now, it doesn't bother you that these assets are illiquid and yield little.

Senior Manager

Characteristics

Age: Fifties
Income: $100,000
Net worth: $500,000
Risk tolerance: Low to medium
Goal: Plan for a comfortable retirement

Asset Allocation

Cash and cash equivalents . . . . 10 to 15%
Fixed-income vehicles . . . . 35 to 45%
Equities . . . . 30 to 40%
Hard assets . . . . 5 to 20%

Financial Profile

Again, you keep your allocation more conservative and liquid than the senior executive who is about your age. You have some of the same concerns as the senior executive. But there are some important differences, too.

While your cash flow has improved since your middle years, you're still less willing to take risks with your principal. Your accumulated assets—or net worth—may not be enough for you to reach your goal of a comfortable retirement. You can't afford to lose any of your assets, and you must rely more on company benefits, particularly your defined-benefit retirement plan.

Investment Strategies

To prepare for retirement, you want more income but less volatility and risk. You allocate more of your assets to cash and cash equivalents to keep your investments less volatile and provide readily accessible cash reserves. You also allocate more to fixed-income vehicles and less to common stocks.

You have even fewer resources invested in hard assets than you did at your career peak. The reason: Your expenses are geared toward basic goods and services. Moreover, you're counting on your company benefits to cover your living expenses when you retire.

Retiree

Characteristics

Age: Sixty plus
Income: $100,000
Net worth: $1.5 million
Risk tolerance: Low
Goal: Preserve capital

Asset Allocation

Cash and cash equivalents . . . . 10 to 20%
Fixed-income vehicles . . . . 40 to 50%
Equities . . . . 25 to 35%
Hard assets . . . . 5 to 15%

Financial Profile

Since you no longer take home a paycheck—or expect to in the future—your tolerance for risk is low. For the same reason, your need for current income from your investments has increased.

And your planning time is shorter, so you can afford to reduce your inflation hedges. Also, you might find yourself needing some ready cash—for unexpected illnesses, for example.

Investment Strategies

You're satisfied with a modest return on your cash, since you want to reduce the volatility of your portfolio and maintain readily accessible cash reserves.

You expect a lower return on your fixed-income investments than you'd get on common stocks. But their lower volatility and higher current income make the trade-off worthwhile.

You still want to keep a significant portion of your portfolio in equities. You like the growth potential.

You also want to stay diversified in the event of a drop in the value of your fixed-income vehicles.

Since you're more concerned about predictable income and your need for inflation hedges is low, you have few funds committed to hard assets.

Besides, most hard assets have low—or no—current income and liquidity, making them particularly unattractive for a retirement portfolio.

Execution Is Everything

You now have an idea of how to allocate your investments according to your assessment of future inflation rates and your own personal profile. Once you've decided how you want to divide up your funds, you must implement your plan. What's the best way?

It depends on the value of your portfolio. If your portfolio is small, you should certainly consider mutual funds. Otherwise, with only limited amounts available to invest, you'll probably find it difficult to achieve enough diversification within each asset category on your own.

For example, you may be able to purchase only four or five individual stocks with the dollars you've allocated to stocks. The probability that the total return from these few stocks will be close to the market average is far less than the possibility that the return from forty to fifty stocks in a mutual fund will approximate the average.

If you have a greater amount to invest, you may want to use a discount broker or retail broker to buy stocks and bonds.

Again, to some degree how you invest—whether in individual securities or mutual funds—will vary according to your own attitude toward risk and the particular investment category. It's hard to diversify adequately with fixed-income vehicles, for instance. Institutions trade some bonds heavily, and commissions are steep on bond purchases of less than $50,000.

But with common stocks, you may achieve enough diversification with $50,000 or less—even if you make *round lot purchases* (that is, purchases of 100 shares or multiples of 100 shares). As you'll see in Chapter 9, mutual funds offer the opportunity to diversify with even less money.

If your portfolio is substantial, you may want to use an investment manager to manage your money. Most reputable money managers, however, will manage portfolios of only $250,000 or more.

Firm Foundation

You know the basics of asset allocation. And you realize that this concept is the cornerstone of a sound financial plan. Moreover, you also have a good idea of how best to diversify your own portfolio. In the chapters ahead, you'll see how to make specific choices within the broad asset-allocation categories that are right for your circumstances.

6 Cashing In

The Case for Cash and Cash Equivalents

*U*sually it doesn't make sense to put all your financial eggs in one basket. But you should put at least some of these eggs in cash—or, more properly, cash equivalents.

Passbook savings accounts, short-term certificates of deposit, money-market accounts, and other cash equivalents offer market rates of return and a high degree of safety.

You may put your emergency cash reserve—and that portion of your investment portfolio you choose to keep in cash equivalents—in a variety of vehicles.

Each one is tailored to fit particular needs, and each one has its advantages and disadvantages. Obviously, you should select vehicles that best suit your needs.

In this chapter, we run through a whole menu of cash-equivalent investments, so you can consider which ones are right for you.

What You Get in Return

First, though, a word about return. The rate of return you earn from cash equivalents changes as the economy changes.

As you may remember, in 1980, you could capture a return as high as 13 percent on a money-market account. By 1989, though, the return on the same type of account had fallen to about 8 percent.

But this dramatic drop shouldn't deter you in the slightest from depositing your money in cash equivalents. When you account for inflation, you'll find that your real return was greater in 1987 than it was in 1980. For example, in 1980, the rate of inflation was actually higher than the return paid on many money-market accounts. So in real terms, your return was not keeping pace with the cost of living.

One other point: Although returns over the last several years have varied considerably, the value of the principal you might have invested in cash equivalents has remained exactly the same. And that's an important consideration.

With cash equivalents, you are in little danger of losing your principal. Your only worry: if our economy were to go completely out of control, much as Germany's did in the 1920s, say, when 4 trillion German marks were worth one American dollar. In that unlikely event, at least we'd all be rowing in the same leaky boat.

An Embarrassment of Riches

What are the most common cash-equivalent vehicles?

If you guessed short-term certificates of deposit, money-market accounts, and money-market funds, you guessed right. Certificates of deposit and money-market accounts are products of banks and savings and loan associations. Money-market funds are managed by brokerage houses and mutual-fund companies.

Safety First

The first $100,000 that you deposit in banks and savings and loans is insured by the Bank Insurance Fund (BIF) or the Savings Association Insurance Fund (SAIF). This amount is backed by the full faith and credit of the U.S. government. The only requirement: The financial institution must be a member of BIF or SAIF. In 1989 Congress established SAIF to replace the troubled Federal Savings and Loan Insurance Corporation (FSLIC). Both BIF and SAIF are administered by the Federal Deposit Insurance Corporation (FDIC). So if you go into a bank, you'll still see "FDIC" on the door. And you may see "FDIC" when you go into a savings and loan.

The federal deposit insurance system was set up in the 1930s to bring stability to the nation's banking system. Be warned, though: There is no law that says a financial institution must be a member of BIF or SAIF. In fact, some financial institutions are chartered under state law, not federal law.

If that's the case, the state may have its own insurance fund. However, in the last few years, some of these state funds have had inadequate resources to protect investors.

Unfortunately, there's no way—short of an audit—to verify that an institution without BIF or SAIF insurance is absolutely solid.

Moreover, as we've seen, only the first $100,000 is insured. So if you want to deposit more than that amount in a bank or savings and loan, you may want to use more than one financial institution. That way, you won't have more than $100,000 on deposit at any one place.

Another consideration: Just because an institution has BIF or SAIF coverage doesn't mean that you have instant access to your cash should your bank or savings and loan be forced to close (as many were during the S & L crisis of the last few years). You might have to wait months before you could actually get your hands on your money—but at least you *will* get your money.

Now that you know how to keep your money safe, let's look at some of the ways you can invest your cash at banks and savings and loans.

No doubt you're thoroughly familiar with checking and savings accounts. So let's move on to certificates of deposit and money-market accounts.

Certificates of Deposit

In the old days, the government dictated the minimum size of certificates of deposit (CDs). It also told banks and savings and loans the interest rates they could pay.

The result? It made no difference whether you purchased a certificate of deposit from a local bank or one in a city 2,000 miles away. The rate was the same.

A few years ago, however, the situation changed.

With the deregulation of the financial services industry, institutions may offer CDs in any amount, for any period, and for any rate of interest. And that spells good news. With a little judicious shopping around, you may boost the amount your money will earn by a percentage point or so, without sacrificing safety.

A red flag should go up, though, if you find an institution that offers a rate of return substantially above the market rate. Often, unusually generous rates signal greater risk.

For example, the institution might not be insured by BIF or SAIF. Or it could be in a cash crunch itself and paying higher rates to attract new depositors.

In this case, your funds could be tied up for months if the institution closes its doors, since, as we've seen, federal insurance doesn't pay off immediately.

Another point: When you're investing in CDs as cash equivalents, stick to certificates of deposit that mature within one year. With longer maturities, your investment functions more like a bond—that is, the longer the term, the greater the inflation risk, deflation risk, and interest rate risk. (See Chapter 5 for more information on these types of risk.)

And remember, even a short-term CD ties up your money for a time. So you should know before investing what penalties—if any—your bank or savings and loan imposes on early withdrawals.

Pay close attention, too, to the annual effective yield a CD pays. (In fact, when comparing CDs, always ask about *yield*—the actual amount your money earns.) Yields depend on the interest rate the bank pays, the method it uses to compound interest—even the number of days in the bank year.

Compounding is the paying of interest on your interest. The more frequent the compounding, the higher the annual yield.

How does the number of days in the bank year influence your investment? At many banks, a year contains not 365 days, as you might expect, but 360 days. Despite this time warp, however, some banks pay interest for the full 365 days. Called "compounding on a 365/360 basis," this practice raises slightly the effective annual yield of a CD.

The bottom line: Shop around for the CD that best fits your needs. It really doesn't matter if the bank is in another city—or even another state. You may buy—and redeem—CDs entirely by mail.

Money-Market Accounts

Many banks and savings and loans offer money-market accounts. And these accounts, like CDs, are insured—up to the same $100,000—by BIF or SAIF. The difference: With a CD, you are guaranteed a stated yield if you hold your certificate to maturity.

A money-market account carries no such guarantee. Instead, you are offered a variable rate, which usually fluctuates with market conditions.

The plus of a money-market account is that you can withdraw your money at any time without penalty. And, usually, you may write checks on the account—a privilege you certainly don't get with CDs. But you'll have to maintain a balance—usually $1,000 to $2,500—to keep the account open.

Again, be wary of any institution that offers an interest rate that is much higher than the rates offered by its competitors.

You've got to be on your toes to make a sound money-market account investment. Because of the wide differences in these accounts, there are many factors to consider when you invest.

It all starts with yield. Institutions offering money-market accounts set their own interest rates, and the federal government has left them free to adjust their rates at will. It's not unusual to find two banks on the same street one-half a percentage point apart. And remember: The bigger your balance, the higher your yield.

If you're rate shopping, you may not want to waste your effort on small gains. Hold out for the good stuff: Some banks, for example, encourage bigger deposits by offering higher rates—or bonuses—on accounts that maintain an average daily balance of $20,000 or more. Sometimes, the sweetening adds up to as much as 0.25 percent.

And don't let the compounding confound you: It has more to do with the size of your earnings than the interest rate itself.

Some institutions compound daily, others quarterly, and still others annually. Say you deposit $1,000 in a money-market account that pays 7 percent. If the institution compounds annually, your account will total $1,070 at the end of the year. Compounding quarterly will add $1.86 to your balance; daily compounding, $2.50.

Obviously, you want your interest calculated and paid into your account as frequently as possible.

Money-Market Funds

Money-market funds—as opposed to money-market accounts—were first introduced by brokerage firms in the early 1970s. But they became popular only in the late 1970s, when interest rates began to soar. Here's how money-market funds work.

Customers buy shares in the funds, which then invest in a variety of short-term securities that earn market rates of interest. (As we'll see in Chapter 9, funds vary according to the type of securities in which they invest.) The funds pay a small portion of the earnings—usually 0.50 to 0.75 percent—as a management fee. Shareholders get the rest.

The net asset value (NAV) of each share is expected to remain at $1. In this respect, a money-market fund is supposed to work just like a bank account. For $1,000, you get back $1,000 plus interest. (See Chapter 9 for an explanation of net asset value.)

And earnings are also paid in shares. Say you invest $1,000 in a fund for one year, and the fund earns 8 percent. At the end of the year, you own 1,080 shares worth $1,080. So, for all practical purposes, this structure is the same as if you'd put money into a bank account.

You may make deposits and withdrawals at any time. But the funds may impose a minimum on the size of the transactions you may make. In most cases, this minimum is $1,000, though some funds call for a minimum of as little as $2.50.

And they also require a minimum balance for keeping your account open. What happens if you don't keep the required balance? The fund could close your account after sixty days (but only after sending you a notice to give you a chance to increase your balance) and mail you the remaining balance. (You continue to earn interest until that time.)

You may open a money-market fund account with only $1,000—and some institutions require only $500. Most funds charge no fees of any kind except for their operating expenses and wire transfers (which we discuss later in this chapter).

The exceptions: Funds that are part of cash-management accounts carry annual fees of up to $100. And funds offered by some brokerage houses levy a fee if your account does not generate a minimum amount in commissions for buying and selling securities.

Money-market funds usually offer a somewhat higher rate of interest than bank money-market accounts, but that advantage is offset by a few drawbacks.

The primary one: The funds aren't insured by a federal agency, although some are covered by private policies.

They are also not quite as accessible as accounts at local banks. To withdraw money, you must make a phone call, write a letter, or write a check. You can't simply go to a nearby automated teller machine, insert a card, and walk away with your cash.

Let's take a look now at the types of money-market funds in which you may invest. Here are three.

General Purpose Funds

These funds are the most common and invest in a wide variety of money-market instruments—Treasury bills, certificates of deposit, and other so-called debt instruments with short maturities.

Government Funds

Government funds invest only in securities issued by the federal government. So they're safer than general purpose funds.

There is a catch, though. Some funds put their money in repurchase agreements that are backed by government securities. And you should know that these funds may not be as safe as those that invest in the government securities themselves.

Funds Free from Federal Income Tax

These funds invest primarily in obligations of state and local governments, the income from which is exempt from federal income tax.

Federal law requires money-market funds to send you a prospectus before you open an account. Once you receive it, you fill out a simple application and mail in your money.

That's all there is to it.

When you want to withdraw your cash, you have several options. The easiest and most popular method: to write a check to yourself or to a third party. Some funds let you write any size check you wish. But most impose a minimum of $250 to $500.

You may also withdraw funds by telephone. Either the fund mails you a check or it transfers money by wire to your bank checking account. Many funds, though, charge a wire-transfer fee, which usually comes to $5 to $15.

Some funds also let you wire money from your bank checking account to your fund. As you might expect, for this service, they don't charge a fee, but your bank might.

How safe are the funds you deposit in these accounts? Even though they are uninsured, you have little reason to lose sleep. Money funds invest only in rock solid vehicles, such as government and high-quality corporate securities.

U.S. Treasury Securities

Finally, you may put money earmarked for cash-equivalent investing in short-term U.S. government obligations, known more commonly as Treasury bills, or T-bills.

You buy these bills directly through a Federal Reserve bank or from a broker or a bank. (If you do buy through a broker or bank, you'll pay a commission, but it's a small one.)

Issued in denominations of $10,000 and up, Treasury bills carry maturity dates of one year or less. You buy the bills at a discount. Here's how it works.

Let's say you were to buy a one-year $10,000 Treasury bill, yielding 6.4 percent. You pay $10,000 for the bill. A short time later, you get a check for $600—an amount representing your discount. At the end of the year, you get $10,000 back. This amount represents the $9,400 you've invested, plus $600 interest.

Federal taxes are due on your earnings (capital and interest) when the T-bill matures. (For this reason, T-bills can prove a good tax strategy for deferring income from one year to the next.)

These securities are as safe as the government itself. And you don't have to pay state and local taxes on your earnings. Moreover, they're totally liquid. You can sell them at any time before they mature.

But, remember, you buy them at a discount based on a predetermined yield. So you might have to recognize a gain or a loss on the sale if you sell them before maturity, particularly if interest rates have changed.

As Good as Cash

One last point about cash equivalents. Even though most cash-equivalent investments pay a fixed rate of return, there's a difference between these investment vehicles and fixed-income instruments. Cash equivalent means pretty much what it says. Your investment is as good as cash—or, in the case of short-term CDs, nearly so.

But, as we've seen, longer-term CDs function more like fixed-income instruments—a subject we tackle in the next chapter.

7 *Gentlemen Prefer Bonds*

Investing in Fixed-Income Instruments

*F*ixed-income instruments, such as long-term certificates of deposit and bonds, make up a large portion of many portfolios.

Long-term certificates of deposit are simply CDs with a maturity of more than a year.

Bonds—the most common fixed-income investments—are more complicated. How complicated? Read on.

Solid as a Rock

In the old days, bonds were the Rock of Gibraltar of investments. They promised steady returns and a reasonable degree of safety. But all that has changed.

These days bonds are almost as volatile as common stocks. The reason: wide swings in interest rates and inflation over the past several years.

Do bonds still make sense for your portfolio? Let's take a look at the pros and cons of these investment vehicles.

First Things First

The first thing you need to know about bonds is this: All bonds—no matter what type—operate on basically the same principle. They're essentially contracts between an issuer (or borrower) and a bondholder (or lender).

The issuer agrees to pay interest at a fixed rate, known as the *coupon rate*, according to a set schedule—usually semiannually.

Also, the issuer must repay the principal, or face value, of the bond when it matures—which can be anywhere from one to forty years from the date it was issued. (Another fact to file away: Bonds that come due in ten years or less are frequently called *notes*.)

There's nothing that says you have to hold a bond until maturity, however. You can usually sell it on the open market at any time.

Return to Sender

While all bonds operate on the same basic principle, they are not all equal investments. Some are riskier than others, and, accordingly, some offer greater rewards in the form of much higher interest. How can you judge which bonds are good buys for you?

First, you need to know that bonds can provide a return on your investment in two ways: current yield and capital appreciation.

What's the difference? *Current yield* is the annual return that a bond pays its holder. For instance, if you purchase a bond with a par—or face—value of $1,000 and a stated coupon rate of 8 percent, you should expect to receive $80 per year from the bond.

As long as the bond is valued at par ($1,000), the current yield and the coupon rate will be the same—8 percent. However, what if the value of the bond changes to, say, $1,100?

The coupon rate, 8 percent, remains the same. It's stated right on the bond. But the current yield changes—from 8 percent to approximately 7.3 percent ($80 divided by the new price of the bond, $1,100).

So current yield actually refers to a percentage: the dollar amount that the bond pays in a year divided by the current price of the bond.

In addition to current yield, you might also realize some *capital appreciation*—or *loss*—in the value of your bond. Capital appreciation or loss can occur in two ways: You buy at par and sell before maturity—or you buy at a price other than par and sell at any time. If you purchase a bond at par and hold it until maturity, you post no gain or loss in principal except in purchasing power.

Capital appreciation, like current yield, is a function of a bond's price. Let's say you bought your 8 percent coupon bond from the issuer at par—$1,000. A year later, because of market forces, the value of your bond rises to $1,100. You collect the $80 in interest, and then you sell the bond.

Your total pretax return from that bond comes to 18 percent—$80 in coupon payments plus $100 appreciation, or $180, divided by your $1,000 initial investment.

Shifting Values

Why do bonds change in value? Two factors affect the price of a bond: a change in the bond's rating or a change in interest rates. Let's look at ratings first.

Bonds are rated by two major agencies, Moody's and Standard & Poor's. These ratings help investors determine an issuer's ability to make the required annual interest payments and to repay the principal when it comes due.

Here's a rundown of these ratings.

Standard & Poor's rates bonds AAA through D, and Moody's rates them Aaa through C. As you might expect, as bonds go further down in the ratings, they carry higher risk.

If an issuer's bond rating is increased—and its bonds are now considered to carry less risk—a new investor would be willing to accept a lower current yield. Why not, since the risk of default is lower?

That doesn't mean that the bond issuer can reduce the interest it pays on bonds already outstanding. If you bought an 8 percent coupon bond at par, you'll continue to enjoy an 8 percent current return.

But if you decide to sell the bond, the buyer will be willing to pay more for it than you did, because it is now considered a safer investment. So the new buyer trades a lower current yield for greater safety. The price he or she is willing to pay for your bond is the price that will bring current yield in line with the current yields of other similarly rated bonds.

If, on the other hand, Moody's, say, lowered the safety rating on your bond, its value—the price you could get for it in the bond market—would drop. The new buyer would demand a higher current yield to compensate for the higher risk.

So, changes in its rating cause the market price of a bond to vary up or down. Savvy investors anticipate downgrades in ratings, and these expectations may influence prices before a new rating appears.

Interest rates also affect bond prices. But fluctuations don't affect investors who hold their bonds until maturity.

If, because of changing investor expectations, other bond issuers similar to yours are forced to pay higher interest, the price of the bond you already hold will probably drop. Why?

Well, for the simple reason that interest rates are higher. An investor could buy a new bond with a higher coupon rate for the same $1,000 you paid for your 8 percent bond.

The change has nothing to do with either issuer's bond rating. It just reflects the fact that, for some reason—market conditions, say—investors in general are less willing to lend money to bond issuers. The issuers must offer a greater incentive—in the form of higher interest—to lure investors.

Let's say you buy your 8 percent coupon bond for $1,000, just as before. But a year later the general level of interest rates has increased to 10 percent. That's the going market rate.

For your bond, which promises to pay $80 a year, to yield a 10 percent return to a new buyer its price would have to fall to approximately $800 ($800 divided by $80 equals 10 percent).

Why do we say "approximately"? Because the value of a bond at any given time also depends in part upon the time remaining until the bond is scheduled to mature.

A change in interest rates will affect the current yield on a bond with twenty years before maturity for all twenty years. In contrast, the current yield of a bond only five years from maturity will be affected for only five years. So a change in interest rates affects the value, or price, of the bond with the longer time to maturity much more than the price of the bond that matures sooner.

Here's another way of looking at it. Let's assume that you buy several $1,000 bonds today, all of which have a current yield of 8 percent but mature over different periods of time. To get an idea of the change that would occur in the price of the bond if interest rates were to rise or fall by 2 percent, look at the following table:

BOND PRICE			
YEARS TO MATURITY	6% YIELD	8% YIELD	10% YIELD
1	$1,019	$1,000	$981
5	1,085	1,000	923
10	1,149	1,000	875
20	1,231	1,000	828
30	1,277	1,000	810

As the chart shows, a 2 percentage point drop in interest rates causes a bond scheduled to mature in one year to increase in value by 1.9 percent ($1,019 minus $1,000 divided by $1,000). The bond scheduled to mature in thirty years, on the other hand, increases in value by 27.7 percent ($1,277 minus $1,000 divided by $1,000).

Here's the important point: If you invest in long-term bonds, you must keep in mind that the market value of the bonds—the price they will command—can vary wildly if you have to sell them before maturity. In investment jargon, the price of these bonds is said to be "volatile."

Another important concept when it comes to bonds is *yield to maturity*. This is simply the compound rate of return you would have to earn on a comparable investment to equal the total return you'll get on your bond—provided you hold it until maturity. Yield to maturity takes into account not just the interest payments you'll receive, but also the net rise or fall in the price of the bond as it moves toward its $1,000 maturity value.

To see how yield to maturity works, assume that you pay $900 for a twenty-year, 6 percent coupon bond that matures in ten years. If you hold the bond until it matures, you'll collect $600 in interest payments ($60 per year for ten years).

But you'll also realize a $100 gain in the value of your bond (the $900 that you paid for it subtracted from the $1,000 that it is worth at maturity). So, your total return from the bond is $700 ($600 in interest plus $100 in capital gain).

This return translates into a yield to maturity of 7.3 percent. Of course, the implicit assumption in any yield-to-maturity figure is that earnings will be reinvested at that rate.

Watch Those Curves

You can see that bonds with the same coupon rate but different maturity dates will have different current yields. Bonds with a longer maturity generally pay a higher current yield. The reason: There is greater risk inherent in longer-term bonds.

For example, on December 31, 1989, the yields available on U.S. Treasury bonds of various maturities were as follows.

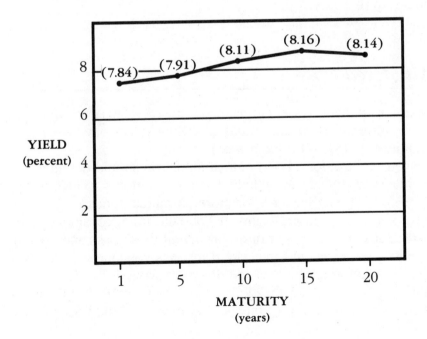

Graphs like this one are known as *yield curves*. Usually, they slope upward as this one does. Before investing in bonds, you should consider the yield curve at specific times, so you can determine whether the additional yield that you receive by extending the maturities compensates for your additional risk.

Note, however, that this yield curve also slopes down. When investors expect interest rates to fall, they are willing to accept a lower long-term rate in order to lock that rate in.

Another point to consider before investing in bonds—especially if you expect interest rates to remain constant: the "real" rate of interest on the bond. And what is the *real rate of interest*? The current yield less the inflation rate. The current yield isn't as important as what you have left after inflation takes its bite.

You must also subtract the taxes you'll pay on the bond's nominal rate of return in order to arrive at the real rate of return.

So, you see, it is extremely important that you concentrate on the real rate of return when investing in bonds. On average, by the way, bonds have produced approximately a 2 percent real rate of return to investors over the last thirty years.

All Mixed Up

As is the case with many types of investments, the secret to successful bond investing is a diversified portfolio. So don't stick with any one issue or any one denomination ($1,000 is the lowest).

Or you may opt for a bond mutual fund. You should definitely use bond mutual funds if you have a limited amount of money to invest—say, less than $50,000. (See Chapter 9 for more on mutual funds.)

What if you have more to invest? You still might consider a bond fund, particularly if the thought of evaluating all those risks and keeping track of all those prices and maturity dates gets you queasy. That way, somebody else can watch the ups and downs for you.

But whether you take the do-it-yourself approach or opt for the convenience of a mutual fund, you should understand the various kinds of bonds and decide which ones best suit your goals and personal financial profile. Here they are.

U.S. Government Bonds

What makes bonds vary are safety and yield. United States Treasury notes, Treasury bonds, and savings bonds are rock solid. Each of these instruments is backed by the U.S. government. So their value collapses only if the government does (in which case your currency wouldn't be worth anything, anyway).

Only the thirty-year Treasuries can be "called"—a subject we'll get to shortly—and even they can be called only after twenty-five years.

Treasury bonds have another plus: You don't have to pay state and local taxes on the interest they earn. The disadvantage: Their yield is generally from 0.75 to 1.50 percentage points less than that of high-grade corporate bonds.

And you have to be able to invest at least $5,000 to buy a note that matures in less than four years. The less-preferred longer maturities cost $1,000.

If the denominations of the Treasuries give you pause, look to U.S. savings bonds. They're every bit as safe as the Treasuries. They can be purchased without a commission charge from most banks and savings and loans. And, since 1982, their yield has been competitive with that of short-term financial instruments, such as money-market accounts.

It wasn't always that way. Savings bonds fell out of favor during the 1970s, when inflation shrank their returns and chased the market away.

The bonds have regained some of their appeal, however, since the Treasury Department began issuing ten-year, variable-rate, Series EE bonds, which come in denominations of $50 to $10,000. The EEs don't pay interest before maturity. Instead, they sell for half their face value, and the interest is automatically reinvested.

If you hold the bonds for at least five years, you receive a guaranteed minimum return or 85 percent of the average yield of five-year Treasury notes during the life of the bond, whichever is higher. But that yield dwindles to a mere 5.5 percent if you sell the savings bonds in one year.

In either case, you pay taxes on the accrued interest when you cash in, unless you choose to report the interest annually. In either case, the interest isn't actually paid until you cash in the bonds.

Corporate Bonds

Bonds issued by corporations are naturally riskier than those issued by the federal government. But their yields can be commensurately higher. As we've seen, historically, high-quality corporate bonds have yielded 0.75 to 1.50 percentage points more than U.S. Treasuries.

Remember, though, that the higher the yield, the greater the risk. Before investing in corporate bonds, look at their ratings in Standard & Poor's and Moody's.

Another factor to consider carefully: Corporate bonds may be *callable*—that is, the issuer may require you to sell your bonds back before they mature. Why? To reduce the issuer's debt, perhaps, or to refinance that debt at lower rates.

Issuers want to reserve for themselves all the leeway possible, so they include what's known as a *call provision* in some bond contracts. This provision spells out the *call price*, which is set at either face value or face value plus a premium.

Having a bond called will prove painful to the pocketbook, since the coupon rate is now worth more than the prevailing rates for new issues. And a callable bond that carries a substantial premium above the call price is more likely to be called.

Two types of corporate bonds can lessen your exposure to the risk of rising interest rates: *floating-rate bonds*, on which rates are regularly adjusted to prevailing interest levels, and *put bonds*, which can be sold back to the issuer at face value during certain periods before they mature.

Hybrids

Because floating-rate and put bonds are hybrids that share some of the safety advantages of short-term securities, their yields are usually lower than those of fixed-rate bonds. There is, however, a way of recouping some of that lost yield, and that's to buy *convertible bonds*. Convertibles offer the higher interest income of bonds, along with some of the capital gains potential of stocks. (See Chapter 8 for information about stocks.)

You can exchange convertibles for a predetermined amount of stock in the issuing company at any time during the life of the bonds. And there are no broker fees, which you'd pay when you buy stock outright. The only drawback: The value of the shares—their *conversion value*—is less than the face value of the bond at the time it's issued.

But if the price of the stock rises enough, it can make up the difference in the conversion value of the bond. That's why many investors choose convertibles that offer only a modest gap between face value and conversion value. They also look for packages with a high fixed-income yield that is competitive with the yield you'd realize from owning stock outright.

We're in the Muni

Municipal bonds are issued by state and local governments or even smaller entities, such as local development districts. You may buy these bonds individually or you may invest in a municipal bond fund.

These bonds have one big advantage: The interest they pay is exempt from federal tax, and, if you buy bonds issued by your home state, you can escape state and most local taxes as well.

You do, however, have to have some money to spend: Municipal bonds usually sell in units of $5,000. And you have to be prepared for less than outstanding yields. Because they're tax exempt, munis yield about 75 percent as much as taxable U.S. Treasury bonds with similar maturities.

Moreover, all munis are not alike. So-called *general obligation bonds* are backed by the taxing power of the issuer—the state of California, say—and are intended to provide capital to that entity. *Revenue bonds*, however, are backed only by the income from the project they are sold to finance—a sewer system, say. So they carry higher risk.

Although governmental units sometimes experience financial trouble, defaults on muni bonds are quite rare—they've amounted to less than 1 percent of the face value of all municipal bonds issued.

If even that little bit of default gives you the willies, you can buy insured municipal bonds, at an additional cost. No, you don't pay for the insurance outright. Rather, the issuer pays the premium and recoups the cost by offering you an interest rate that is usually one-tenth to one-third of a percentage point lower than those offered on uninsured bonds.

Understandably, insurance reassures the rating boards as much as it does the rest of us. An issue that might rate BBB without the protection often garners that coveted AAA rating with it.

Zero-Coupon Bonds

Zero-coupon bonds are securities that make no periodic interest payments but instead are sold at a deep discount from face value. You receive a rate of return by the gradual appreciation of the security, which is redeemed at face value on a specified maturity date. The difference between what you originally paid for the bond and the amount you receive when the bond matures is called "original issue discount."

For tax purposes, the IRS maintains that you must report part of the discount as taxable interest income each year even though you do not actually receive the cash until maturity.

For this reason, zeros make the most sense if you're seeking a diversified portfolio for Keoghs, IRAs, and other savings plans where the tax is deferred.

There are many kinds of zero-coupon securities. Some are issued at a deep discount by a corporation or may be created by a brokerage firm when it strips the coupons off a bond and sells its *corpus*—or body—and the coupons separately. This technique is used frequently with Treasury bonds, and the zero-coupon issue is marketed under such names as *CAT* or *TIGER*.

Zero-coupon bonds are also issued by municipalities. Buying a municipal zero means you don't have to worry about paying taxes, since the interest is tax exempt. (Of course, since the interest *is* tax exempt, there's no tax benefit to using them in a tax-deferred IRA or Keogh plan).

People frequently use zero-coupon securities to plan for a specific investment goal. For example, a parent knowing that a child will enter college in ten years can buy a zero that will mature in that time and be assured that the money will be available for tuition. Similarly, you can provide for retirement in twenty-five years by buying a twenty-five-year zero.

Because zero-coupon securities pay no current interest, they are the most volatile of all fixed-income securities. That is, when interest rates rise, zeros fall in value more dramatically than bonds paying interest currently.

However, when interest rates fall, zero-coupon securities rise more rapidly in value. The reason: The bonds have locked in a specific reinvestment rate that becomes more attractive if rates fall further.

But, as is always the case with bonds, interest rate fluctuations have no effect if you hold the bond to maturity.

Mortgage-Backed Securities

Mortgage-backed securities, such as those issued by the Government National Mortgage Association (GNMA), have become a much more important part of the bond market in recent years.

These instruments—called Ginnie Maes—are basically pools of home mortgages. Each month as the mortgagee makes his or her mortgage payment, you receive interest and principal on the original amount you invested. And, if the mortgagee decides to repay the mortgage, the payment of that amount is accelerated to you.

The government does not ensure that the market value of GNMAs won't fluctuate. But it does guarantee the payment of interest and principal by the mortgagee. In other words, if a mortgagee defaults, the government—not the investor—loses.

However, you can still lose money on an investment in Ginnie Maes if you must sell them when their market value is lower than the price you paid.

Bear in mind also that mortgagees have the right to repay their mortgages at any time. If mortgage rates rise, most mortgagees probably won't pay early. They'll want to retain the benefit of their low rate. But if rates fall, the mortgagee may repay the loan. You, then, would have to reinvest the funds at a time when available interest rates are probably lower.

Because of this risk, GNMAs, although government backed, pay a rate of return higher than those available on regular U.S. Treasury bonds. Before making a Ginnie Mae investment, you should decide whether this additional premium is large enough to offset your risk.

Costs in Purchasing Bonds

You can purchase bonds through most brokerage houses, as well as through specialized bond houses. There is no charge for buying a newly issued bond. But you will be charged a handling fee when you buy previously owned issues or when you sell one of your own bonds before maturity.

The handling fee may come in the form of a commission. Or the fee may appear as a markup in the price of the bond.

Some bonds—U.S. Treasuries, for instance—are very liquid, so the commissions charged on them are usually small. One discount brokerage house charges $34 on the purchase of U.S. Treasuries regardless of the size of the transaction. But many municipal bonds and thinly traded corporate bonds may have substantial markups.

Often you won't be able to determine the exact amount of the markup, because it is not recorded on the brokerage "advice," or invoice. So be careful. It is not inconceivable that you could pay as much as 5 to 6 percent when purchasing a thinly traded municipal bond.

Junk Bonds

If you can stand to be a bit of a daredevil, there are gains and yields aplenty in buying what only high rollers want: low-grade corporate bonds, known euphemistically as *high-yielding bonds* and colloquially as *junk bonds*. Any issue rated BB+ or lower is a low-grade corporate bond.

These instruments have earned their monikers. Over the last decade, junk bond defaults have averaged 1.52 percent of the total dollar amount of low-grade bonds outstanding. The default rate on all corporate bonds, for the sake of comparison, is a mere 0.08 percent.

To compensate for that higher risk of default, low-grade corporate bonds sell at substantially higher yields than their high-grade cousins—about three percentage points higher.

High-risk bond investments such as these aren't for the novice. But for those who understand the game they're playing, and who play it well, the rewards can be high.

Stocking Up

Now that you know the ins and outs of bonds, let's turn to an area that is more familiar to most people—stocks.

8 *Taking Stock*

Strategies for Investing in the Stock Market

*R*ewarding, terrifying, and complex.

That's the stock market. Stocks are probably the securities that investors think they know the most about. Everybody has an uncle or a grandma who "could have bought IBM" when it was selling for just a few dollars a share.

It's so easy, in retrospect, to make money in the stock market. It's also easy to lose.

In general, however, the optimists have it right. Over the long term, stocks have been better than any other financial asset at rewarding investors with superior returns.

But not every investor goes into the market with an equal chance. The more you understand about what you're doing, the more likely you are to do well.

The first step in gaining this understanding is to master the fundamentals. And that's what this chapter is all about.

High Flying

The tables in Chapter 5 showed exactly how much better stocks have performed over the years. They compared the actual returns of five types of financial assets over the sixty-year period from 1926 to 1988. And they contrasted these returns with the average inflation rate during this period.

The result: Small company stocks posted an average return of 12.3

percent and common stocks 10.0 percent, compared to 5.0 percent for long-term corporate bonds, 4.8 percent for long-term government bonds, and 3.5 percent for U.S. Treasury bills.

"That's great," you say. "Now I know where to put my money." Well, yes and no. Although the average return produced by stocks over the long term has been more than respectable, you should not plunk down your hard-earned cash quite yet.

The reason: The return you would have enjoyed during any single year during this period would have fluctuated dramatically.

This fact is hardly surprising. As we saw in Chapter 5, riskier investments usually have a higher potential return. But all stocks are not equally risky.

We've mentioned only two types of equities: small company stocks and common stocks. But most financial analysts divide stocks into four separate categories. Here they are, in ascending order of risk.

Types of Stock

Income Stocks

These stocks produce steady income in the form of dividends. The companies that pay consistent dividends are usually those in mature industries, such as utilities and railroads. And these companies are unlikely to grow very fast. Here's why. Demand for their products is fairly stable. And the companies are paying out a good chunk of their income in dividends.

These stocks make sense if you need the current income that dividends bring. Income stocks are also the least risky you can buy, so they fit into a more conservative portfolio.

Growth-and-Income Stocks

With these securities, you receive a respectable dividend and have a reasonable expectation for growth.

Should you invest in growth-and-income stocks? The answer is "yes" if you have a low tolerance for risk and want a relatively stable return. Also, these stocks are a good choice when you need some income to pay your current expenses but also want to finance long-term goals and objectives.

Blue-chip stocks—which we discuss later in this chapter—fall into this category.

Growth Stocks

These are the stocks of faster-growing companies, such as those listed annually in the *Inc.* 100. More volatile in price than stocks in the first two categories, they carry higher risk to your principal, are cyclical—or seasonal—and seldom pay dividends. The reason: These companies usually reinvest their earnings.

Growth stocks make sense if you're comfortable with risk and have other sources of income. And they can help you build capital for the future—but you have to be prepared for a possible loss of principal.

Aggressive Growth Stocks

These stocks behave the same way growth stocks do—but more so. They are issued by young, fast-growing companies involved in, say, high technology or medical technology. Again, the companies reinvest their earnings, so they pay few or no dividends. And their share prices are volatile. For that reason, your chances of losing principal are high—but you have a correspondingly great opportunity for success. These stocks belong in your portfolio if you want to build wealth and are comfortable with a great deal of risk.

Wall Street Speak

No matter where you are, it helps if you speak the language. That's true of the stock market, too. So, to help you get along on Wall Street, here's a checklist of terms you should know.

Common Stock

The definition of common stock: units of ownership in a corporation. As a stockholder, you actually own part of the company. By contrast, bondholders have simply loaned the company money.

Because you are an owner, you typically have the right to vote on important matters, such as choosing corporate directors and changing company bylaws. And you're entitled to receive dividends from the company.

But what happens if the company goes out of business, and its assets are liquidated? You could be out of luck. Holders of common stock are the last to get their money back. They must fall in line behind secured and unsecured creditors and owners of bonds and preferred stock.

In exchange for this risk, though, you can usually expect greater appreciation in the value of your securities than you'd get with either preferred stock or bonds.

Preferred Stock

Preferred stock also represents ownership in a corporation. And, as an owner of this stock, you're entitled to dividends at a set rate. You get paid before common shareholders at dividend time and—if it comes to that—when the company liquidates. Preferred stock does not ordinarily carry voting rights.

Most preferred stock is *cumulative*. So if dividends are "passed"—that is, not paid—for any reason, they accumulate. And they must be paid before common dividends. A passed dividend on *noncumulative* preferred stock, however, is usually gone forever.

Your preferred stock might fall into one of several categories. If your stock is labeled *participating* preferred, you—like common shareholders—get to share in profits that exceed the declared dividend. Or your stock might be *nonparticipating* preferred. In this case, you're entitled to your dividend and nothing else.

Another type of preferred stock: *adjustable-rate* preferred. As its name implies, this stock pays an adjustable dividend. Either the company can adjust the rate at its option, or the rate changes at an interval—usually quarterly—that is stated on the stock.

How is the rate determined in this case? The corporation bases the new rate on Treasury bill or other money-market rates.

When you own *convertible* preferred stock, you have the right to exchange it for a fixed number of common shares. This feature makes the trading price of convertible preferred somewhat unstable in comparison to *nonconvertible* preferred, which functions more like a fixed-income bond.

Blue-Chip Stock

Everyone's familiar with the term. But what type of stock actually falls into this category?

Well, there's no printed directory of companies that qualify. But the generally accepted definition of "blue chip" is common stock of companies that are well known and have solid histories of growth, profit, and dividend payments.

Blue chips usually have low yields. And their prices are less volatile than other common stocks.

New Issues

New issues fall into two categories. Either they are initial public offerings (IPOs)—that is, stock offered to the public for the first time by companies that were formerly private—or they are additional blocks of shares issued by public companies. New issues are always registered with the Securities and Exchange Commission (SEC).

New York Stock Exchange

The largest and oldest (established in 1792) stock exchange in the United States, the New York Stock Exchange (NYSE) also is known by the monikers Big Board and the Exchange. The NYSE is really an unincorporated association.

Currently, the NYSE's voting membership totals 1,366 "seats," which are largely owned by partners or officers of securities firms. Traders buy and sell stocks and other financial instruments at *trading posts* on the floor of the exchange.

The number of securities firms represented on the Big Board is about 550. And 150 of these are so-called *specialists*. What's a specialist?

These are the traders responsible for making sure that the market in the securities of specific companies remains orderly. So any trades in a given stock on the NYSE must go through that stock's specialist.

About thirty exchange members—known as *floor traders*—buy and sell only for their own accounts. The majority, though, trade stock for the general public.

More than 1,600 corporations, mostly large firms, are listed on the NYSE.

American Stock Exchange

Until 1921, the American Stock Exchange (AMEX) was known as the Curb Exchange. And today, many people still refer to the AMEX as the Curb.

For the most part, the stocks and bonds that are traded on this exchange belong to small and medium-sized companies.

Over the Counter

Over the counter describes stocks that aren't traded or listed on an organized exchange, such as the NYSE or the AMEX. But the phrase also refers to a specific market where dealers, instead of trading on the floor of the exchange, make transactions through a computerized telephone network.

Traditionally, over-the-counter stocks have belonged to smaller companies that fall short of the strict listing requirements demanded by the NYSE or the AMEX. In the last few years, though, many companies that do meet the Big Board or AMEX standards have remained with over-the-counter trading.

Here's why. These companies like the fact that their stock is traded by many dealers rather than one person. As we've seen, the NYSE requires all trading in a stock to go through a single specialist.

The National Association of Securities Dealers (NASD) writes and enforces the rules that govern over-the-counter stock trading.

NASDAQ

NASDAQ—the National Association of Securities Dealers Automated Quotations System—is owned and operated by the National Association of Securities Dealers.

NASDAQ is a computerized system that provides brokers and dealers with price quotations for securities traded over the counter. It also provides quotations for many New York Stock Exchange listed securities. NASDAQ quotes are published in the financial pages of most newspapers.

Options

Options are contracts to buy or sell a given stock at a given price within a certain time. If you don't exercise your option by a specific date, it expires and you lose your money.

Traded on the organized exchanges, options are used by sophisticated investors and traders for a variety of investment purposes. Approach them with caution. And seek the help of a professional adviser.

How Do You Buy Stocks?

The key to investing in the stock market is diversification—which only means spreading your investment dollar over an adequate number of different stocks, so that you may offset losses in the value of some stocks against gains in others.

How much diversification? That depends on the degree of risk you think is prudent for the appreciation you're likely to get. If you invest in just one stock, and its market price doubles, you double your money. If, on the other hand, you invest in 100 stocks and the value of just one of them doubles, you've made a nice little gain, but that's all.

On the other side of that coin, however, is the possibility that the value of your stock will fall—potentially all the way to zero. If you own just the single stock, you suffer a huge loss. But if that stock is just one of 100, you can afford the small loss.

Here's a rule of thumb for diversification: It's difficult for anyone with less than $50,000 to diversify adequately by buying individual stocks. Our advice: Rather than buy single stocks, turn to mutual funds. When you buy a single mutual fund, you are really buying a diversified portfolio of stocks that are consistent with the fund's stated investment objectives. (We cover mutual funds in the next chapter.)

If you have $50,000 to $250,000 to invest in the market, you can achieve some measure of diversification. So you have a choice. You can stick with mutual funds, or you can purchase stock through a retail or discount broker.

What if you have more than $250,000 to invest in the market? Should you be so fortunate, you can achieve diversification on your own. Of course, it might not be a bad idea to hire a professional investment adviser to help you out.

When it comes to buying stock, most investors use one of three methods to determine which securities to buy.

Fundamental Analysis

Using this approach, you analyze a stock's underlying value—its "fundamentals." Here are the measures you should employ.

The Stock's Historic Trading Range
Look at the stock's current price versus its price over the past twelve months, then over the past five years. Ascertain the reason the stock is selling so low or so high and make your decision to buy or sell accordingly.

The Industry
Determine the characteristics of the industry to which your prospective pick belongs. For example, does the company do business in a mature or emerging industry? If it's in an emerging industry, the possibility of stock price appreciation is greater.

Also, is the industry in which the company does business stable or volatile? A volatile industry means a greater chance of sharp fluctuations in stock prices.

Return on Equity
Return on equity is perhaps the most important measure of a company's performance. Here's how to calculate it.

At the start of an accounting period (a fiscal year, say) you divide a company's common stock equity (its net worth) into its net income. You use the net income figure after the company has paid its preferred stock dividends—but before it pays common stock dividends. You'll find this number in the company's annual report.

Return on equity lets you know how efficiently a company is using its resources. And by comparing percentages for different periods, you can see trends and determine how well the company is doing against the competition.

Earnings per Share
Look at how well a company has done in the last ten years for an idea of what it is capable of earning. Ask a broker for the firm's estimate of earnings in the next twelve months.

Price/Earnings Ratio
To determine a stock's price/earnings (P/E) ratio—also known as the *multiple*—you divide its price by its earnings per share.

You should know, however, that P/E ratios come in two varieties. The P/E ratio either uses an analyst's predictions of future earnings—a forward P/E—or actual earnings from the latest year—a trailing P/E.

Take a stock that is selling for $40 a share. It has projected earnings next year of $4, so its forward P/E is 10. But the same stock that earned $2 last year has a trailing P/E of 20.

Why are P/E ratios so useful? They let you know how much you're shelling out for a company's earning power. When you see a high P/E, you know investors are willing to pay more for a stock's earnings. The reason: A high P/E—one with a multiple greater than 20—usually means investors expect earnings to grow rapidly.

High P/E stocks are typically those of rapidly growing, newer companies. And, as you might expect, you take on a lot more risk trading them than you do when you trade low P/E stocks. That's because the potential for disappointment—earnings that don't reach high expectations—is so great. The company may still be doing well, just not as well as optimistic investors had hoped, so the price of the stock falls.

Where do you find low P/E stocks? They're usually in slow-growing, mature industries, in blue-chip companies, and in stock groups that, for one reason or another, aren't currently in favor. As a general rule of thumb, low P/E stocks offer higher yields to investors. In fact, high P/E stocks often pay no dividends whatsoever.

The trailing P/E is listed along with the stock's price and trading activity in daily newspapers.

Book Value per Share

This measure is the company's net assets divided by the number of shares outstanding. It can be a useful starting point in arriving at underlying value.

However, remember that book value is based on historical cost and may not represent either liquidating value or replacement cost.

Debt-to-Equity Ratio

Debt-to-equity ratio can be measured in two ways.

Total liabilities divided by total shareholders' equity. This measure shows how well owners' equity can cushion creditors' claims in case a company liquidates.

Total long-term debt divided by total shareholders' equity. This is a measure of *leverage*—the use of borrowed money to boost the return on owners' equity.

Tip: One measure of a company's relative health is its debt-to-equity ratio compared with the debt-to-equity ratio of other companies in its industry.

Dividends

Dividends are earnings distributed to shareholders. The amount is decided by the board of directors and is usually paid quarterly.

Technical Analysis

The second method of determining which securities to buy is technical analysis.

Technical analysts use computer models to track a stock's price and trading volume and to detect changes in trends based on a comparison of average prices over a certain period of time and/or average volume over the same period.

The Efficient Market

Now for the third way of making stock purchasing decisions. In the early 1900s, French mathematician Louis Bachelier took a look at the Paris Securities Exchange and concluded that it was a game of chance. His *Theorie de la speculation* sparked the long-running debate over whether the market is "efficient."

The efficient market theory—or "random walk theory," as it is sometimes called—holds that no investor can beat the market over the long run.

The Black and White of It

If you're a proponent of the random walk theory, you'll find it very simple to choose individual stocks. Just open up your newspaper to the financial section and throw darts. This method works as well as any other under this theory.

However, if like most people, you're an advocate of fundamental or technical analysis, you'll find it a bit more difficult to select individual securities. There are simply too many choices for you to become sufficiently knowledgeable about all of them. So you may find it helpful to subscribe to one of the many investment newsletters on the market.

These newsletters are as hot as ever. There are now about 1,200 published in the United States. And more than one million people pay $12 to $1,000 a year for subscriptions to them.

Another source of information on individual stocks: your stockbroker. Many full-service brokerage firms have research departments. But you must decide whether the additional information is worth paying higher commissions.

Dollar-Cost Averaging

Dollar-cost averaging is an easy investment technique to use. You simply invest a fixed dollar amount at set intervals in a particular stock, a group of stocks, or a mutual fund.

Since the price of the securities you buy will vary with market and economic conditions, sometimes your money will buy more shares and sometimes fewer. But, over the long run, the cost of the shares that you accumulate will more closely approximate an average cost than if you purchased the same number of shares each time you invested.

Let's say, by way of illustration, that you decided to invest in Amalgamated Paper Clip Corporation on the first day of each quarter. Last year, Amalgamated's stock sold at $10 per share the first time you bought it, $12 the second time, $14 the third time, and $16 at your last purchase.

If you had used dollar-cost averaging and invested, say, $1,000 at each purchase, at the end of the year you would own (not counting fractional shares) 316 shares of Amalgamated stock at an average cost of $12.66 per share ($4,000 divided by 316 shares).

But let's say you had decided instead to buy 100 shares at each purchase, regardless of the price. Now, at the end of the year you would own 400 Amalgamated shares at an average cost of $13 per share.

Reinvestment Programs

Dividend reinvestment programs are also a way to practice dollar-cost averaging. You've heard of these programs, or the "buy, hold, and reinvest strategy"? Dividend reinvestment programs allow you to use your dividends to purchase additional shares of stock—sometimes at a discount. About 1,000 corporations, many of them on the New York Stock Exchange, now offer these programs.

The benefit of reinvestment programs: Most of the companies that offer these programs charge no brokerage or service fees. Even those who do charge levy only a nominal fee—typically, $3 a transaction. You'd pay at least $25 to $30 if you used a broker.

Foreign Affairs

What about foreign stocks? One reason people invest in these stocks: Stock markets in foreign countries have performed spectacularly in recent years.

The safest way to invest in foreign markets is through mutual funds. But some investors insist on picking their own stocks.

One problem with choosing individual stocks is the scarcity of information. There is no counterpart to the Securities and Exchange Commission in many countries. And when you invest in foreign stocks, you can fall victim to swings in the currency markets. Also, you pay higher brokerage commissions on foreign shares than you do on domestic shares.

Most investors in foreign stocks confine themselves to American Depository Receipts (ADRs). These are receipts for the shares of a foreign-based corporation. They're sold in the United States and held in the vault of a U.S. bank. And they entitle the shareholder to all dividends and capital gains from the stock.

Most ADRs are sold over the counter, but a few are traded on the New York Stock Exchange. (Canadian stocks are traded freely in U.S. markets.) If you don't purchase ADRs, you must buy stock in overseas companies on foreign exchanges.

Look Before You Leap

No doubt about it. The stock market has rewarded investors with superior returns. Still, it isn't simple to make money in the market. Be cautious and learn as much as you can—about the market and individual stocks—before investing.

9 *Mutual Benefits*

Choosing the Best
Mutual Funds

*M*utual funds are far and away the most popular investment vehicle for most Americans. The popularity of these funds is not undeserved. They offer many advantages. You get expert management of your money, for one. Your money is handled by people who devote their full time and attention to the task.

You also get diversification. When you invest in a mutual fund, you purchase an interest in a multimillion-dollar securities portfolio.

And you get convenience. Putting money in a mutual fund is almost as easy as depositing money in your corner bank or savings and loan. Moreover, you can often switch investments from one mutual fund to another within a fund family with one telephone call.

Should you include mutual-fund shares in your portfolio? If so, how should you go about selecting a fund? The answers are provided in this chapter.

What Is a Mutual Fund?

Many investors include both *open-end mutual funds* and *closed-end companies* in their definition of mutual funds, although, technically, the two are different legal entities. Both, however, accumulate pools of money from investors and invest these dollars in a wide range of vehicles, such as domestic and foreign stocks, bonds, options, and money-market instruments.

Open-end companies constantly sell new shares and repurchase or redeem outstanding ones. So the amount of money under their management is always changing.

With closed-end companies, the amount of money under management is relatively fixed. These companies raise money as ordinary corporations do—through public offerings. Also, once they're issued, the shares of closed-end companies are traded just like any other stocks—on the New York or American stock exchange or over the counter.

Closed-end companies and mutual funds share one important characteristic: As we'll see, they can both be classified by their investment objectives.

The Price Is Right

If you look at your newspaper's listing of mutual funds, you'll see listed under the price the letters *NAV*, which stand for net asset value per share.

Net asset value per share is calculated by subtracting a fund's total liabilities from its total assets, then dividing the result by the number of shares outstanding.

Open-end funds usually sell or redeem their shares at NAV less any applicable redemption fees or deferred sales charges. But closed-end funds sell for an amount that is higher (that is, they carry a premium) or lower (they sell at a discount) than their NAV. It all depends on what the market thinks of the stock. Historically, most closed-end funds have traded at a discount.

In other words, the stock price of closed-end companies—like the stock price of other companies—is determined by supply and demand.

One other point to keep in mind: If you invest in either a closed-end or open-end fund, it is not the same as investing in, say, a bank certificate of deposit. With a CD, the amount of your principal won't fluctuate. With a mutual fund, there is no such guarantee.

Evaluating the Funds

The single most important criterion in evaluating a fund: its performance record. This record lets you compare how a fund you're considering stacks up against other funds with similar objectives.

No matter what kind of fund you choose, market professionals say you should not necessarily buy the hottest fund of the moment. The funds that do well when the market is rising often do poorly when it begins to fall.

Our advice: Look for funds that have been consistently good performers over the years—those that have done better than the broad stock indexes in both up and down market cycles. This consistency provides the best test of a fund's ability to handle money over the long term.

Caution: Past performance is one of your best objective indicators of how a fund will do. But always keep in mind that it does not guarantee future performance. And its usefulness as an indicator may diminish if conditions change—if, for example, the fund managers change.

Few Things in Life Are Free

Obviously, mutual-fund managers don't provide their services for free. The cost of operating a mutual fund, including management fees, is charged to the fund, reducing return on investment. In addition, some funds impose an initial sales charge (a front-end load), a deferred sales charge (a back-end load), and a redemption fee.

Since funds have different charges for buying, holding, and redeeming shares, it makes sense to find out about a fund's fee structure before you invest.

The best sources of information on charges: the fund's prospectus and a supplementary document known as the "Statement of Additional Information." Ask for a copy of both, as well as the latest annual and interim reports to shareholders.

Here's a checklist of the fees you may encounter.

Annual Expenses

The managing expenses of a fund, including its management fee, are paid for by the fund. These charges generally add up to 0.5 to 1.5 percent of the value of your fund shares.

You'll find these expenses described in the fund's prospectus. You'll also see prior years' costs as a percentage of net assets and on a per share basis.

Front-End Loads

When you buy mutual-fund shares from a stockbroker or other salesperson, you might pay a *front-end load*—that is, a commission on the shares you purchase.

Here's an example. Say you instruct your stockbroker to invest $3,000 in a mutual fund whose shares have a net asset value of $50 each.

Your $3,000 will get you 60 shares, right? Wrong.

To purchase shares in some funds, you pay an initial sales charge, which is levied on the total amount you invest. In this case, the sales charge is 8.5 percent and adds up to $255. So only $2,745 of your money actually goes to purchase shares.

If you buy more shares in the same fund from a broker or salesperson, chances are you will pay a reduced sales commission. The reason: Many funds offer discounts on sales charges, based on the total dollars you invest.

Because of the sales commissions many investors steer clear of load funds and opt instead for low-load and no-load funds. You usually buy shares in these funds directly from the mutual-fund company or its sponsor.

With low-load funds, expect to pay an initial sales charge of 0.5 percent to 4.5 percent. No-load funds levy no sales charges, but a few impose a redemption fee of 1.0 percent.

You should know that there is no evidence that load funds perform any better than low-load or no-load funds. So unless you have a reason for buying a load fund—you need investment advice, say—purchase directly from the fund or its sponsor and save on commissions.

Another tip: In deciding whether to opt for a load, low-load, or no-load fund, consider how long you plan to tie up your money.

If you intend to put your money in a fund for only a short time—a year or less, say—consider a low-load or no-load fund. Why? A load fund has to earn a higher total return to perform as well as a no-load fund. And the shorter the time frame, the more difficult it is to achieve this return.

Back-End Loads

Some funds impose back-end loads or contingent deferred sales charges when you take your money out. These fees vary widely but are usually based on how long you hold your shares. For example, if you pull out in the first year of your investment, you pay more than if you pull out after four years.

Funds that impose back-end loads typically charge 6 percent if you withdraw your money within one year. This percentage usually decreases 1 percent each year until it reaches zero after six years. Since back-end loads decrease over time, they usually are less than front-end loads. Often they are combined with 12b-1 fees.

12b-1 Fees

Many of the mutual funds now on the market that charge no front-end load or a low load levy an annual 12b-1 fee. This fee takes its prosaic name from the Securities and Exchange Commission rule that allows its use. It may be used by the fund sponsor to cover the cost of compensating salespeople and advertising the fund.

Front-End Loads or 12b-1 fees

Many mutual funds now offer investors a choice: You can pay a front-end load or pay the 12b-1 fee. Paying the front-end load may make sense if you're investing a large sum. That way, you'll pay a lower percentage load.

Choosing to pay the 12b-1 fee, by contrast, might be more appropriate for you if you prefer to pay "over time" and do not mind paying more in total dollars in exchange for the privilege.

All in the Family

A *mutual-fund family* is a group of two or more mutual funds under the auspices of the same sponsor organization. In most cases, the goals of the funds differ. For example, one may be a growth fund, the other an income fund.

One reason to invest with a fund family is convenience. With a family, you can move your money from one investment vehicle to another—sometimes with no more than a telephone call—as you expect market conditions to change. For example, if you expect the market to turn down, you can transfer money from, say, a growth stock fund to a bond fund or even to a money-market fund.

Another advantage to a family: If you've invested in a fund that originally charged a front-end load, you usually don't have to pay another sales charge if you transfer to another fund in the same family. However, you may have to pay an exchange fee. And some fund families limit the number of transfers you can make.

Investment by Objective

The funds you choose will depend—among other factors—on your career, financial situation, and family obligations. You need to ask yourself the same questions before investing in mutual funds as you do when you make any investment.

For example, you should consider what your financial commitments will be in the future for college costs, retirement, and other necessities. Can you afford to take some risks now, or is preserving your money more important to you?

Once you have answered these questions, look for investments that suit your needs. Fortunately, doing so isn't very difficult. Mutual funds offer an increasingly broad range of choices to meet investment objectives.

You can buy aggressive but risky funds that aim for maximum appreciation of capital. Or you can purchase conservative funds that are structured to minimize the risk to your principal.

You can purchase mutual funds that invest in common stocks, preferred stocks, or convertible securities—or those that invest in U.S. government or state and municipal bonds. And you can buy funds that match your conscience: Some fund managers exclude certain investments from their portfolios for political, social, or ecological reasons.

Specifically, you may purchase stock funds that aim for aggressive growth, steady growth, or growth and regular income. Or you may buy a fund that purchases only international stocks or stocks in specialized industries.

Among bond funds you may choose U.S. government bond funds, mortgage or Government National Mortgage Association (GNMA) funds, high-grade corporate bond funds, high yield funds, and municipal bond funds that are free of federal tax and sometimes state and local taxes.

Your choice of a mutual fund depends very much on your goals and objectives. Here are some of the kinds of mutual funds in which you may want to invest.

Income Funds

Income funds invest primarily—if not exclusively—in stocks that pay healthy dividends. So managers of these funds put your money into the shares of companies in mature industries. Because these funds are among the least risky you can buy, they fit nicely into more conservative portfolios. (See Chapter 8 for more information about income stocks.)

Growth-and-Income Funds

Growth-and-income funds buy stocks that pay a dividend and have reasonable potential for growth.

Growth-and-income funds make sense if your tolerance for risk is low, and you want a relatively stable return. They also make sense if you need some income to pay current expenses but also want to finance long-term goals and objectives. (You'll find more information about growth-and-income stocks in Chapter 8.)

Growth Funds

Growth funds are somewhat riskier than growth-and-income funds, because their return is primarily based on future growth, rather than current yield. They usually provide some dividend income, albeit a small amount.

These funds can help you build capital for the future—as long as you're prepared to take the risk of losing some of the principal that you invest.

So opt for growth funds if your tolerance for risk is high, and you don't need current income from your investments. (For more about growth stocks, turn to Chapter 8.)

Aggressive Growth Funds

Aggressive growth funds are among the riskiest you can buy. Managers of these funds have as their aim maximizing capital gains. So they invest in stocks of growth companies that pay few or no dividends.

As a rule, stocks of these companies go through wide swings in price. Consequently, this type of fund generally performs very well during an up market, but exposes you to greater risk than do more conservative funds when the market heads down.

Also, managers of aggressive growth funds may buy and sell stocks more often than managers of more conservative funds. Since *portfolio turnover*—the percentage of a fund's assets that are bought or sold each year—is high, brokerage costs are also high.

Moreover, many of these funds generally stay fully invested in the market. They may not, for instance, put their assets in money-market investments even if they expect the market to head south. If the market does turn down, you could sustain a heavy loss.

(See Chapter 8 for more about aggressive growth stocks.)

Sector Funds

Sector funds specialize in buying shares of companies in one particular segment of the economy. Examples include technology funds, health-product funds, leisure funds, and so forth. The idea for investors: Switch into different sector funds, depending on which segment of the economy you think will be "hot."

Worldwide Funds

These funds let U.S. investors tap into the world economy. Among these funds: global funds, which buy stocks and bonds of companies from around the world, including the United States; international funds, which exclude U.S. companies; regional funds that specialize in one area of the world—the Pacific Basin, say; and country funds that specialize in the stocks and/or bonds of companies in one country.

Money-Market Funds

Money-market funds use their shareholders' money to invest in a variety of short-term securities earning market rates of interest. The funds' operating expenses include a management fee—usually ranging from 0.50 to 0.75 percent of the fund's average net assets.

Money-market funds are somewhat similar to a bank account. There are usually no capital gains or losses. If you put $1,000 in, you would expect to get $1,000 out—plus the earnings of the fund after expenses. (See Chapter 6 for the details on money-market funds.)

Fixed-Income Funds

These funds invest in bonds and preferred stocks. Some funds invest solely in municipal bonds, so you don't usually have to pay federal income taxes on the income you receive. (See Chapter 7 for more information on bonds.)

Balanced Funds

Balanced funds attempt to give you the best of all worlds. They invest for both current income and long-term capital appreciation.

To achieve this end, managers put money into a variety of investment vehicles—from common stocks and bonds to money-market instruments. You should evaluate these funds on the basis of their *total return*—that is, the combined return from current income and capital appreciation or depreciation.

Asset-Allocation Funds

These funds may invest in equities, fixed-income securities, and money-market instruments. The mix depends on how the investment manager views the outlook for economic and securities markets worldwide.

Precious Metal Funds

Many of these funds limit their investments to shares in companies that mine gold and other precious metals. (See Chapter 13 for more information on investing in precious metals.)

Dollar-Cost Averaging

Whatever types of funds you choose, consider following dollar-cost averaging. As you saw in Chapter 8, with this method you put an equal amount of money into the fund at regular intervals, once a month, say. That way, you buy some shares when prices are high and some when prices are low.

Some people prefer dollar-cost averaging to plunking down a large sum of money when they think the market is low. Here's why: When you follow the latter course, you're attempting to time the market's highs and lows, and it's the rare individual who can consistently predict those.

Cashing Out

Deciding when to pull your money out of a fund is more difficult than deciding when to put your money in. Our advice: Hold your shares as long as the fund is meeting your objectives.

Let's look at the reasons for cashing out.

First, you may want to switch investments as your tolerance for risk changes. For example, as you get older, you may not be able to afford to take as many chances with your money. So you may want to move from a growth fund to an income fund.

Other reasons for changing funds: a change in fund managers, an increase in fees, or maybe even the size of the fund (you think it's grown too large or isn't large enough). Still another reason: Your investment objectives shift, so the fund's mix of assets is no longer right for you.

Or maybe your mutual fund isn't performing as well as it has in the past. You can get a better return elsewhere, so you take your money and invest it in another fund that meets your investment objectives.

Timing Is Everything

You made a handsome profit with your mutual fund. And now you're ready to take some of your money out. How do you go about it?

The prospectus for your fund will tell you. Some funds require no more than a telephone call—a plus, since you can cash out precisely when you want to. But most require that you put your request in writing. If your fund does allow telephone redemptions, you must make arrangements in advance. The alternative is to put your request in writing.

If you want to redeem shares by mail, simply send a letter to the fund's *transfer agent*. This is the organization—in most cases, a bank—

that the fund designates to handle and keep track of all its shareholder transactions.

The letter should include the name of the fund, your account number, the number of shares or dollars you want redeemed, and where the check should be sent. There are sometimes additional requirements if you want the check sent to an address other than your address of record. There may also be other requirements if you actually hold certificates.

You may also request—either by telephone or in writing—that the fund wire the money directly to your bank account. If you want this service, you must provide the transfer agent with your bank account number and the bank's wire number. Be prepared to pay a wire-service fee of about $5 to $15.

Another point: Most funds require that written requests include your signature. Not only must you sign the request, but you must have your signature guaranteed for authenticity by a trust company, a federally insured commercial bank, or a brokerage firm that is a member of a major stock exchange. Institutions usually guarantee signatures free of charge for account holders. The idea, of course, is to prevent fraud.

If you write, send your letter by registered mail, return receipt requested. That way, you'll know when the transfer agent received it. And you can make sure that your shares were redeemed on the proper date.

In most cases, the transfer agent sends your money to you the day after your shares are redeemed. But some funds take longer. And, in fact, the Securities and Exchange Commission allows funds to take up to seven days to pay.

Tip: If you redeem only a portion of your shares, be sure to specify which shares you are selling—the ones you bought at $20 a share, say, or the ones at $25.

Uncle Sam taxes you on your gain. And he assumes that the shares you sell are the first shares you bought unless you specify otherwise.

Our advice: Reduce your tax bill by first selling your highest-cost shares. If you follow this strategy, save all your fund statements and redemption slips in case you are audited.

Variety Is the Spice of Life

As you can see, mutual funds give you almost unlimited choice in investment vehicles—or combinations of vehicles. And they offer the added benefits of diversified portfolios and professional management of your money. These are the reasons most investors use funds to carry out at least a portion of their asset-allocation strategy. You should, too.

10 *The Good Earth*

How to Invest in
Real Estate

*I*f you're like many people, you like the idea of investing in real estate: It's an asset you can see and touch.

But the growing array of real-estate vehicles can make investment decisions seem overwhelming. Is real estate right for your portfolio? And, if so, what kind?

Let's take a look.

What Are Your Options?

There are three principal ways you can invest in real estate. First, you can invest in securities of real-estate companies—via real-estate investment trusts, say.

The second way to invest in real estate is through real-estate syndications—that is, partnerships that are formed to buy and manage properties.

The third way is through direct investment. In other words, you purchase residential rental property or commercial real estate on your own.

What is most important is not the type of vehicle, but the property itself. And where property is concerned, the most critical characteristics are "location, location, location" and "price, price, price."

To reduce your risk, you should make sure that the people managing your potential investment have good track records. Check their credentials before you fork over your hard-earned dollars.

The bottom line: Whether you purchase securities, buy a partnership interest, or invest directly, you should look for good properties and experienced management.

What else should you know? Read on.

Securities of Real-Estate Companies

If you decide to invest in the securities of real-estate companies, your options are to put your money into real-estate investment trusts (REITs), real-estate mutual funds, real-estate mortgage investment conduits (REMICs), or master limited partnerships (MLPs).

Let's take a look at each of these vehicles.

Real-Estate Investment Trusts

Real-estate investment trusts combine the best features of the Wall Street stock market with Main Street's realty markets.

These are liquid investments traded daily on the stock exchanges. But they also offer all the benefits of otherwise illiquid income-producing real estate.

Here's how they work.

Investing in a REIT is similar to investing in a mutual fund. You pool your money with that of other investors to buy and/or finance income-producing properties, such as office buildings.

Rental income from these properties goes to the REIT to pay its expenses. The remainder goes to you in the form of dividends. So does the interest the REIT may receive from any mortgages it writes. (Some REITs—known as mortgage REITs—take investors' funds and write mortgages. In effect, they act as bankers—charging interest to owners for use of the funds and distributing the net income to the REIT investors.)

Gains from the sale of properties are also passed along to you as dividends. As dividends increase, so usually does the price of your REIT shares, but share prices could fluctuate due to interest rate changes, expectations for earnings, and other factors.

Through the combination of dividends and price appreciation, REITs can reward investors with an average total return of 6 to 8 percent annually. But beware: As you might expect, REITs are not always this successful.

One large REIT, for instance, invested heavily in real estate in oil-producing states. When real-estate prices there plummeted, the REIT collapsed. The result: Investors may have lost every penny. Again, what matters in real-estate investments are the underlying properties.

Most REIT shares are easy to buy and sell. You do it the same way you buy and sell shares of corporate stock—through a broker.

About a third of all REITs are listed on the New York and American stock exchanges. The rest are traded over the counter. The price per share averages less than $30.

The biggest advantage of many REITs over other forms of real-estate investing: liquidity. Usually, you may sell your shares at any time, but the price you receive may vary considerably with the market value of underlying assets. So REITs are, for the most part, a very liquid way of investing in a traditionally illiquid asset. Also, REITs usually allow you to spread your risk by buying into a diverse portfolio of properties.

So if you have limited assets, need liquidity, and think real estate is a sound investment, REITs may be for you.

If you decide to put some of your investment dollars in a REIT, you may choose among three basic types: equity, finite-life, and mortgage.

Let's look at the pluses and minuses of each.

Equity REITs
Equity REITs own a variety of properties: shopping centers, office buildings, apartment houses, warehouses, even horse-racing courses. Most REITs specialize in one or two types.

A handful of equity REITs, however, are so-called *blind pools*—that is, they own no properties at the time of the initial offering. The trusts often take a year to complete their acquisitions, and they keep shareholders' money in money-market funds until then. Also, once the initial offering is completed, REIT share prices tend to drop to make up for the front-end costs of raising capital.

You should be cautious in investing in a blind pool. But if you have confidence in the trust's managers, you shouldn't necessarily avoid them.

The prospectus—which you should read carefully before investing in *any* new offering—will tell you if the REIT you're considering is a blind pool.

Some equity REITs pass along to their shareholders the interest they make on mortgages, plus the rents they collect. Others use these funds to buy more properties.

Usually, you're better off buying older equity REITs than newer ones. The reason: You have properties that are producing income, and management is experienced; so, the income stream and resulting dividend are easier to predict. Also, the first investors in REITs pay hefty set-up fees. If you buy shares later on, you may have to pay broker's commissions, but you bypass these start-up costs. That's why share prices tend to "settle" after the initial offering.

Finite-Life REITs

Introduced in 1974, finite-life REITs (FREITs) were created to solve a problem with real-estate trusts—that is, the discount in the price of the shares from the trust's appraised value.

Conventional trusts keep buying and selling properties, but they never fully liquidate their portfolios. So investors treat a trust's appraised value as a promise instead of a reality, and they do not pay face value for the holdings.

Finite-life REITs have a deadline—usually ten to fifteen years—for selling all their properties and distributing the gains to shareholders. As the trust nears its liquidation date, the price of the stock should rise—a reflection of the value of the properties that will soon be sold.

You should know, though, that the trustees can change liquidation dates in order to keep the trust from having to sell properties in a down market. So the shares may keep selling at a discount.

Mortgage REITs

Mortgage REITs specialize in making mortgage loans. There are, however, variations on this theme. For example, we know of one small REIT that concentrates on making second mortgages on homes. Another specializes in wraparound mortgages.

Mortgage REITs perform just like other interest-sensitive stocks. When interest rates fall, share prices rise, and vice versa.

Because mortgage REITs pay fat dividends, they're good candidates for IRA and Keogh investments, but they do carry the risk of defaulting.

Real-Estate Mutual Funds

Real-estate mutual funds primarily hold shares of REITs and other real-estate related companies. Like other mutual funds, they offer liquidity, diversification, professional management, and, generally, the backing of a financial institution that the public is familiar with and can trust. They offer other advantages as well, including relatively low sales charges, compared to a typical limited partnership purchased through a broker, a small minimum investment ($100 to $2,500), and similar yields to REITs.

Real-Estate Mortgage Investment Conduits

The REMIC—an acronym for real-estate mortgage investment conduit—is a brand-new investment vehicle authorized by the 1986 Tax Reform Act.

When our legislators created the REMIC, their idea was to make it the vehicle for issuers of mortgage-backed securities. In other words, the REMIC would replace the old collateralized mortgage obligations, or—as they are sometimes known—CMOs.

CMOs are similar to mortgage-backed securities, such as those backed by the Government National Mortgage Association (Ginnie Mae). But, unlike Ginnie Maes, CMOs are subject to double taxation. That is, Uncle Sam treats the interest paid on the underlying mortgages as income to both the issuer *and* the investor.

Enter REMICs.

With the REMIC, Congress eliminated the double taxation problem by treating the security issuer as simply a conduit. Think of a partnership or an S corporation, both of which pass income and losses directly through to partners or shareholders without paying any tax themselves. That's how REMICs work, too.

But—a word of caution—REMICs can also produce disadvantages for investors. Because they are so flexible, issuers may use them to design riskier investments. With a REMIC, as with other securities, make sure you know what you're buying.

Master Limited Partnerships

Still another way to invest in real estate is through a master limited partnership (MLP).

MLPs—like any other limited partnerships—are subject to no separate federal income tax. Profits (and losses) are reported on the individual returns of their partners. But MLPs—unlike other limited partnerships—are traded on a securities exchange.

So MLPs combine the tax attributes of limited partnerships and the liquidity of stocks and bonds. A good deal, you say, and you're right. Unfortunately, this good deal also caught the attention of the IRS. As a result, Uncle Sam changed the rules. He now taxes publicly traded partnerships formed after December 17, 1987, as corporations. And that means partners in these entities may no longer report their share of profits and losses on their individual returns.

The good news? The IRS carved out an exception to these corporate treatment rules. Say 90 percent of the partnership's gross income comes from interest, dividends, gains from the sale of capital assets, gains from the sale of certain trade or business assets, income or gains from certain oil and gas activities, and real-estate rents. In this case, the IRS still treats the MLP as a partnership.

Real-Estate Syndications

Real-estate syndications, or real-estate limited partnerships, still may make good investments—even with the advent of the 1986 Tax Reform Act, which sharply curtailed the use of passive losses from tax shelters. (See Chapter 11 for more on passive investments.)

Real-estate syndications, like real-estate investment trusts, may invest in a host of properties—hotels, motels, office buildings, nursing homes, and so on.

Their advantages: They offer most of the benefits of owning real estate, including tax breaks. But you escape the burden of managing the property and the personal liabilities of an owner.

Still, real-estate syndications are limited partnerships. And when you invest in a limited partnership, you often turn your dollars over to someone else to manage for five or more years.

Real-estate limited partnerships come in two forms: those designed to produce income and growth and those geared toward producing tax deductions. The safest and only ones that really make sense today? Those designed to produce income and capital appreciation.

Partnerships generally are riskier than REITs, because of the lack of liquidity and lack of diversification. With partnerships, you get current income and a good possibility of price appreciation when the partnership sells out. (Watch out, though, for fees at both the front and the back end—fees the sponsors take to organize the syndication and to participate in any profits when the property is sold. These costs, which you can find out about in the prospectus, can amount to 15 to 50 percent of the selling price.)

Income syndications often buy properties with cash, instead of financing their purchases with mortgages. So, because there is no leverage, there is no related debt service. The result: income rather than a loss. And these partnerships can also generate partially tax-free income.

Here's how. Say your share in a limited partnership produces revenues of $10,000, expenses of $7,000, and depreciation of $3,000. For tax purposes, the partnership breaks even. But for cash purposes, you post a $3,000 profit.

Should you choose a REIT over an income-oriented syndication? There's something to be said for both investments.

Some REITs carry low management fees (the fees are included in the syndication or REIT per-share price). And, of course, REITs are generally liquid.

The advantages of syndications: Their return is based on the underlying value of the property. So they generally aren't affected by the vagaries of the stock market. And they can shelter some cash flow or pass along any tax losses to investors (subject to the passive loss limitations we discuss in Chapter 11).

If you want to test the waters—and can afford it—you should carefully study the syndicator's track record. The offering prospectus will contain this information.

What if you want out early?

Traditionally, you had to get permission to sell from the general partner. And the market for limited partnership interests was thin.

But in recent years, a secondary market for these partnerships has developed. So getting out is easier.

One reason for the growth in the secondary market for partnerships: volume. Americans invested more than $53.7 billion in partnerships in the three years ending in 1986. That's more than was invested in the previous thirteen years.

Another reason is investor disenchantment. A soft real-estate market and a few bankruptcies have made some investors skittish about partnerships.

Be aware, though: As we've seen, the partnerships with the best potential for resale are those structured to generate income, not tax deductions.

One way to sell a real-estate partnership interest is the same way you buy one: through your stockbroker. Also, the syndicator of the partnership may purchase your interest back from you. Or another partner may be interested in boosting his or her stake.

But take care. If you sell your limited partnership interest, don't expect to get back what you paid. You could make a bundle, or you could get nothing. A rule of thumb: Count yourself lucky if you get back as much as 50 to 75 percent of its value.

Also, you probably need to enlist an accountant or investment adviser to help you calculate the value of your "used" partnership.

Direct Ownership

Let's face it. Not everyone is cut out to be a landlord. Many people have neither the time nor the temperament to cope with dripping faucets and broken windows.

And making money buying and selling properties isn't the "sure thing" it was in many locations just a few years ago. True, some markets, such as southern California, seem to head in only one direction—up. However, most real estate markets are cyclical. The Northeast is generally strong, for example, although metropolitan New York and Boston properties are not increasing at the rate of previous years and are even "soft" in some areas. Houston, which in recent years has been a case study in the ability of real-estate values to decline, is now clearly in a recovery mode. The message is clear: Don't buy assuming your principal is guaranteed and, if possible, be prepared to ride out the cycle.

Having said that, we should also point out that buying and selling property directly can still yield the biggest rewards for investors—if you're in the right place at the right time. Just be aware that direct ownership also entails the biggest risks.

For instance, you buy a small apartment building. You figure the rents you collect will pay off your mortgage. A few years down the road, you'll sell the building at a profit.

How can you lose? Easily.

For one, a number of factors—an increase in supply over demand, say—may suddenly cause rents in your area to plummet. But you must still pay off your mortgage. And that cash will come out of your own pocket.

Because real estate is such a risky and time-consuming proposition, it's a good idea not to go into it alone. In fact, only if you have plenty of cash to spend on repairs and ample time to devote to details, such as faulty plumbing, should you try direct ownership.

And you should go in with realistic expectations. Many people who buy apartments or houses lose money. They find their rental income just isn't enough to cover mortgage payments, so they need the added plus of tax breaks just to come out even.

And the tax breaks for rental property are a lot less favorable now. (We cover the tax benefits of real-estate ownership in Chapter 11 and the vacation home rules in Chapter 12.)

How do you figure out if a real-estate deal is a good one? And what should you look for in valuing property? Here are some ideas.

Never—and we mean never—buy real estate without studying the market where you plan to buy. For instance, in some areas of the country, condominiums are strictly a losing proposition. In other locations, they sell briskly. Ideally, you should live in an area for several years or research it thoroughly before you even consider purchasing property there. A firm grasp of local conditions can prevent you from making costly mistakes.

Another tip: Try to purchase property that is close to shops, schools, entertainment, and public transportation. Keep in mind, too, another traditional rule of thumb. It's better to buy the worst house in the best neighborhood than the best house in the worst neighborhood.

Also, make sure your property generates enough current income to cover your debt and provides good potential for long-term appreciation.

Some people say that if you purchase an apartment building with fewer than five units, you're not making an investment—you're buying a job. Also the more apartments a building contains, the lower the risk due to vacancies. For example, you lose less on a percentage basis if one of six apartments stands empty than if one of two apartments goes unrented.

And, of course, have the property inspected by experts for structural, termite, or any other damage before you buy. You need to know how well the current owners maintained the property. Are the heating and cooling systems and kitchen appliances all in good working order?

The fact is, if you're in for major repairs, you need to know before you plunk your money down. Also, if major repairs *are* needed, you may negotiate a lower purchase price. Inspectors charge no more than $100 to $200. And it is money well spent.

Farms and Ranches

Before investing in a farm or ranch, you ought to consider this fact: There are more than 2 million farms and ranches of every conceivable kind in the United States. There is irrigated cultivation and dry land cultivation, row crop or permanent crop farming, grazing livestock or concentrated livestock, and combinations of crop and livestock.

The point is, you can't just invest in agriculture. You have to decide what kind is right for you. So let's discuss some factors that you ought to consider.

Land has traditionally served as an inflationary hedge. During the 1970s, for instance, land values increased by more than 200 percent across the country, while consumer prices rose by 100 percent. So given a stable economic climate, continuing growth in world demand for food products, and sustained inflationary pressure, farm and ranch land should prove an attractive investment for preserving capital.

But to realize any income from an agricultural investment, you've got to sell the product. Skill in marketing farm commodities—an extremely sophisticated process—usually determines the difference between profit or loss.

Another point to consider: Farm and ranch land is not highly liquid.

So you have to think of it as a long-term investment. You don't want to be forced into a fire sale when land prices, for whatever reason, are down.

Moreover, unlike most paper securities, your agricultural investment is subject to risks such as floods, drought, disease, and insect pests. Good management for your property—often the exception rather than the rule in agriculture—is absolutely essential. If you aren't a knowledgeable manager yourself, you'll need a highly skilled, capable operator.

We don't mean to be discouraging—just realistic instead of romantic about what's involved in making a profitable farm investment.

This Land Is My Land

Another option for real-estate investors: undeveloped, or underdeveloped, land. By *undeveloped*, we don't necessarily mean that the land is unused now—although it could be. But it might also be farmland or woodland.

Undeveloped, or underdeveloped, land is simply acreage that—as far as investors are concerned—is not currently put to its best potential use. To be useful as an investment, the land should have the potential for development or subdivision within a reasonable time frame—say, ten years or so.

One disadvantage to this type of investment: the absence of any current cash return during the time you own the land.

Of course, you may be able to rent farm parcels while you're awaiting development, but this type of property rarely brings an annual rent of more than 5 percent of its market value. That return might pay the taxes, but it won't create a good cash flow.

And sometimes the sale of timber, mineral rights, hunting rights, easements, and other "partial" interests may also help offset your property tax payments and interest expenses.

Many Happy Returns

Now you know some real-estate investment basics. And, chances are, some of you want to know more. So let's take a look at the tax advantages of real-estate ownership.

11 Write It Off, Write It All Off

The Tax Benefits of Real-Estate Ownership

*T*he major lures of a real-estate investment are current income and the possibility that your property will dramatically appreciate in value. But the tax benefits are inviting, too.

By reducing your income through deductions—and paying less in taxes—you increase the total return on your investment.

What may you still write off, since the 1986 Tax Reform Act changed the rules of the game? Here is a rundown.

When a House Is Not a Home

When you purchase investment property—an apartment building, say—the government allows you to write off the cost of that property over a specified number of years. This gradual write-off is known as *depreciation*.

The 1986 Tax Reform Act stretched out the time required to write off investments in residential rental property and commercial real estate. Under the old law, you deducted a portion of the cost of your investment property each year for 19.0 years using an accelerated method of depreciation. Under the current law, you write off residential rental property over 27.5 years and commercial real estate over 31.5 years under the straight-line method of depreciation.

What's the difference? Under the accelerated method, depreciation deductions were speeded up, so you received larger write-offs during the early years of ownership. The straight-line method is less favorable. Under it, depreciation deductions remain the same each year.

Wearing Away

Depreciation is—by definition—a tax deduction you take for the effects of decay, corrosion, and wear and tear. Since land does not decay—at least not in the eyes of the IRS—the law allows you to write off only the price of buildings, not the cost of the land on which they stand.

When can you begin claiming your depreciation deductions? Uncle Sam won't permit you to depreciate property until it's either on the rental market or, in the case of a factory, say, ready for use. So the answer depends, in part, on when your building is—in IRS lingo—"placed in service."

For example, you build a small office building. The price tag: $400,000—$315,000 for construction of the building and $85,000 for the land.

You put the building on the rental market on March 1. A reasonable person, you assume that you calculate your depreciation deductions from that date. Wrong. The law mandates that you treat the property as if you'd placed it in service in the middle of the month.

This rule for investment property—known as the *midmonth convention*—applies to both residential and commercial rental property.

It requires you to figure your depreciation deduction in the first year of ownership by adding up the number of months the property was actually placed in service. And, for the first month, the law considers all real estate as placed in service in the middle of the month.

What does this rule mean to you? You started leasing the building in March. So you're entitled to nine and one-half months of depreciation for the first year.

Your deduction adds up to $7,917—that is, the building's cost of $315,000 divided by 31.5 years, with the result multiplied by the fraction 9.5 months over 12.0 months.

Tip: The law also allows investors to depreciate residential rental property and commercial real estate over 40 years. At first glance, this method seems far less desirable than using either the 27.5- or 31.5-year depreciation periods. After all, you get to write off much less each year. But it can have an advantage for investors, specifically those subject to the alternative minimum tax (AMT).

Uncle Sam levies the AMT on those who pay little or no tax despite their high incomes. As a rule, the more depreciation and other deductions you claim to drive down your taxable income, the more likely you are to be subject to the AMT, a flat tax of 21 percent.

If you use the 40-year method, depreciation deductions aren't added back to your income when you calculate your AMT liability.

(See Chapters 25 and 26 for more on the AMT.)

At Your Expense

Investors in real estate—like homeowners—may deduct mortgage interest. But homeowners may write off interest on only their principal residence and one other house. As an investor, you are subject to no such limit. You may deduct mortgage interest on as many pieces of property as you like. But—as you'll see next—you are bound by some restrictions.

Outer Limits

In the old days, the amount you could write off in rental losses—chiefly resulting from mortgage interest, depreciation, repair costs, utility bills, and so on—was unrestricted. But now the amount may be limited by the passive loss rules.

These rules say that you may deduct passive losses only from passive income. What's passive income? Income from real-estate investments generally meets the test. And so does income from limited partnerships. But dividends and interest do not—even though the dictionary may define this type of income as passive.

The good news: Uncle Sam will phase in this rule gradually for investments made before October 22, 1986. Even if your passive losses exceed your passive income, you may still deduct a portion of them during the phase-in period.

In 1989, you could still deduct from your regular income 20 percent of the excess passive losses over your passive income. You may write off 10 percent in 1990—but zero in 1991.

However, you may carry forward any excess passive losses—that is, passive losses you are unable to deduct currently—to succeeding years. You use these carryforward amounts to offset future passive income.

As we've emphasized, you may deduct passive losses only from passive income. But the law makes one exception when it comes to rental property. You may deduct losses that add up to more than your passive income—up to $25,000 from your ordinary income if you meet these two requirements: You actively participate in the management of the property, and your income falls within certain limits.

Under the rules, you actively participate if you have at least a 10 percent ownership stake in the property and are involved in management decisions in a bona fide way.

To participate in a bona fide way, Uncle Sam says, you must approve tenants, establish rental terms, and approve expenditures. If you make these important decisions, the government doesn't care if you use a rental agent to carry them out for you.

What happens, however, if you don't actively participate in the management of the property? You may not deduct losses up to $25,000 from your regular income. You may deduct rental losses only from income generated by other passive investments.

The other limit on passive loss deductions depends on your income. As it goes up, the amount of loss you may claim on rental property goes down. Here's how:

- You may write off as much as $25,000 in losses on your rental property if your adjusted gross income (AGI) is less than $100,000.
- You must reduce the amount of the $25,000 cap by 50 percent of the amount by which your AGI exceeds $100,000.

Your AGI—for purposes of the cap—is total income before you subtract any rental or other passive losses or your itemized deductions.

Say, in October 1990, you and your spouse buy a small house that you rent out yourselves. In your first year of ownership, you run up a $25,000 rental loss. How much may you write off?

As we've seen, if your AGI is less than $100,000, you may deduct $25,000 in rental losses as long as you actively participate in rental operations.

But if your adjusted gross income totals more than $100,000, your deduction begins to phase out. And, once your income tops $150,000, it disappears entirely. (For single people, the same limit applies as for a married couple filing jointly. For married couples filing separately, these levels are cut in half.)

How does the phase-out work?

Say your AGI for the year adds up to $130,000. You subtract the $100,000 income ceiling from your $130,000 AGI to get $30,000. Next, you multiply 50 percent times $30,000 and subtract this amount—$15,000— from $25,000.

The result: You may write off only $10,000 of your real-estate rental loss.

When it comes to rental real estate, Uncle Sam makes some exceptions to the active-participation rules we just discussed.

What happens if you meet one of the exceptions? Strange as it may seem, the IRS no longer considers the activity a rental activity. And that means you don't get to use the $25,000 loss allowance. Instead, you must apply the material participation tests to see if the activity is passive. If you meet the tests—that is, if you are involved in the activity on "a regular, sustained, and continuous basis," your activity is not considered passive, and your losses aren't limited.

The exceptions?

- You rent your property for an average period of seven days or less.

    This exception means most hotels and motels are exempt from the rental property rules. Also, say you own a mountain getaway that you rent for an average of less than seven days. Your vacation house no longer qualifies as rental property.

- Your average rental period is 30 days or less and you or an employee provides "significant personal services" to rental customers.

   For example, you would meet this exception if you ran a bed and breakfast where the average rental period is 20 days, and you hire a manager who cooks and cleans for your guests. (You should know that significant personal services don't include maintenance, routine repair, trash collection, and security.)

- You make the property available free of charge to a partnership or S corporation in which you're a material participant.

   Say, though, you charge the S corporation or partnership rent. In this case, says Uncle Sam, the rental income is nonpassive, but losses from the property qualify as passive.

Here's another helpful rule. Say you own and rent a vacation house. But you also live in the house part of the year. In this situation, you don't fall under the passive activity rules. Rather, your deductions are subject to the limitations we discuss in Chapter 12. That's because the vacation home rules supersede the passive activity rules.

As these exceptions and rules show, you must examine thoroughly the way you rent real estate. If you're uncertain which rules apply in this complicated area, you should consult with your tax adviser.

Are You at Risk?

Real estate, just like other investments, is now subject to the government's strict at-risk rules. These regulations further limit the amount of losses you may write off. The at-risk rules dictate that your deductions may not top the total of

- Your cash contributions to your real-estate business
- The adjusted basis (cost minus depreciation) of your property contributions to the business

- Any amount you borrowed for the business—but only if you have personal liability for the debt or pledge personal assets as security

However, the rules make an exception for "qualified nonrecourse financing"—financing secured only by the property itself. If the property is financed with qualified nonrecourse financing, the amount of losses you may claim is increased by the amount of the financing.

Say, for example, that you buy a building. You put $25,000 down and finance $75,000 using a qualified nonrecourse loan. You may write off losses up to $100,000—that is, the amount of your down payment plus the loan amount.

Credit Where Credit Is Due

Two real-estate investments that can pay off particularly handsomely are older buildings and low-income housing projects. Here's the reason: The law grants sizable tax credits to people who rehabilitate old buildings and invest in low-income projects.

But here's the kicker. You may use these credits only to offset taxes on passive income—not to offset taxes on ordinary income, such as salary or dividends.

However, the law does give you one break. It says that you may use these credits to offset the tax on up to $25,000 of ordinary or nonpassive income. And this rule holds true regardless of whether you actively participate in the management of the property.

To qualify fully for this break, your AGI must add up to less than $200,000. The benefit of this $25,000 break is phased out between $200,000 and $250,000 of AGI.

So, once your AGI reaches $250,000, the special dispensation is gone. And you may use the credits only to offset taxes on passive income.

However, for low income housing property placed in service after 1989, the phaseout of the $25,000 break doesn't apply. In other words, even if your AGI exceeds $250,000, you may still claim low-income housing credits to offset the tax on up to $25,000 of your ordinary income.

What happens if you claim both the rehabilitation and low-income housing credits and are not subject to the phaseout of the $25,000 allowance? You may use the credits to offset taxes on only up to $25,000 of income—not $50,000.

There's also another obstacle to overcome—an upper limit on general business credits you claim. The rehabilitation and low-income housing credits both qualify as general business credits. The ceiling on the amount of business credits you may claim is $25,000 plus 75 percent of any tax you owe over $25,000.

Moreover, you qualify for the credit only if the amount you spend on rehabilitation tops $5,000 or the "adjusted basis" of the building, whichever is greater. How does the law define the adjusted basis? This is the amount you pay for the building minus your depreciation deductions.

Here's an example. Say you purchase a building for $50,000 and write off $10,000 in depreciation. So your adjusted basis for purposes of the rehabilitation credit is $40,000. That means you qualify for the credit only if you spend at least $40,000 fixing up the building.

There's another catch: When you calculate your future depreciation deductions on the building, you have to take into account the amount of the credit you claim.

Assume you own a Certified Historic Structure with an adjusted basis of $40,000. You shell out $100,000 to rehabilitate the building.

Under the law, you may take a credit of $20,000 (20 percent of $100,000). But you must calculate future depreciation deductions on the building on an adjusted basis of $120,000—that is, $40,000 plus $100,000, minus your $20,000 credit.

It's Worth It

Mastering the complex rules on real-estate taxation is not easy. But it *is* worthwhile, because investing in real estate still helps to slash your federal tax bill. And that fact means you'll have more investable dollars to meet your objectives.

12 *Home Away from Home*

Making Your Vacation Home Pay

Why do most people buy vacation homes? Second homes can fulfill many financial planning goals—a comfortable life-style, say, or a pleasant retirement.

Vacation homes are also valuable investments. And they can serve as the real-estate portion of a diversified portfolio.

How can you make a vacation home pay?

Let's take a look.

You Need a Vacation

Vacation homes offer opportunities for appreciation. If you buy one in the right place, its value can go up significantly.

You stand the best chance to gain if your second home is easily accessible. Look for a house that is no more than an hour or two away from a major city. Also, houses located on or near water are traditionally good bets. Their capital appreciation is usually high, and so is their rental income.

Here's another idea: Scout for property in areas where land development is restricted by law—a house adjacent to a land preserve, for example. Since builders are forbidden to erect new homes on the site, there will never be a glut of houses on the market.

It's Taxing

If your vacation home appreciates in value, that's terrific. But apart from appreciation, second homes offer other financial benefits, most of them related to taxes.

And Uncle Sam doesn't much care what you use for a vacation home— a cabin in the woods or a town house in the city. Virtually any dwelling unit that contains basic living accommodations qualifies.

In the following sections, we explain how you can use your vacation home to earn extra income and to reduce your federal income tax bill.

But first you should know that as far as Uncle Sam is concerned, your second home fits one of these three categories:

- A vacation home for you and your family
- Rental property
- Some combination of the two

The tax treatment your property gets depends on which category it falls into.

A Vacation Home

A vacation home that you and your family use personally (and never rent out) gets the same IRS treatment as your first home—that is, your mortgage interest and property taxes on it are tax deductible. Other expenses, such as utilities and repairs, of course, are not.

Caution: Mortgage interest is fully deductible only on your principal residence and one other home. Also, the same restrictions apply to mortgage interest deductibility on a second home as on your primary residence. (See Chapter 16 for details.)

Rental Property

Let's assume that you rent out your second home and never use it yourself. You may depreciate the home—that is, deduct from your income a portion of its cost each year.

For example, if your home was bought and placed in service between 1981 and 1987, you may write it off over 19.0 years. If you buy and place it in service now, you must write it off over a period of 27.5 years.

In addition to the home itself, you may depreciate furniture and appliances used in the home. And the depreciation rules let you write off the cost of these items much faster—over seven years for post-1986 property and over five years for pre-1987 property.

You may also deduct operating expenses. Among the operating costs you may write off: insurance, utilities, and maintenance. You may also deduct expenses such as commissions, advertising, professional fees, repairs, and supplies—any costs that you would normally deduct for profit-oriented activities.

That's not all. You may also write off your state and local property taxes and mortgage interest. In fact, given all the expense involved in maintaining a second home that you rent out, you'll be likely to have a loss on your hands at the end of the year.

Uncle Sam will happily share that loss with you, but only within the limits of the passive loss rules. As we saw in Chapter 11, the IRS generally considers the rental of real estate a passive activity. And you may subtract passive losses only from passive income.

There is, however, an exception to the rules: You may write off up to $25,000 in losses if you actively participate in the rental operations and you meet certain income requirements.

Tip: Let's assume you do not have enough passive income to absorb a loss. And your income is too high to qualify for the $25,000 exception.

You may then want to make sure you violate the personal use rules by using the home more than fourteen days. (See our discussion of mixed use next.) Then your property will qualify as a second residence, and you may still deduct your mortgage interest in full.

Part Personal, Part Rental

If you're like most people, you want to have your vacation home and rent it, too. The tax treatment of combination property depends on the proportion of rental and personal use your vacation hideaway gets. The deductions you take may be limited, and you must allocate expenses in proportion to the amount of rental and personal use.

As we've seen, the passive loss rules apply to rental activities. But these rules are really the second hoop you must jump through. The first is a limitation on personal use days.

If you personally use the home for more than the greater of fourteen days in the year or 10 percent of the days that it is rented, you may not claim a loss from the property. You'll never even reach the second hoop. You are allowed deductions, but only up to the amount of rental income you receive from your property.

The consolation prize: You're allowed to carry the excess deductions forward to succeeding years to offset income from the same property.

Let's say you rented your home for 200 days. You could use it yourself for as many as 20 days—10 percent of 200—without jeopardizing its generally more favorable tax status as rental property. Occupy it for 21 days, though, and Uncle Sam reclassifies the property as a personal residence for the entire year.

Fine Lines

The law gets quite picky about what constitutes personal use. In Uncle Sam's view, you've used your vacation property for personal purposes if on any portion of any day your property is occupied by

- Someone who is related to you by blood
- Someone who holds an equity interest in the vacation home
- Someone with whom you have a barter arrangement that lets you use another home for a comparable period of time
- Someone to whom you rent your vacation home at a rate that is

less than "fair market value"—which, according to the law, is the going rate for similar homes in the area

And note: If you rent your home to a relative—or a person who has some equity interest in the property—the IRS looks upon this transaction as personal use. This strict rule applies even if the rent you charge is the going rate for your area.

An exception to this rule: If you rent your home at fair market value to a relative who uses it as a principal residence—say, a condo for your parents—the use is not considered personal.

All Work and No Play

Vacation homes require maintenance, and if you're there doing repairs, it's not much of a vacation. So, Uncle Sam says, any day that you spend in the home for the "principal purpose" of making repairs or maintaining the property will not count as a personal use day.

Beware, though: If you're audited, the IRS will scrutinize "all the facts and circumstances" to determine if your "principal purpose" was repair and maintenance. It will look at the amount of time you devoted to repair and maintenance activities, the frequency with which you did the work, and the presence of companions.

If, for example, you often take friends along—particularly the same friends—while you're performing repair and maintenance work, the IRS will probably suspect that there's more vacation than work to your visits.

Allocate, Allocate

Remember: You can use your vacation home within the fourteen-day or 10 percent limits described earlier in this chapter and still claim most of the deductions you would get for rental property. However, you must allocate expenses between the two uses, personal and rental.

This rule applies even if you use the home yourself just one day out of the year, say, the Fourth of July. You must then allocate one day's worth of your vacation home's total expenses to personal use. The allocation isn't difficult—except that there are two formulas, depending on the type of expenses.

Here's how the formulas work.

First, for all expenses other than property taxes and mortgage interest: Calculate the number of days the property was rented at a fair market value. Then count the number of days that you used the property personally. (Don't count repair or maintenance days as either rental or personal use.)

Add these together to get the total use days.

Multiply your total expenses (excluding taxes and interest) for the year by the fraction of rental days over total use days. The product of that multiplication is the amount you may deduct as rental expenses—subject, of course, to the passive loss rules.

Second, for property taxes and mortgage interest: Allocate these expenses to the rental period in the proportion of rental use days to the total days in the year, rather than to the total days you actually used the property.

This second method of allocation—which has been sanctioned by the courts but not by the IRS—is usually more advantageous for taxpayers. So, until the conflict is resolved, you should probably use it. The exception: You might find when you run your own numbers that allocating expenses in the proportion of rental use days to total use days serves you better.

Obviously you should use the method that works best for you. The important point: For now, you have a choice. (In the example later in this chapter, we show you how using one method over the other can add up to thousands of dollars in tax savings.)

The need to allocate expenses is one consequence of using your vacation home as both personal and rental property. Another complication is the order in which you must deduct expenses—an order that is mandated by law:

- First, adverstising and commission charges
- Next, taxes and interest
- Next, operating expenses
- Last, depreciation

This order becomes important when you exceed the personal use limitation and your rental expenses are limited to rental income. The government effectively forces you to offset income first by those expenses (except advertising and commissions) that you could deduct in any case. Then, if there is any income left, you are allowed to write off other rental expenses.

Special Cases

More Than Two? If you're fortunate enough to own three or more homes, you get a choice. Each tax year, you may designate which one—other than your principal residence—you want the IRS to treat as your second home.

Provided you exceed the personal use limitation test for this home, you may deduct the mortgage interest. The IRS treats the interest on any other residences as personal interest, which won't be deductible at all after 1990. (See Chapter 16.)

Rented Fourteen Days or Less? If you rent your second home for fourteen days or less, all you can deduct are mortgage interest and property taxes. Of course, as we've seen, you may deduct interest on only one home in addition to your personal residence, and you must meet the personal use test.

The good news? The rental income you collect isn't taxable. And this is one rule that can work to your advantage.

Say your vacation home is located in an area that commands unusually high rents for a very short period—the site of the Super Bowl, for instance. You may rent out your property for a huge sum for fewer than fifteen days and enjoy the income—tax free.

Profit by Their Example

Confused by all the rules? Here are some examples to help you understand them better.

Let's assume that your principal residence is in New Jersey, and you also own a vacation home in Florida. Your annual expenses on your second home are

Property taxes . . . . $ 3,000
Mortgage interest 12,000
Operating expenses 4,000

CASE 1: You use the property personally and never rent it

What are the tax consequences? For starters, none of your operating expenses are deductible. But you can write off your property taxes in full. And mortgage interest is deductible, too, if you designate this house as your second home.

One word of warning, though: For mortgages signed after October 13, 1987, the law allows you to deduct the interest only if the loan is secured by the home and only to the extent your debt doesn't exceed the lesser of the fair market value of your home minus the total acquisition debt or $100,000.

(For the full details on mortgage interest deductions, see Chapter 16.)

CASE 2: You rent the house and never use it personally

It's the end of the year, and you add up your income and expenses from the property for the year. Here's your statement for tax purposes:

Rental income $20,000

RENTAL EXPENSES:

Property taxes . . . . $ 3,000

Mortgage interest 12,000

Operating expenses 4,000

Depreciation 8,000

Total expenses $27,000

Loss . . . . $ 7,000

Since you never use the house personally, your $7,000 loss is fully deductible—subject to the passive loss rules, of course.

CASE 3: *You rent the home for 90 days during the year and use it personally for 10 days*

Again, assume it's the end of the year, and you're tallying up your income and expenses from the property. Here's your statement for tax purposes:

Rental income $10,000

RENTAL EXPENSES:

Property taxes .... $ 740
($3,000 × 90/365)

Mortgage interest 2,960
($12,000 × 90/365)

Operating expenses 3,600
($4,000 × 90/100)

Depreciation 7,200
($8,000 × 90/100)

Total expenses $14,500

Loss .... $ 4,500

What are the tax consequences in this case? You used the home personally for fewer than fifteen days, so the loss is deductible—subject, again, to the passive loss rules.

But you must allocate expenses to rental use. For taxes and interest, we've allocated based on the total days in the year. Operating expenses and depreciation, meanwhile, are allocated based on the total days of use.

The rest of your operating expenses and depreciation are not deductible. But the balance of your property taxes—$3,000 minus $740, or $2,260—is fully deductible.

What about interest?

The balance of your mortgage interest of $9,040 ($12,000 minus $2,960) is considered personal or consumer interest. Congress is phasing out deductions for consumer interest, so this amount is deductible only in limited amounts during the phaseout period of 1987 through 1990. (See Chapter 16 for the details.)

Losing $9,040 in interest deductions will obviously hit you hard at tax time. Here are two possible solutions to the problem: Change the method of allocation you use, or increase your personal use.

If you were to adopt the "total days" method of allocating taxes and interest, here's what your statement would look like:

Rental income	$10,000
RENTAL EXPENSES:	
Property taxes	$ 2,700
($3,000 × 90/100)	
Mortgage interest	10,800
($12,000 × 90/100)	
Operating expenses	3,600
($4,000 × 90/100)	
Depreciation	7,200
($8,000 × 90/100)	
Total expenses	$24,300
Loss	$14,300

Now you're much better off. The $14,300 loss is deductible subject to the passive loss rules. And even if these rules restrict the amount you may write off in the current year, you may at least carry the unused loss over to future years. Nondeductible personal interest, on the other hand, is lost forever.

The $300 balance of property taxes ($3,000 less $2,700) is fully deductible. And you have only $1,200 in interest ($12,000 less $10,800) that is treated as personal interest.

Another alternative is to increase your personal use from ten days to, say, fifteen days. This is an important option, so let's consider it.

CASE 4: You rent the home for 90 days during the year and use it personally for 15 days

Here is the result:

Rental income	$10,000
RENTAL EXPENSES:	
Property taxes ($3,000 × 90/365)	$ 740
Mortgage interest ($12,000 × 90/365)	2,960
Operating expenses ($4,000 × 90/105)	3,430
Depreciation ($8,000 × 90/105)	6,860
Total expenses	$13,990
Loss	$ 3,990

The bad news: The loss is not deductible, because you've used the home for more than fourteen days.

The good news: The loss carries over to succeeding years and can offset future income from the same property.

And here's even better news: The balance of mortgage interest of $9,040 ($12,000 less $2,960) is deductible in full, and you may also write off the balance of taxes of $2,260 ($3,000 less $740).

(As you can see, in this case, it's better to use the 365-days allocation method for interest and property taxes. Doing so reduces the non-deductible loss.)

Last Resort

The keys to making sense of the Byzantine tax rules on vacation homes:

- Decide how you want to use the property.
- Balance your investment goals against your recreational goals.
- Project the taxable income and cash flow.
- Determine how the tax results would change with some fine tuning to your rental or personal use.

Remember, you may be able to enjoy your home and capture tax deductions from it, too.

13 *Buy Now, Profit Later*

How Other Investment Vehicles Stack Up

As we've seen, you can and should allocate your assets among a variety of investment vehicles—from cash and cash equivalents to natural resources and tangibles.

Natural resources and tangibles are hard assets—that is, investments you can see and feel. Oil and natural gas are examples of natural resources. Rare coins are examples of tangibles.

Should you include natural resources and tangibles in the hard-asset portion of your portfolio? Following is our guide to the pros and cons of these investments.

Before we begin, though, a word about collectibles. Though art, books, rugs, antiques, and many other items also fall in the tangible-asset category, we don't include a discussion of them in this book. The reason: Most people buy collectibles for love—that is, for personal enjoyment—not money.

Oil and Gas

There are three ways you can invest in oil and gas—through stock in energy companies, a stake in private or master limited partnerships, or a "working interest."

A simple way to participate in the oil and gas industry is to buy energy stocks, which make up about 18 percent of the Standard & Poor's 500 composite stock index. A major advantage of this strategy is liquidity. You can buy and sell any amount whenever you want.

The downside: Energy stocks may not directly reflect changes in oil and gas prices. And they're subject to the vagaries of the stock market as a whole.

You can participate more directly in this industry through the second investment route—oil and gas "programs" or drilling partnerships. We address private partnerships in this section.

The purpose of oil and gas programs: to explore or drill for oil or purchase producing oil wells. Usually these programs come in the form of joint ventures or "untraded" limited partnerships.

Each program is a distinct operating business, varying in size from $1 million up to $300 million. Partnership units usually cost a minimum of $5,000 to $10,000.

Who offers these programs? They're put together and offered to investors either by independent oil companies or by oil investment managers.

Before we look at the four types of oil programs available today, a word about shelters. As you know, you may no longer write off your losses in passive investments against your ordinary income. (See Chapter 11 for a complete rundown on this new rule.) So it increasingly makes sense to invest in one of these partnerships only if you think your eventual return justifies the risk.

Now, here are the four types of programs.

Exploratory Programs

These partnerships try to discover new petroleum reserves. Since exploration usually takes place in untested areas, the success rate is often not very high.

Moreover, an exploratory well must be developed after it is discovered. So, chances are, you may be tapped for more money before the partnership produces a positive cash flow.

If everything goes well, return on capital may be extraordinary. Keep in mind, though: It may take a long time to collect on your investment, and these deals are pretty risky.

Development Programs

These programs set up wells near existing oil reserves in areas where production is already under way. So chances of success are higher than in exploratory programs. And you can expect a faster return on your investment.

As you might expect, the return on your capital is often less than you'd get with successful exploratory programs.

Balanced Programs

Balanced programs include both exploratory and development wells in about the same proportion. They try to combine the advantages of higher yields produced by successful exploratory wells with the early cash flow and lower risk of development wells.

Income Programs

Unlike either exploratory or development programs, income partnerships purchase producing properties rather than develop drilling sites. So the risks are considerably less.

Income programs also do not offer the same tax benefits. Most of their tax write-offs come from the depletion of their oil reserves rather than from development drilling costs.

The principal advantage of these programs: You get income over the life of the oil well, which might be ten years, or the gas well, which may last fifteen years. As the oil or gas is removed from the well, the income falls until the well is abandoned as commercially unproductive. Since these programs produce income with not too much risk, they appeal to a larger number of people.

If you're thinking about an investment in oil and gas partnerships, make sure you look for a reputable financial adviser who has experience in evaluating these programs. And ask if he or she has performed an in-depth review of the investment.

Now on to the third way to invest in oil and gas: working interests.

Only a few tax shelter benefits survived tax reform. One of the survivors: working interests in oil and gas properties. How does the law define a working interest? It's one in which partners pay a share of development and operation expenses.

Your losses in these partnerships are not subject to the normal limitations on losses from passive investments. (See Chapter 16 for information on these limitations.) So you may deduct them from your regular income. And you don't have to participate in the actual operations yourself to do so.

Gold

For the pharaohs, it was the price of admission to heaven. For the Old Testament kings, it was royal treasure. For the buccaneers, it was bounty.

Over the years, gold has not lost its appeal.

The advantages of investing in gold: Since it has intrinsic value, it is a hedge against inflation and political uncertainties. Also, gold is a liquid investment. There is an active market for gold, so you can sell it any time you want.

The disadvantages: The price of gold is volatile. Gold's price is determined by the Zurich Interbank price, the London "fixing," and the spot or near-due-delivery contract price on the New York and Chicago futures exchanges.

Here's how the pricing works.

Soon after the banking day begins in Zurich, the prices at which early trades were made are published worldwide. Later in the morning— and again in the afternoon—representatives of five merchant banks meet in the London offices of N. M. Rothschild to set the price. The amount they agree upon is the London fixing.

At about the time of the London afternoon fixing, trading in futures contracts, including the contract for next delivery (spot), opens in the Commodity Exchange (COMEX) in New York and in the International Monetary Market (IMM) in Chicago. After the business day ends in Europe, the COMEX and IMM quotes become the key prices for traders all around the world.

The real turning point for gold investments was December 31, 1974, the day Uncle Sam lifted a long-standing ban on private investment in gold by U.S. citizens.

Today, you can invest in gold in a number of ways. You can purchase bullion—gold bars or ingots—or coins directly. Or you can buy certificates from a dealer who holds on to the gold for you.

You can purchase gold futures. You can buy gold mining stocks—or invest in mutual funds that invest in gold mining stocks.

Let's take a look at each option.

Gold Bullion

You can buy bullion outright and hold it for the long term, either in a depository in the United States or in a foreign banking center, such as London or Zurich.

Gold Certificates

Gold certificates—which you purchase from brokers, dealers, or bankers—are a convenient way to own gold. They represent your ownership of a specific quantity of the metal that is stored in a bank or vault. They're convenient because you never have to take possession of the heavy metal itself. Also, with gold certificates, you don't pay the state and local taxes that are normally imposed on the purchase of gold.

Gold Coins

Buying gold coins is far more practical. Among your choices: the Canadian maple leaf, the U.S. gold eagle, the Mexican peso, and the Chinese panda.

All these coins are sold for a small premium above the value of their gold content. Usually a dealer sells one-ounce coins for a premium of 5.0 to 7.0 percent above the day's spot market price of gold and repurchases them at 2.5 percent above spot. The smaller denomination coin you buy, the larger premium you'll have to pay.

Gold Futures

A futures contract is simply an agreement for a buyer to buy and a seller to sell a fixed amount of a commodity—in this case gold—on an agreed-upon date in the future at an agreed-upon price.

The standard futures contract calls for delivery of 100 troy ounces of gold on a settlement date as far as thirty months in the future. But, in practice, fewer than 1 percent of these contracts result in actual delivery of gold.

Gold Mining Stocks

Of course, if you buy gold directly, you get no current return. Shares in gold mining companies can be another story. They frequently pay dividends—some of them quite generous.

Companies in the United States and Canada are small, their deposits are of a relatively low grade, and their production costs are high. So the profits they can make are limited.

These North American companies do have some pluses, though. Unlike some foreign concerns, they operate in a stable and noncontroversial political climate. And the price of their shares is sensitive to changes in the price of gold. In fact, shares of these companies often fall or rise more dramatically than the price of gold itself.

And what about foreign companies? You invest in many of these concerns not by buying common stock but by purchasing depository receipts. The receipts entitle you to receive dividends but not to participate in the company's policy-making decisions.

The value of both the depository receipts and your dividends depends on the exchange rate on the foreign currency.

Mutual Funds That Invest in Gold Mining Stocks

Several mutual funds now offer portfolios of gold-related investments. These funds usually invest in domestic and foreign mining stocks. (See Chapter 9 for more information on mutual funds.)

Other Precious Metals

Most people who invest in metals put their money in gold. But you can also invest in silver and platinum—and in much the same way.

Again, your options are bullion, coins, certificates, metals futures, mining stocks, and mutual funds that invest in mining stocks.

Coins

Investing in coins that are no longer minted is risky business—and not the kind you should enter into without considerable education and skill.

If you are new to numismatics—that is, coin collecting—your first step should be to find a reputable dealer. Our advice: Seek out someone who has been in the business at least ten years, and ask for references from other investors.

Horror stories abound of dealers who claim their coins are a much higher grade, or condition, than they really are. And grades are what coin investing is all about.

Gems

Gems you buy to wear are seldom of investment quality—that is, unless the gem in question is the Hope diamond.

The fact is, when you buy a gem, or a piece of jewelry containing a gem, the dealer takes a sizable markup—sometimes as much as 100 percent. Unfortunately, if you try to sell the stone, dealers usually offer you less than wholesale prices.

Unlike stocks and bonds, there is no readily quoted market for gems, because no two stones are identical in quality or value.

With diamonds, you take into account carat or weight, cut, color, and clarity. Even the color of white diamonds is graded. A change of one letter grade can add—or subtract—hundreds of dollars per carat in the price.

With few exceptions, colored stones cost less than diamonds, but they are far more risky as investments. There is no universally accepted grading system for colored stones, as there is for diamonds.

Your best—indeed, only—hope is to get an independent written appraisal of the gem from a reputable gemologist.

To sum up, if you are acquiring jewelry—or even gems—for pleasure, you aren't likely to come up short. But don't deceive yourself that you are making a surefire investment. Unless you are an expert, gems are for buying, not for selling.

Stop and Look

Investing in hard assets can pay off. But this is one area where you must do your homework. Make sure you understand the ins and outs of any of these investments before plunking down your hard-earned cash.

PART THREE

Debt Management

14 Red Alert

What You Need to Know About Debt Management

*D*ebt management?

Sure. People talk about managing their assets in order to increase their net worth. A debt is just the flip side of an asset. Reducing debt is another way of boosting your net worth.

In fact, managing debt is just as important to your financial well-being as deciding how and when to invest and what to invest in. Managing debt means knowing when it makes sense to borrow and when it doesn't, whom you should borrow from, and what form your borrowing should take. It's as complex a subject as asset allocation, so let's break it down into manageable chunks.

In this chapter, we'll consider who should borrow, when, and why. In later chapters we'll take up types of debt and alternative credit sources.

On Loan

Think of a loan as a purchase. If you can't afford it, don't buy it.

When you take out a loan, you are simply agreeing to pay a lender for the use of that lender's cash. If you can't afford to buy the cash—that is, if you don't have the income or resources required to repay the loan principal and interest while still meeting your other obligations—then you shouldn't borrow.

Of course, your financial profile comes into play, too. For example, if your earnings expectations are high, borrowing may make sense for you.

137

So let's say that you can afford to pay back the loan. And let's say, too, that you're bullish about your future earnings. Does this mean going into debt is a good idea?

Why and How to Use (and Not to Use) Credit

Let's look at a situation that most of us are all too familiar with. As we do, we'll raise the kinds of questions you ought to raise the next time you consider taking on debt.

Congratulations. You finally found the car you've been looking for at the price you wanted to pay. The color is right, the options are great, and the dealer has it in stock. Now it's time to buy.

So, how are you going to pay for this dream buggy? Cash or credit— or some combination of the two?

For some people, the answer is easy. They don't have the cash, so borrowing is the only option open to them. Other people have such poor credit ratings that cash is their only answer.

But let's assume that these easy answers don't apply to you. You've got the cash, or at least some of it. And your credit rating is good.

In other words, you could borrow. So you've got other issues to consider—your financial profile, for one, and your tax situation, for another.

The after-tax cost of the loan may depend on your tax bracket. The higher your bracket, the cheaper it may be for you to borrow. That, as you probably know, is because the interest deduction is worth more in tax savings to individuals in the top tax bracket.

On the other hand, the interest on auto (and other consumer) loans is only partially deductible under the tax law, unless you're borrowing against the equity in your home. Consequently, except in this one circumstance, there's less and less difference between the after-tax and pretax cost of a loan. By 1991, when the deductibility of consumer credit costs is scheduled to end, there will be no difference in pre- and after-tax credit costs. (For more on deductions, see Chapter 16.)

Here's another issue, one that people frequently neglect to consider: the investment costs of not borrowing.

Say that you have the cash for the car. Are you still better off borrowing and leaving the cash invested where it is?

To answer that question you need to know what investment returns are available to you and at what level of risk. If these returns, adjusted for risk, are higher than the cost of borrowing, then borrowing is the more attractive option.

But remember to compare apples and apples. To see what we mean, let's abandon our car example and discuss more generally how you should calculate whether it makes financial sense to borrow.

With a loan, you usually know exactly what to expect as far as your pocketbook is concerned. That is, you know for certain that you will have to pay interest and principal at regular intervals.

But all investments are not equally predictable. Cash flow and appreciation from some of your investments might not materialize as you expect. Dividends may not be paid when due, and a market downturn could erode your investment's value.

To compensate for this additional risk, the return you expect from these investments should be significantly greater than the interest rate on a loan. And, as we've seen, if this isn't the case, you're probably better off using cash than borrowing.

But let's look at an investment where you do have the same degree of certainty you have with a loan—a certificate of deposit (CD). In this case we are comparing apples and apples—two very predictable situations. Now how does the return from your CD compare with the interest charges on your loan?

First, keep in mind that the interest rate on your loan will almost certainly top the interest rate paid on the CD by at least two to three percentage points.

Also, what about comparative returns? Clearly, it makes sense to use $3,000 of your hard-earned dollars on which you are earning just 5 percent interest to pay off a credit-card debt on which you're being charged 19.6 percent.

But remember: With credit-card debt, it costs you nothing—that is, you pay no up-front charges—to take out a loan in the future. So, if you pay off your debt, then find that you need or want to reobtain the loan, the cost is zero.

And with some types of debt, you do pay up-front charges for the privilege of borrowing. For example, mortgages involve points, title search fees, administration fees, and other costs that can add up quickly—say, to 3 to 5 percent of the loan amount.

So keep in mind: Before you rush off to pay all your debts, consider the costs of reobtaining that debt.

Also consider the cost of borrowing for future major expenditures. Here's an example. Let's say you can't stand debt. So you gather together all your present cash and investment balances and use the money to pay off your home mortgage. Six months later, your faithful auto dies.

Now you have to buy a new car. But you don't have enough cash left. So you're forced to finance your new auto with an expensive and not fully deductible auto loan.

If you hadn't paid off your home mortgage, you'd be paying interest on your less expensive and fully deductible home mortgage and using cash for your new car.

And Now?

Remember: There are some good reasons to borrow. As we've seen, you may not be in a position to do so later if you use all your cash to pay off a loan.

Or you might just want to establish credit. Keep in mind the old rule of thumb: The best time to borrow is when you don't need the money.

So, now you know how to think about whether you should borrow, provided that you have the choice. Let's move on to other debt-management issues, such as where to borrow and when.

15 *Back to Basics*

The Right Way to Borrow Money

*G*etting turned down for credit hurts. Usually it hurts your pride. But, on occasion, it can also wreak havoc with your carefully laid financial plans.

This chapter tells you the right way to apply for credit. And it provides the information you need to borrow wisely.

Getting Credit

Getting a loan is relatively easy for most people. Lenders decide whether you are a worthwhile risk by looking at two sources—your loan application and a credit bureau report.

When you fill out your loan application, it helps to know which categories are the most important to lenders. Despite the numerous items on the application, only a few really determine the final outcome.

Your stability is still a major factor for most lenders. But these days, job hopping and relocation are increasingly common. So the length of time you've spent with a particular company or lived in a particular house or apartment isn't as critical as it once was. Similarly, renting rather than owning your own home is no longer a red flag for the majority of lenders.

Here are the other major considerations.

Other Creditors or Debt
You're more than halfway there if you've had a previous loan from the lender to whom you're applying and you paid on time. You also get high

marks for having (and handling responsibly) bank credit cards and department store charge cards.

Income and Debt-to-Income Ratio

The higher your income, the better you'll do. So, report all sources of income. What's even more important, however, is your debt-to-income ratio. If more than 40 percent of your gross income goes to pay your monthly debt obligations, you may be denied credit.

Occupation

Job categories that imply stability, responsibility, and a college education score best.

On File

So, you've never seen a copy of the credit report that lenders use to determine if you are a good credit risk? Most people haven't.

But you can—and should—get a copy of this report. The last thing anyone wants is to be turned down for a loan because of erroneous information. It's better to iron out any problems before you apply for a loan—not after.

There are more than 2,000 credit bureaus across the country. Sometimes sponsored by a city or town chamber of commerce, these bureaus act as clearinghouses for collecting information on people's credit histories. Most cities and towns have at least one.

To find out which credit bureau has your records, look in the yellow pages under "credit reporting agencies" or ask your banker or a retailer with whom you have a charge account.

The federal Fair Credit Reporting Act—which we discuss later in this chapter—requires credit bureaus and credit reporting agencies to provide you with either a copy or a summary of your report. Credit bureaus will usually mail you a copy of your report on request, though some make you visit their offices and review your report there.

Expect to pay about $10 for a copy of your report. But if you have been turned down for credit in the past thirty days because of information contained in the credit bureau's file, you can review your record free of charge.

Most credit bureau reports contain two types of information: information the credit bureau gathers itself and information purchased from private companies.

These companies—such as TRW, Trans Union, and Credit Bureau Inc.—collect credit information, store the information in computers, then sell the computerized reports. For example, TRW maintains credit information on more than 133 million consumers. (And there are only 144 million consumers in the entire United States.)

What are you likely to find in your credit report? There is—for starters—information on your outstanding debts. Automobile loans and lines of credit are listed. So are balances due on bank credit cards, government-backed student loans, and small-business loans.

The reports also show how promptly you pay your bills, either by recording recent payments or assigning a grade given by the creditor.

Sometimes, credit bureau reports contain the name of your employer and your salary, as well as information from public court records—bankruptcy filings, legal judgments, tax liens, and, in some cases, even divorce settlements.

What won't you find in your report?

The reports contain no overall rating of your credit. That judgment is left to the people or institutions to whom you're applying for credit.

Also, not all creditors report information to credit bureaus, so you may not find all your accounts listed. For example, you probably won't find a mention of your American Express account, because American Express reports only its most delinquent customers to credit agencies.

Nor do credit reports contain information on checking and savings accounts, race, religion, sex, personal life-style, or criminal records.

Most of the information in credit bureau reports is accurate. But what happens if you find a mistake? Your credit bureau must investigate and—if you're in the right—notify creditors to whom you have recently applied.

If the credit bureau sticks by its guns on a disputed item, you can write a brief statement explaining your side of the story. This statement will be included in the report.

It's always a good idea to write a statement for your report. If nothing else, you will demonstrate to lenders that you care about your credit.

The Law Is on Your Side

A number of federal laws—the Fair Credit Reporting Act, the Equal Credit Opportunity Act, and the Fair Credit Billing Act—apply to credit transactions.

Let's take a look at your rights under each.

Fair Credit Reporting Act

The Fair Credit Reporting Act grants you the right to see what information the credit bureau has on you and to know who has received your report in the past six months.

The act also ensures that information that you dispute will be reinvestigated and corrected or removed if it is inaccurate or unverifiable. And it says that you may place a statement in the report if you continue to dispute the accuracy of an item after reinvestigation.

Finally, the law says, bad debts and other negative information remain part of a credit report for no more than seven years. Bankruptcy filings are listed for no more than ten years.

Equal Credit Opportunity Act

The Equal Credit Opportunity Act was enacted to make sure women receive the same treatment from creditors as men. Under this act, creditors must judge you on an equal basis with all other credit applicants—regardless of your sex or marital status. You have the right to obtain a credit card in your own name if you are a married woman and to have child support and alimony counted as income at your request.

The law prohibits creditors from asking questions about birth control or child-bearing plans. And it requires them to tell you their reasons for denying you credit.

Fair Credit Billing Act

This law gives you the right to file a written complaint with a company or institution that granted you credit within sixty days after the bill you question was mailed to you. The creditor must acknowledge receipt of your complaint within thirty days and reach a settlement with you within ninety days.

Until the matter is resolved, the creditor may not collect the disputed amount from you. Nor—until it is settled—may the creditor report any negative information about the dispute to credit reporting agencies.

Taking Credit

If you have a good credit history, you could be eligible for any amount of credit. What are some potential sources of money? Let's take a look.

Installment Loans
Banks make installment loans. So do credit unions, finance companies, automobile manufacturers, even big financial institutions.

You can use installment loans to pay for big-ticket items, such as a car or a boat. But before you sign on the dotted line, compare rates.

Line of Credit
With an unsecured line of credit, you can borrow money in large or small chunks up to a predetermined limit. A few banks offer limits as low as $500, but usually the range is between $5,000 and $25,000.

As the word *unsecured* indicates, you do not have to pledge collateral to back up this kind of loan. But because the loan is unsecured, you pay higher interest rates than you do on secured loans.

Once approved, though, you can tap the credit line as often as you want, for whatever you want—college tuition, home improvements, a vacation—simply by writing a check. Many banks also permit overdrafts— covered by your line of credit—on regular checking accounts.

Repayment requirements vary, as do interest rates. Usually you'll also have to pay a nominal processing fee.

Brokerage Firms
Brokerage firms make personal loans to their customers, sometimes at a rate of interest that is lower than is available elsewhere. The one requirement: You must pledge the securities held in your brokerage account as

collateral for the loan. But you may borrow up to half of your account's value.

The danger with these loans is that the brokerage firm may order securities in your account sold if the securities decline in value.

Insurance Policies

Your insurance carrier will loan you an amount equal to the cash value of your life insurance policy. And you don't have to repay the money. You pay interest, but the amount you borrow simply reduces the benefit that is paid upon your death.

Older life insurance policies that charge interest of 5 to 7 percent are an excellent source of low-interest borrowing.

Card Tricks

One California man applied for 1,173 credit cards. He got all of them—and a listing in *The Guinness Book of World Records.*

No one, naturally, needs—or should have—1,173 credit cards. Indeed, most people are best off with only one or two. How many—and which ones—are right for you? In a minute, we'll take a look.

First, though, a word about nonprofit organizations. Many nonprofits—colleges, universities, environmental organizations, and so on—are entering into cooperative arrangements with financial institutions to issue credit cards bearing their names.

You still make your payments to the bank each month, but the nonprofit organization gets a few cents for every dollar you spend. It's a painless way to help out a favorite charity or organization.

Eat, Drink, and Be Merry

Credit cards are a way of life for most of us. In fact, they are so much a way of life that there are some things we can't do without them—rent a car, for example.

If you do not drive or travel frequently, you probably can get by with just one card—a bank card. But an airline ticket and a few nights in a hotel can quickly eat up the credit line on a typical bank card. So if you travel extensively or run up a large expense account, you need a travel-and-entertainment card, such as American Express, Diners Club, or Carte Blanche.

These cards don't have any spending limits. With most travel-and-entertainment cards, you pay the entire amount due each month.

With bank cards, it's a different story. Typically, your terms are

- Up to thirty-six months to pay
- Interest rates ranging from 10 to 22 percent, depending on the issuer and the state where it's located
- Small minimum monthly payments—usually about 5 percent of your balance
- Low annual fees (a tiny number of banks still issue free cards)
- Credit lines that range from $500 for first-time cardholders to $5,000 or more
- No interest on new charges that are paid within twenty to thirty days of receipt of the bill

If you pay your bills on time, these bank cards can be a source of short-term interest-free credit. They're also a source of emergency cash.

Moreover, because the credit card business is highly competitive, many institutions offer incentives so you'll sign on with them. Among these lures: the award of points for every dollar you spend. With these points, you get free merchandise, discounts on products, and so forth.

Adding It Up

Bank and department store credit cards are more expensive than other forms of credit. You must pay interest on any unpaid balance from previous bills.

And with interest rates ranging as high as 22 percent, a credit card can be surprisingly costly. For example, if your average monthly unpaid balance over a year totals $5,000, and the bank is charging 18 percent, you'll pay $900 in interest. And, with the advent of tax reform in 1986, a good portion of that interest is no longer deductible. (See Chapter 16.)

Take note, too: The method the bank uses to calculate finance charges often has more effect on the charges than does the interest rate.

Here are the three methods banks use.

Adjusted Balance Method

The bank assesses finance charges after subtracting payments for the billing period. If the payments are almost equal to the unpaid balance, finance charges are low.

Previous Balance Method

You get no credit for payments you made during the billing period. If the unpaid balance is high, finance charges will also be high—regardless of the payments you've made.

Average Daily Balance Method

The bank adds up the balances for each day in the billing period, then divides by the number of days in that period. Purchases you make during the billing period are added to the daily balance.

Clearly, it pays to find out how your finance charges are computed.

At a Premium

So-called *premium cards* carry annual fees of $50 to $250, compared with $25 to $50 for standard cards. What do you get for the additional fee?

A much higher line of credit, for one. Regular Visa cards and MasterCards carry average credit lines of $1,500, but on premium cards the line may start at $5,000 and go as high as $50,000.

Other extras with all prestige plastic include more generous check-cashing privileges and, in some cases, no-fee traveler's checks and credit life insurance.

But before you sign up, you should evaluate whether you'll make use of these added attractions. If not, it may not be worth it to pay the higher fee.

It's in the Cards

When considering any card, be sure you won't be cramped by a credit limit that is too low. And find out what the interest rate is on unpaid balances. Remember: You can avoid finance charges if you pay your balances each month.

Keep in mind, too, that you should shop competitively for credit cards. The differences in interest rates, how the rates are computed, and annual fees can be substantial from one bank to another and from state to state.

In South Dakota, for example, banks are free to set whatever rates and fees they feel the market will bear. But in North Carolina, state law limits interest rates on credit cards to 18 percent per year and annual fees on standard cards to $20.

Cards with no annual fees used to be common, but no more. Texas and Missouri forbid fees by law, but some banks make up for that loss: A St. Louis bank charges 22 percent interest on the first $1,000 balance and 10 percent on amounts over $1,000.

Since the state your card is issued in makes absolutely no difference to retailers, it makes good sense to shop around for the best deal.

Keep in mind: Not all applications disclose interest rates. If yours doesn't, ask. Take a close look, too, at how many days' grace you have before you begin to pay interest charges. Most cards offer twenty to thirty days, but some have shorter periods and others have none. So if you pay on the installment plan, you may find yourself paying interest on purchases as soon as you make them.

Also make sure there are no *transaction fees*—fees that are charged each time you use your card.

Write It Down

It's a must to keep a list of your credit card accounts and numbers. That way, if a card is lost or stolen, you can notify the credit card company immediately.

What about the companies that offer for a small annual fee a notification service when you register your charge cards? Since federal law restricts maximum liability on lost credit cards to only $50—and since most companies waive even this amount—the need for these services is questionable.

Even if your cards disappear and you don't have a list of their numbers, you can find your account numbers on recent statements.

Give Me Credit

"Money is a terrible master but an excellent servant," P. T. Barnum once noted. Using credit wisely is one way to make money work for you.

Remember: You shouldn't borrow frivolously. But you shouldn't hesitate to use credit judiciously to meet some of your objectives.

16 The Taxman Cometh

Your Interest Deductions

*T*here are only two ways to reduce the cost of borrowing: One is to pay a lower rate of interest. The other is to share the cost with Uncle Sam. In this chapter, we tell you how to let Uncle Sam foot part of the bill.

Changes, Changes

In days gone by, interest was interest, and, with few exceptions, all interest was deductible. But today life is no longer so simple. Some interest is deductible, and some is not.

The Internal Revenue Code describes many types of interest expenses. But there are only five kinds most of us need to worry about: mortgage interest on your first and second homes, business interest, personal interest, investment interest, and interest from "passive" investments. (We'll explain this last category—a new one—later in this chapter.)

What are the rules governing each? You need to know if you are to borrow intelligently. So let's run through them.

Mortgage Interest

You may write off interest on your home mortgage—as long as the loan is for your primary residence. You may also deduct mortgage interest on one second home.

So most taxpayers may still fully deduct their home mortgage interest. You just make sure that the house is used as security for the loan and the mortgage is recorded. Also, say you signed a mortgage October 14, 1987. In this case, the interest is fully deductible even if the loan is a second mortgage or a home-equity mortgage.

Not everyone, however, can deduct interest in full. Let's review the rules.

Say you own three or more residences. The IRS classifies mortgage interest on any home other than your first or second according to how you use both the additional house and the loan proceeds.

For example, say your third residence is a beach cottage that you reserve for your personal use. Uncle Sam classifies interest on the loan you take out to buy the cottage as personal interest. (We cover personal interest later in this chapter.)

Now say you use the cottage as security on a loan and use the proceeds to buy corporate bonds. In this situation, you must write off the interest on your loan as investment interest.

If you purchased a new home, refinanced an existing home, or incurred additional mortgage debt after October 13, 1987, the IRS divides your deductible mortgage debt into acquisition debt and home-equity debt.

What's the difference?

According to the rules, acquisition debt is secured by your primary or secondary residence. You incur it when you buy, build, or substantially improve your home. In addition, debt you incur when you refinance an old mortgage—up to the amount of the refinanced debt—qualifies as acquisition debt.

Your primary or secondary residence also secures home-equity debt. But, in contrast to acquisition debt, you don't use the loan to buy, build, or substantially improve your home.

You should also know that a single loan can qualify as both acquisition and home-equity debt.

Here's an example:

Say you refinance your mortgage and use part of the loan to pay off your original mortgage. You use the remainder to pay off your auto loan. In this case, your loan qualifies partly as acquisition debt and partly as home-equity debt.

You may deduct in full interest on a home-equity loan—or on the home-equity part of a combined acquisition/home-equity loan—under this condition: The debt must not top the lesser of the fair market value of your home less your total acquisition debt, or $100,000 ($50,000 if you are married and file separate returns). It makes no difference if you own two homes. The cap on your home-equity debt may not top $100,000.

It obviously makes sense, from a tax point of view, to maximize your acquisition debt. If you think you may need more money later, borrow it when you buy the house.

There is a cap on how much mortgage interest you may decuct on acquisition debt. Under the rules, you may write off mortgage interest on acquisition debt of up to $1 million. The cap falls to $500,000 if you're married and file separately.

Taxpayers who signed their mortgages before October 14, 1987, however, are not subject to the $1 million ceiling.

Say, though, that your pre–October 14, 1987, acquisition debt came to more than $1 million. Say, too, that you incurred more debt after that date—you wanted to add a bathroom to your home, for example. In this case, you become subject to the ceiling.

There's also another issue for homeowners to consider. You may be able to deduct all the interest you pay on a refinanced mortgage for regular tax purposes. However, you may not be allowed to write off the full amount when you compute your alternative minimum tax (AMT).

What is the AMT? It's a flat tax of 21 percent, and it's the government way of making sure every taxpayer—no matter how many deductions he or she takes—pays a fair share. In other words, if you have deductions that cut the regular tax you owe much below the amount your income suggests you ought to pay, you may be subject to the AMT. (See Chapter 25 for more on the AMT.)

So how do you figure out the deductibility of a refinanced mortgage when it comes to the AMT? Here's an example: Say your house costs $100,000. The outstanding balance on your existing mortgage comes to $90,000. You refinance the loan for $145,000. How much of the interest on this new loan may you deduct when you compute your AMT?

First, calculate the difference between your previous mortgage balance and your new loan. In this case, it comes to $55,000 ($145,000 less

$90,000). You may not write off the interest on this additional $55,000 when it comes to the AMT.

Here's a simple way to figure out how much interest is deductible for AMT purposes: Divide your previous mortgage balance—$90,000—by the amount of your new mortgage, $145,000. The answer—in this case, 62 percent—is the amount of interest on your refinanced mortgage you may deduct under the AMT.

The AMT rules also allow you to write off interest on money you borrow to "substantially rehabilitate" your home. There's just one condition: The loan must be a mortgage secured by the house. The IRS doesn't define "substantially rehabilitate." But you can rest assured, it means only major renovations.

Business Interest

Business interest is fully deductible, whether you do business as a multinational corporation or a sole proprietorship.

Say you own a small deli. You take out a loan of $4,000 to purchase a state-of-the-art meat slicer. Uncle Sam lets you write off all the interest you pay on the loan.

There is, however, one exception to this rule that applies to employees, but not to people who own and operate their own businesses. Current law states that you may not deduct interest on loans that are related to your activities as an employee.

Here's an example: Say you are employed as a sales representative for a big steel company. You borrow $12,500 to purchase a car you use for business.

Under current law, you may not deduct interest on the loan for the car as business interest. Rather, the interest is classified as personal interest. That's bad news, because personal interest is subject to restrictions on deductibility—as you'll see next.

Personal Interest

In the not-so-distant past, the law allowed you to deduct all "personal" interest—the interest you paid on car loans, credit cards, charge accounts, and so on. But no more.

The change in the tax law means that buying on the installment plan is, for most people, more expensive than ever before. The only good news: Congress did not put the kabosh on interest deductions all at once.

Rather, it decided to phase them out gradually. The following table shows you the amount of personal interest expense you may deduct for tax years after 1986:

YOUR PERSONAL INTEREST DEDUCTIONS

YEAR	AMOUNT DEDUCTIBLE
1987	65%
1988	40
1989	20
1990	10
After 1990	0

Say the year is 1988, and you rack up $500 in personal interest expenses—$183 on your department store charge accounts and $317 on your bank cards. You may write off only 40 percent of your interest expense—or, in this case, $200.

In 1989, your personal interest expense again adds up to $500. But in that year you may deduct only 20 percent of this expense, or $100. So your after-tax cost of borrowing increases as the years pass.

The disallowance of personal interest deductions is prompting some people to carry less debt. And it is encouraging others to bundle their debts into those categories of loans—mortgages and home-equity loans, for example—that still qualify for interest deductions.

There are three ways to tap the equity in your home: refinancing your mortgage, taking out a second mortgage, and signing up for a home-equity loan.

We'll cover refinancing in Chapter 17.

With a second mortgage, you receive a check for the full amount you've borrowed. Home-equity loans are technically second mortgages. But, generally, when you take out a home-equity loan, you borrow money as you need it by writing a check or using a credit card. Second mortgages generally run five to fifteen years, while home-equity loans often run longer—some are even open ended.

Before you rush out to get a loan secured by your house, think about whether the savings you realize on your tax bill are worth the risk. Putting up your house as collateral for a loan is serious business. There is more to consider than the deductibility of interest.

Say you decide to pay for a new car with a home-equity loan. That's fine. But if you fall behind in your payments, you stand to lose your house instead of your car.

There is also the expense to consider. Many banks charge to process and approve your credit line or second mortgage. These "loan origination fees" can add up to 2 to 3 percent of the amount of the loan. And you pay those fees up front. You may also have to shell out closing costs of $200 to $400.

As if loan origination fees aren't enough, there's also the prospect of a recording fee. In order for the interest on your first or second home to be deductible, the loan must be secured by the property. That means that if you fail to make good on your mortgage payments, the bank can foreclose on your home.

In order for the loan to be legally secured by the house, most local laws provide that the security interest—be it a mortgage, a deed of trust, or whatever—be recorded at your local title office. And there's almost always a recording fee. This generally applies to home-equity loans, too.

Home-equity loans are particularly dicey. Unless you are extremely well disciplined, you may take on more debt than you should simply because you now have a credit line that makes tens of thousands of dollars instantly available to you.

Consider this example. You use your equity line to purchase an expensive new car. If you had taken out a standard car loan instead, you would have to pay the principal back in three to five years.

But your equity account makes amortizing the loan your responsibility: You can take as long as you'd like to repay. Your car may be on its last legs—and still not be paid for.

Another potential trouble spot: rising interest rates. When the rates go up, you may find you can no longer make your payments.

It doesn't hurt to set up a home-equity line of credit just to have cash available for emergencies. But proceed with caution.

Here's another idea for writing off your consumer interest. Borrow the money you need from yourself—that is, from your own savings. Then pay back the principal plus interest just as you would to a bank. You are effectively getting a deduction on your loan interest, because you are not reporting interest income on the amount you took out of your account.

Say you buy $4,000 worth of new furniture for your living room. The store offers you plenty of time to pay, but at a hefty rate of interest, and the interest you pay will not be deductible.

Instead, you take $4,000 out of your savings account and set up a plan to pay yourself back $200 per month plus interest for 20 months. Through smart and disciplined money management, you are effectively getting a "deduction" for interest on the funds you borrowed from yourself.

Another strategy: Lease rather than buy.

Here's an example of how leasing can pay off. You're a taxpayer in the 28 percent bracket and are in the market for a new car. You settle on a midsize model with a purchase price of $15,000.

Your down payment adds up to $2,250, or 15 percent of the purchase price. And you agree to pay a lender $330 a month for 48 months. The installment loan rate: 11 percent. The total amount the car will cost you: $18,090.

Your colleague in the next office is also in the 28 percent tax bracket. He, too, is in the market for a new car. And he, too, finds one with a price tag of $15,000. But he opts to lease rather than buy.

His monthly lease payments are $290, which means he is out of pocket $13,920 over a period of 48 months—or $4,170 less than you will pay to purchase your car outright.

In addition, he invests the $2,250 he had set aside as a down payment in a money-market account paying 6 percent compounded monthly. His earnings over 48 months: $609.

His total cost, then, is $13,311—that is, his lease payments of $290 a month for 48 months minus the $609 in interest he earned.

What about you?

You are out $18,090, but, at the end of 48 months, you own a car with a resale value of $3,000. (Of course, resale values fluctuate depending on the type and model of car.) Also, you benefit from interest deductions.

In 1987, your interest expense adds up to $1,270, so you deduct 65 percent of that amount on your personal return. In 1988, you write off 40 percent of $958, and, in 1989, 20 percent of $611. In 1990, you take an interest deduction of 10 percent of $223.

Your tax savings (assuming a top tax rate of 28 percent): $231 in 1987, $107 in 1988, $34 in 1989, and $7 in 1990.

Your actual cost for the car, then, is $14,711—that is, $18,090 (your out-of-pocket expense) minus $3,000 (the resale value) minus $379 (your tax savings). The bottom line: You would have saved money—$1,400, to be exact—by leasing.

Caution: This example is just that—an example. If you plan to continue to use your automobile for a fifth, sixth, or even seventh year, you may be better off buying than leasing.

Here's why: If you buy, you have only the cost of repairs. If you lease, though, your lease term will have expired. So you must lease a new car—and make new lease payments.

Investment Interest

What qualifies as investment interest? Appropriately enough, it is defined as interest you pay on a loan, such as a stock margin account, that you take out to buy an investment. For the most part, you're allowed to write off investment interest only to the extent of your investment income.

Say, for example, the year is 1990 and you earn $4,000 from your investment in XYZ corp. You pay your stock broker $1,500 interest on the margin account you used to buy the shares. You're allowed to write off the full $1,500. Now, say your earnings totaled only $1,000. That's the maximum amount of investment interest you could deduct.

Uncle Sam does give you a break, though. If you're unable to deduct part of your investment interest in any one year, you may carry it forward to other tax years. Let's return to our example. You had $500 in investment-interest expense that you couldn't deduct. Under the law, you may carry this amount forward as long as you need to—until, that is, you have enough investment income against which you may deduct it.

Remember: Investment income includes gains from the sale of investments, as well as periodic earnings.

You may also convert investment interest to mortgage interest. All you do is borrow against your first or second home. As long as your loan doesn't come to more than $100,000, you may fully deduct the interest.

But take care: It doesn't matter if you're borrowing to buy a second home or a share of stock—putting up your home as collateral is always serious business. Think through the pluses and minuses carefully before you decide to do so.

Passive Investment Interest

We've just seen that you may deduct investment interest only to the extent of your investment income. The same applies to passive activity interest. You may write it off only against passive activity income. That means, of course, if you don't have passive activity income, you can't collect the interest deduction.

But there's good news, too. You also may carry passive activity interest forward indefinitely. Unlike the case with investment interest, however, you get an additional break. The year you sell or otherwise dispose of a passive activity, you may write off all the passive activity interest you weren't able to deduct earlier. (For a complete discussion of passive losses, see Chapter 11.)

What qualifies as a passive investment? The IRS definition is any trade or business in which you do not "materially participate." *Material participation*—in Uncle Sam's eyes—means you are involved in operations on a "regular, continuous, and substantial basis."

The government uses a so-called *facts-and-circumstances test* to determine if you materially participate.

Here are some of the factors Uncle Sam considers.

Is the activity your principal business?

If you spend sixty hours a week operating a retail store, the government concedes that you are materially participating in the store's operations. In general, if you can prove that a business is your principal business, you will almost surely pass the test.

Is your home near the business?

Say you invest in a small coal mine a hundred miles away from your home and never visit the property. Most likely, you are not a material participant. But, if you mine coal on land that is part of or near your principal residence, Uncle Sam will probably conclude that you pass the material participation test.

Do you have knowledge or experience in the business?

Say you invest in a cattle-breeding business. But your knowledge of cattle breeding is limited to your fondness for sirloin. Chances are, the IRS will rule that you don't materially participate in the management of the business.

Are you a limited partner?

The government always considers a limited partnership to have no material participants.

Are you involved in a rental activity?

Most rental activities are passive investments. So interest expense on rental real estate is treated as passive interest. (See Chapter 11 for information on the exceptions to this rule.)

Paper Trails to You

How the IRS treats the interest you pay on borrowed money depends, for the most part, on how you use the cash. In fact, there's only one exception to this rule: the interest on mortgage or home-equity loans.

But for any other kind of loan, different rules apply. And they can get sticky, because as the use of your borrowed funds changes, so does the tax status of the interest charged.

Let's say that you take out a bank loan for a new family car. The car is a personal asset, so the interest on the loan is personal interest. And it's deductible only to the extent indicated on the personal interest deductions table earlier in this chapter.

But suppose you borrow $25,000 and deposit it in your checking account. Later you use some of it to buy stock, some of it to get a dune buggy for your son, and the rest to purchase a typewriter for your business.

In the eyes of the IRS, this single loan generates three types of interest: investment interest on the stock purchase, personal interest on the dune buggy, and business interest on the typewriter. As you already know, different rules govern the deductibility of each of these types of interest.

And if you had bought a limited partnership instead of the stock? The IRS would count the interest on that part of the loan as passive interest, and it would get still a different tax treatment.

In the case of a simple loan you take out with a single purpose in mind, there's not much question about how the interest is treated.

As we all know, however, tax matters are rarely simple. You may borrow the money and not spend it right away. Or, as in our example above, a loan might have two or three different uses at different times. So, the IRS has established some rules for deciding how it classifies interest charges.

Let's say you borrow some money but don't spend it right away. Instead, you deposit it in a savings account. The IRS says that if you deposit the proceeds, the interest you incur on the loan is investment interest. And it remains investment interest until you make your first purchase.

At the point at which you finally get around to buying something— a computer for your business, for instance—the interest becomes business interest. But watch out. There's a trap here.

If you buy the computer within thirty days of receiving the money or depositing it in the bank, the IRS says it won't question your use of the loan. It is, in this case, clearly a business loan.

If you wait longer than thirty days, though, you could create trouble for yourself. That's because the IRS will classify the interest based on the first purchase actually made—even if that purchase is not the reason you borrowed the money.

Say you want to be ready to buy a particular stock when it hits a certain price. So you borrow $5,000 and add it to your money-market account.

Three weeks pass, and your washing machine goes kaput, so you write a check for $600 for the purchase of a new one. Another month passes before your stock hits its price, and you buy shares worth $5,000.

Because you waited more than thirty days to spend the loan, the IRS no longer allows you simply to designate how you spend the proceeds. Instead, it counts the washer as the first purchase from the borrowed funds.

So the interest you incur during the first month is investment interest. After that time, Uncle Sam designates the interest on the first $600 you borrowed as personal interest, eligible for only a 10 percent deduction in 1990 and no deduction at all thereafter.

Only the interest on $4,400 (the $5,000 you borrowed less the $600 the IRS says you spent on the washer) counts as investment interest, eligible for a 100 percent deduction against your investment income.

As you can imagine, the possibilities for complications are endless. So how do you avoid this paper maze? Here are a few tips.

- Keep separate accounts for personal, business, and investment use.
- Pay off old debts that you incurred for more than one purpose and start anew with segregated accounts.
- Make sure debts you pile up for investments can be traced. How? Observe the thirty-day rule. Or, take out the loan with a check payable to a third party—your broker, for example.
- Use a home-equity loan, but don't exceed the limitation.
- Try not to write checks on stock margin accounts, unless you are using the money only to purchase more stock.

Bear in mind one other point. The classification of a loan can change. When you use a loan to buy a business asset, you may lose the business interest deduction if you later sell or transfer the asset to a nonbusiness use.

Suppose you borrow money to buy a delivery van for your flower shop. The interest is fully deductible as business interest.

Six months later, you stop making deliveries and begin using the van as a second family car. At that point the outstanding balance of the loan becomes a personal loan, and subsequent interest charges are classified as personal, too. They're no longer fully deductible in 1990.

If a year later you sell the van and use the proceeds to buy stock, any remaining interest on what had been a personal loan now becomes investment interest eligible for greater tax deductions.

Watch Out!

When it comes to deducting interest expense, keep these points in mind. You should classify the interest into one of the five types. Also, don't forget to keep track of investment interest and passive losses that Uncle Sam says you may carry forward.

Finally, consider restructuring your debt—through a home-equity loan, say—to maximize the interest you may deduct.

Remember, your objective should be to minimize the after-tax cost of borrowing. Taking the time to familiarize yourself with the rules governing interest deductions pays off.

17 *Choices, Choices*

Your Guide to Mortgage Loans

*B*uying a house or condominium involves not only finding the right property but finding the right mortgage. Fortunately, the choice isn't as confusing as it was in the recent past. Since interest rates are lower, the types of mortgages have dwindled.

But the number of mortgage lenders has increased. No longer is your corner savings and loan the only place to shop for mortgages. New entries in the mortgage-granting game include insurance companies, retailers, and manufacturers.

What mortgage is right for you? And which mortgage lender? The answers depend, in large measure, on your personal financial profile.

Let's take a look.

The Real You

Say you're in your twenties. Your income would not make a Rockefeller jealous, but you have great expectations. For you, an *adjustable-rate mortgage* (ARM) that offers a reduced first-year rate—and reduced first-year payments—may be just the ticket.

But let's say you're in your fifties and looking forward to retirement on a fixed income. You're probably better off with a *fixed-rate mortgage*, even though it costs a bit more.

When it comes time to evaluate what type of mortgage is best for you, you should also consider how long you plan to stay in your new home.

If you intend to stay a short time—say, less than five years—you probably should opt for an ARM, especially one that fixes the rate for three to five years. But if you plan to stay put and are worried that interest rates may rise, you might want a fixed-rate mortgage with its guarantee of stable payments.

Look, too, at your willingness to accept risk. Are you willing to gamble on the belief that interest rates will drop? If so, you may want to take your chances with an ARM.

If, however, not being able to budget a definite mortgage payment from year to year makes you lose sleep, you should probably go the fixed-rate route.

The Basics, Please

We'll get to types of mortgages shortly, but first a few basics.

One key to getting the mortgage that's right for you: shopping around. Keep in mind, though, that not all lenders offer all types of mortgages. Our advice: First, choose the kind of mortgage you want; then seek a lender. Here is a checklist to help you identify potential sources of mortgage money:

- Savings and loan associations
- Savings banks
- Mutual savings banks
- Credit unions
- Commercial banks
- Mortgage companies
- The seller of the house you want to buy

Big Business

If the mortgage you need is quite large—more than $200,000 for a single-family house—you'll have to get a so-called *jumbo mortgage*. Some lenders specialize in these larger mortgages—but not all lenders offer them.

Expect to pay a premium for a jumbo. Here's the reason: Loans that top $153,250 for single-family houses can't be sold in the secondary mortgage market—that is, to investment bankers or government agencies, such as the Government National Mortgage Association (GNMA).

So the lowest rates are available on mortgages that total less than $153,250. Loans over that amount usually cost a half to a full percentage point more.

Also, expect lenders to offer one rate on mortgages between $150,000 and $250,000, and another rate on loans in excess of $250,000.

Tip: Some lenders offer lower rates on jumbo mortgages to borrowers who make down payments equal to more than 20 percent of the purchase price.

Compare Rates

Whether you choose an adjustable-rate or fixed-rate mortgage, you'll want to compare rates. What's the most effective way to compare?

Most newspapers regularly publish a list of current rates. So does *Money* magazine. Since rates can change rapidly, though, you might want to canvass lending institutions in your area.

You can also check rates with local title insurance companies and escrow agents. They often compile lists of rates available from area lenders.

Or ask your real-estate agent for the names of companies that maintain sources of low-rate mortgages in computerized data bases.

All Locked Up

Some lenders make you lock in a rate when you apply for a mortgage. Others make you accept the prevailing rate the day your application is approved. And some give you a rate the day you close or let you lock in your rate a few days before the closing. Others give you a choice among these options.

Time Is Money

The traditional wisdom was that it made sense to finance a house with the largest mortgage and longest possible term you could find. That way, your hefty interest payments ensured maximum tax deductions for a long time. But increasingly home buyers are opting for fifteen-year fixed-rate mortgages. The payments are higher, but interest rates are lower. And you build equity in your house faster.

Also, tax rates are now lower. You used to save as much as 50 cents in taxes for every dollar in mortgage interest you wrote off. Now you save only 28 to 33 cents, tops.

For instance, suppose you need a $100,000 mortgage. Not long ago, a thirty-year mortgage carried a rate of 9.75 percent, while a fifteen-year mortgage was going for 9.25 percent—a full half a percentage point less.

For the fifteen-year mortgage, you'd have to pay $170 a month more—$1,029 a month, instead of $859 for the thirty-year mortgage. But your total payout would be $185,220, instead of $309,240. So you would save $124,020 by paying the mortgage in half the time.

But saving taxes and interest are only part of the story. If you can't afford the higher monthly payments, a fifteen-year mortgage is obviously not for you. Even if you can afford it, you may be able to invest the extra money you'd pay more productively.

The bottom line: You have to run the numbers and take into consideration your own unique circumstances.

How Much Down?

How much should you put down when it comes to buying a house? Of course, most first-time home buyers don't have a choice. They need to borrow at least 80 percent if they're to buy a house at all. If you do have a choice, though, you should consider your options as you would any investment.

Let's say that you're in the market for a new home, and the going rate on mortgages is 9 percent. Should you make a large down payment or a small one?

The answer depends, in part, on how much you can earn on your money and your tax bracket. You want to calculate your actual after-tax cost of borrowing. So you reduce the mortgage rate—9.00 percent—by your tax bracket—28.00 percent. The result is 6.48 percent.

If you can earn more than 6.48 percent after taxes on your money, make a small down payment, and put your money to work elsewhere. Your return exceeds the cost of borrowing.

Of course, your decision on how much to put down also depends on your personal financial profile. For example, you may be so averse to debt that you'd prefer to plunk down as much as you possibly can. And you may sleep better knowing your house will be free and clear—and paid for—in the shortest possible time.

To the Point

When you buy a house, you pay points, or loan origination fees. *Points* are the price you pay just for getting a loan. One point equals 1 percent of your mortgage.

But some lenders allow you to forgo paying points if you're willing to pay higher rates. You pay only title insurance and appraisal fees when you purchase the property.

Now that you know the basics of mortgage shopping, let's look more closely at the different types of mortgages available.

Fixed-Rate Mortgages

Fixed-rate mortgages are currently the most popular. With this type of mortgage, the interest rate you pay is slightly higher than on other kinds. But that rate does not change—ever. And people who believe interest rates will rise find this feature appealing.

Should you take out a fixed-rate mortgage? The answer, again, depends in large measure on your personal financial profile.

The key questions to ask yourself: How important to you is the security of a fixed rate? Do you expect your income to increase over the next few years? If you don't think your income will rise with interest rates, your best bet may be a fixed-rate mortgage.

As a rule, though, it makes sense to opt for a fixed-rate loan when interest rates are relatively low and an adjustable-rate mortgage when rates are relatively high.

Adjustable-Rate Mortgages

Certainly, it's tempting to lock in lower interest rates with a fixed-rate mortgage. But an adjustable-rate loan may still be right for you.

Why? With an adjustable-rate mortgage you pay an initial rate of interest that is below that of a fixed-rate loan. How much below varies.

When fixed-rate mortgages were in the 12 to 14 percent range, ARMs were available at 2 to 3 points less. In the recent past, ARMs were only 1 to 2 points lower than fixed-rate loans.

But you shouldn't let that initial savings go to your head. The reason: If interest rates rise quickly, your ARM can become more expensive in no time flat.

As we've seen, ARMs make the most sense for people who don't expect to live in their new home for more than a few years. Some examples: people who are buying a "starter" home and plan to move on and up as soon as their income increases, military personnel, and corporate candidates for relocation.

They also make sense if you expect interest rates to remain stable or decline. But as we all know, predicting interest rates is far from an exact science.

You should exercise caution in choosing any kind of ARM. There are all sorts of adjustable-rate mortgages and all sorts of financial indices for lenders to monitor.

The Federal Trade Commission (FTC) has issued a list of tips for mortgage buyers to consider before signing on the dotted line. In shopping for any type of adjustable-rate loan, the FTC cautions, you should look at the following:

- The initial interest rate
- How often the rate may change
- How much the rate may change
- The initial monthly payments
- The mortgage term
- The index to which changes are tied

Also, you should know that some ARMs involve *negative amortization*. And negative amortization can come as a nasty shock in periods of high inflation. Under a negative amortization mortgage, you don't pay more each month if interest rates rise. Instead, the lender increases the amount of the total loan.

In other words, the amount you pay each month stays the same. But instead of decreasing the mortgage on your home each month, you could actually be increasing it as rates continue to climb.

Negative amortization loans are low-cost alternatives that make home-ownership available in inflationary times. They involve the expectation that the underlying value of the home will also rise, so you can eventually recover the balance of your loan when you sell your house. The downside: Real-estate prices may not increase enough to keep pace with the increase in your mortgage balance.

Balloon Mortgages

Balloon loans are sometimes called *partially amortized loans*. With a balloon loan, your final payment is much larger than your other payments.

Here's how a balloon mortgage works. Say you buy a new house for $170,000 and take out a mortgage for $125,000. The terms: 11 percent interest and a seven-year balloon.

Your monthly loan payment is calculated as if you financed the loan over a regular term—twenty years, say. So, in this case, your mortgage payments add up to $1,290 a month for seven years. At the end of seven years, you pay the loan off in full or refinance.

Who should get a balloon mortgage? A person who expects a big infusion of cash sometime in the future is a likely candidate. So is someone who intends to refinance.

Graduated Payment Mortgages

A graduated payment mortgage (GPM) offers lower monthly payments at first. Then payments steadily rise until they level off after a few years. Graduated payment mortgages—also known as *JEEPS*—are designed for young people whose income is expected to grow as their careers advance.

If you plan to take on this type of mortgage, you should be as sure as you can be that your income will keep pace with your rising payments.

Wraparound Mortgages

A wraparound mortgage takes its name from the fact that it "wraps around" your first mortgage. A wraparound is really a second or junior mortgage. You make payments on a new mortgage to the wraparound lender, who, in turn, makes scheduled installment payments on the original, senior mortgage.

What's the difference between a senior mortgage and junior mortgage? If you default on your loans, the senior mortgage is paid off before the junior or second mortgage—that is, the issuer of the senior mortgage gets first dibs on your property.

Wraparounds are a convenient way to get additional credit without first having to pay off your existing mortgage. But you should, of course, be careful about taking on more debt than you can handle.

And There's More

We've described the types of mortgages you're *likely* to encounter. But in today's rapidly changing economic environment, you never know what new type of financial product might come your way.

For instance, some lending institutions have recently introduced the "biweekly" mortgage. With this type of arrangement, you make half your normal monthly payment of principal and interest every other week. By accelerating payments, and effectively making 13 months of payments rather than 12, you reduce the amount you owe much faster than you would ordinarily—and build equity at a correspondingly faster clip. So you could pay off a biweekly $100,000 mortgage at 9.25 percent in slightly more than twenty-one years rather than thirty.

Ask your realtor or lender to alert you to any new wrinkles in the mortgage market that you might find advantageous.

To Refinance or Not to Refinance

If mortgage rates are now much lower than the mortgage you have currently, it may be time to refinance. It doesn't take long for some homeowners to recoup the additional costs they pay when they get a new loan.

If you go to your current lender for refinancing of the same principal amount, you might be able to get your mortgage interest rate lowered without rewriting the loan. But most banks sell fixed-rate mortgages in the secondary market—that is, to the Government National Mortgage Association and the Federal National Mortgage Association.

If your loan has been sold, you'll have to go through another mortgage closing—and pay all the closing costs and bank fees over again.

How can you tell if refinancing is worth it for you? Closing costs average about 2.5 percent of the loan amount. Generally, refinancing is worthwhile if there is a difference of at least two percentage points between the interest you are paying now and the interest you could get with a new loan.

Let's say you have a $60,000, twenty-year mortgage at 15 percent, making your monthly payment $790. You refinance at 12 percent. The monthly payment on the same $60,000 would be $660. You save $130 a month by refinancing.

To figure how long it would take you to recoup the cost of refinancing, all you do is divide the closing costs by your monthly savings.

For example, if your closing costs on the $60,000 mortgage were about average—say, $1,500—you would divide $1,500 by your monthly savings of $130. And you would learn that it would take a little less than twelve months for you to recover your costs.

Before making a final decision on whether to refinance, you need to know some additional facts. For example, even if you are refinancing with the same lender, you will have to pay for such items as home reappraisal, legal fees, document preparation, and recording. If you go to a new lender, you'll have to pay for a new credit report, a new title search, and title insurance as well.

See, too, if you have to pay a penalty for prepaying your current mortgage. Some states forbid these penalties, others do not. The penalties can be hefty—six months' interest is common. And that kind of penalty on a 15 percent, $60,000 mortgage can add another $4,500 to your closing costs.

If your present lender balks at giving you a lower-rate mortgage, go elsewhere: a different bank or savings and loan or a mortgage company.

The last word: Interest rates may drop further from their current levels. Do some research. Read and listen to the experts. Then decide on whether now is a good time to refinance.

Remember, no one is perfect at predicting turns in interest rates. You have to make up your own mind.

PART FOUR

Insurance– Your Safety Net

18 *Risky Business*

What You Need to Know About Insurance

When you sit down with a professional financial planner, "risk management" is usually one of the first topics of conversation.

Financial planners know that failing to address your insurance needs can invite financial disaster. So, one of our most critical jobs is to identify your exposure to risk and help you decide which risks to retain and which to transfer.

This is no small decision. When you retain a risk, losses come out of your own pocket. When you transfer a risk, the insurance company pays some or all of the loss.

No hard and fast rules dictate which risks you should live with and which you should hand off to someone else. The decision depends entirely on your own circumstances and, to some extent, your temperament—as the following two examples illustrate.

Say you are a forty-five-year-old senior executive. You earn a handsome $300,000 a year and maintain a cash reserve of $75,000. You are in the market for car insurance.

You opt to purchase only personal injury liability coverage for your 1984 automobile. The reason: You save $1,000 annually in auto insurance premiums.

When you inform your insurance agent of your decision, he points out that you're out a good deal more than $1,000 if an uninsured motorist smashes into your car and totals it. To you, though, with your cash reserve, it's an acceptable risk.

Now let's say you're a freshly minted MBA with a $50,000 salary and

$50,000 in education loans to repay. You choose full coverage on your brand-new car.

Why? You exhausted your cash reserves during your two years in graduate school and can ill afford to replace the car, a graduation gift from your parents. So you decide to pay insurance premiums rather than risk having to absorb any losses that might stem from a collision with an uninsured motorist.

Make the System Work for You

Personal financial planners examine each client's exposure to risk through a three-step process. This system will work for you, too.

Here's how it goes.

STEP 1: Identify the risk.
Risks fall into six general categories: health, disability, death, vehicle, real estate, and liability. You pinpoint potential losses in each of these categories. Then you evaluate how these losses may change over time or with financial circumstances.

In the six chapters that follow, we address the insurance coverage you need to shield yourself from these risks.

STEP 2: Make an informed decision about whether to retain or transfer the risk.
As a rule, you should transfer the risk for potentially severe losses—such as the destruction of a house—to an insurance carrier. It's smarter to pay a small amount each year in insurance premiums to protect yourself from a potentially huge loss.

You should not, however, cover potentially small losses with insurance. A *small loss* is one you are able—and willing—to cover out of your current income or personal savings. For example, you may shrug off a $10,000 loss. But, to the person in the next office, a $10,000 loss could spell financial disaster.

STEP 3: If you transfer the risk, then determine the
amount of coverage you need and purchase a comprehensive
policy that covers all unacceptable situations.
Your goal is to eliminate your exposure to unacceptable risks in both an effective and a cost-efficient manner.

Consider the comprehensiveness of each type of policy. Which events are covered? Which are excluded? Look for policies that take care of all risks that you want to transfer, but watch out for plans that cover risks you are willing to shoulder.

And shop around. That way, you will pay no more than is absolutely necessary for the insurance protection you need.

19 *The Picture of Health*

How Your Health Insurance
Can Keep You in the Pink

With the high cost of medical care today, you have to worry about what will happen to your personal finances if you or a family member is stricken with a long illness.

These days, few people emerge financially unscathed from a medical tragedy. Still, it is possible to preserve most of your resources—if you plan carefully.

Begin by taking stock of your health-care coverage.

Types of Coverage

Until the last decade, most health insurance was provided by commercial carriers and nonprofit organizations, such as Blue Cross and Blue Shield. Increasingly, though, people are opting for coverage by health maintenance organizations (HMOs) and preferred provider organizations (PPOs).

If your employer offers you a choice—or you're self-employed—you should understand fully the differences between these types of coverage. And you should carefully examine any plan before you sign up—or you could find yourself without vital protection at the worst possible time.

180

Basic Plan

The insurance industry defines a *basic plan* as a policy that includes hospital, surgical, and physicians' expense insurance. But, in reality, most individual policies and group plans provide basic coverage *plus* major medical.

The amount you pay for medical insurance depends on your age, sex, occupation, health—even your zip code. Why zip code? Your zip code identifies where you live, and insurance premiums are higher in communities where hospital costs are high.

Most health-care policies include a deductible amount. You pay, say, the first $200 of your medical expenses for the year. Then the insurance company picks up the remaining amount. The typical deductible for a basic health plan is $200 to $500.

Coinsurance is another common feature of health-care plans. A *coinsurance clause* says that you and the insurance company jointly cover your medical expenses.

Usually, a coinsurance agreement calls for the insurance company to pay 80 percent of your medical costs. You pay the remaining 20 percent. Most plans require a co-payment for certain prescriptions and doctor visits when you receive the services.

You're Covered

Here's a rundown of the kinds of health-care coverage available.

Hospital Expense Insurance

If you're covered by a medical plan, chances are your policy includes hospital expense insurance. These benefits go to pay for your hospital stay.

Policies cover room and board, nursing care, drugs, lab fees, X rays, and medical supplies. Included, too, are outpatient services, such as preadmission tests.

Traditional health insurance plans—like those in place at many large companies—limit hospital expense coverage to a specified period of time, in most cases anywhere from 20 to 120 days. Newer plans specify the total dollar amount they'll cover.

Surgical Expense Insurance

You know that surgical expense insurance covers the cost of operations. But you may not know that these policies don't cover all related procedures.

Policies from most well-known carriers list the types of operations covered and the maximum amount they will pay for each. They typically pay the "usual, customary, and reasonable" fees for surgical procedures. Your doctor will have a list of the fees considered usual, customary, and reasonable.

In some states, the physician may accept this amount as payment or may ask you to pay the difference between this amount and the actual fee. In other states, the physician must accept what the insurer pays, and doctors may not ask patients to pay any additional amount.

Caution: Some insurance carriers recommend that you do not sign any agreement to pay more than the usual, customary, and reasonable fees. Rather, you should refer the matter to the carrier, and it will negotiate a reduced amount with the physician.

Some carriers will write a letter to the physician asking why the fee exceeds the usual and customary amount. If the doctor successfully argues that the medical situation required the delivery of extraordinary services, the insurance carrier may pick up the tab.

Physicians' Expense Insurance

These policies pay for only a specified number of in-hospital visits. You should check your plan for limitations. Also, note whether your policy covers the cost of office visits.

Major Medical Insurance

Major medical insurance picks up where your basic coverage—hospital, surgical, and physicians' expenses—leaves off. Benefits go to pay for care provided both in and out of the hospital.

Say, for example, that your hospital expense insurance limits coverage to twenty-one days. You've been in the hospital twenty-five days.

Your major medical plan takes effect once you've exhausted your other benefits and pays for the extra four days in the hospital.

Most major medical plans pay 80 to 100 percent of your medical expenses over a deductible amount (which can range from $100 to $1,000 a year).

Typically, they cover everything from artificial limbs to intensive care services, reconstructive surgery, and prescription drugs. Sometimes, the plans cover mouth and gum diseases, as well as oral surgery, but, in most cases, the treatment must be provided in a hospital.

Among the items not covered by most major medical plans: routine dental work, cosmetic surgery, routine physical examinations, eye exams, eyeglasses, and hearing aids.

Special-Purpose Health Insurance

In the last couple of years, advertisements for special-purpose policies have become a staple on television and radio.

Some of these plans cover only accidents or certain illnesses, such as cancer. Others pay only when you're hospitalized. The usual benefit is $50 to $100 per day for every day you're in the hospital. The policies may also pay you a flat amount for certain injuries—$5,000 if you lose an arm or a leg, $10,000 for the loss of your vision, and so on.

However, there's a long list of exclusions, and some plans require you to be in the hospital ten days or more before payment begins. The likelihood that you'll be in the hospital this long is small. Likewise, the chance of your falling victim to a specific illness is slight.

In most cases, special-purpose policies aren't necessary. Your existing health insurance should cover your costs if you're injured or suffer from a specific illness.

Dental Insurance

Dental insurance policies are now common and frequently offered as a fringe benefit by employers. These plans cover common dental expenses, such as X rays, fillings, extractions, root canals, crowns, and even expensive orthodontic work.

Clearly, you should sign up for dental insurance if it is available to you as a fringe benefit and paid for by your employer. But you shouldn't necessarily purchase the policies yourself.

The reason: Since everyone incurs dental expenses and the bills are fairly predictable, dental coverage is more of a prepayment plan than an insurance policy. Your dental insurance premiums may add up to more than your dental bills.

For a single person, plans usually cost about $15 to $20 a month. Family coverage costs about $10 to $15 a month more.

Extended and Home Care Insurance

Statistics show that one out of every four Americans who reaches age sixty-five will eventually receive nursing home care. For people between sixty-five and seventy-five years old, the median nursing home stay is fifty-three days.

And such a stay is not cheap. The national average cost per day in a skilled care facility is $91. And in some locations it's much higher. The Massachusetts average, for instance, is $149.

Who pays for this care?

You do. But insurance is available that will cover most nursing home costs and the cost of professional care in your own home following a hospital or nursing home visit. Also, some life insurance policies are starting to offer nursing home coverage while you are still alive. Ask your insurance agent about policies, but do your own homework and don't look at just one plan. Shop around.

The benefits vary tremendously from plan to plan. Some reimburse just a small flat daily rate and include numerous restrictions. Most require prior hospitalization before they begin paying, and all of them have lifetime benefit limits. Some plans exclude coverage for mental illness.

Premiums remain the same once you're issued a policy. However, the amount you'll pay depends on your age—the older you are when you buy a policy the more you'll fork over in premiums. At age fifty-five, you'll pay about $180 a year for a no-frills policy that reimburses $40 per day after you've been in the facility for twenty days. At age seventy-five, the same policy will cost you approximately $1,200 a year. And the annual cost for a much more comprehensive plan at that age can run $2,400 or more.

What About Health Maintenance Organizations?

Health maintenance organizations—HMOs for short—are prepaid health-care plans that provide all your medical care.

To attain this end, the organizations employ or contract with physicians in every specialty—from internists to oncologists to psychiatrists. They also contract with hospitals and other health-care facilities.

Most HMOs require you to use their doctors and services, except in emergencies. But the structures of HMOs differ. For starters, some are run for profit, others are nonprofit. Some cost more than traditional health insurance, others less. Also, some so-called *open-ended* HMOs operate more like traditional health insurance plans and allow participants to sometimes see physicians who are not employed by the HMO.

Most HMOs give you a choice of coverages for a flat monthly fee. The broadest coverage pays for everything—from hospital and physicians' fees to prescription drugs. With limited coverage, you'd pick up part of the tab for your medicines and outpatient visits. The majority of plans pay if you have to go to a non-HMO-affiliated hospital in an emergency or need specialized care not available at the HMO.

Most people subscribe to HMOs through their employers, although you can sign up individually. If your company offers an HMO as an alternative to traditional health insurance, consider this option carefully.

Many HMOs are well run and provide excellent care. They give you the cost advantage of no deductibles and no coinsurance. With most plans, you just pay a nominal fee—$3, say—per visit and per prescription.

But you shouldn't sign on blindly. Some plans are not so well run. And with scores of new HMOs forming every day, industry insiders speculate that a shakeout may be likely.

If you enroll in an HMO that is financially unstable, you could be in for real problems. Consider the case of the Illinois schoolteacher whose HMO went bankrupt. A doctor at the HMO diagnosed that the man had a malignant brain tumor and referred him to the Mayo Clinic.

The Mayo Clinic treated the teacher, then sent bills for its services to the HMO. The HMO went belly up, the teacher died, and his family was left with thousands of dollars in medical costs.

So if you are considering enrolling in an HMO, study its finances carefully. Ask for copies of its financial statements for the last few years and compare these with the financial statements of other HMOs in your area. Look at the ratio of assets to liabilities, and make sure the balance sheet indicates a strong organization well able to care for its customer base.

Another question you need to ask to decide if a particular HMO is right for you: What are the reputations of the doctors it employs? Does your own doctor practice there?

One criticism of most HMOs is that they provide you little leeway in the choice of a personal physician. Many people have a family physician. If they switch to an HMO, they could not see that physician unless they were willing to foot the bill themselves.

Also check out the reputation of the HMO within the medical community. And ask each HMO you're considering why you should join its plan rather than its competitor's.

Some other questions to ask: Does your HMO cover accidents when you're out of town? What kind of coverage does it provide in these situations? What if you need a specialist not retained by your HMO? Will the HMO plan pay for outside second opinions? Does your HMO cover organ transplants?

Also ask whether or not you may continue as a member if you are laid off from your job. And make sure you know what happens to your coverage should you move to another state.

What About PPOs?

A preferred provider organization (PPO) typically works like this: Physicians and hospitals agree to provide a company's employees with services at a discount rate. In return, they're likely to receive a steady flow of new patients.

Generally, when a corporation's employees are enrolled in a PPO, all or most of their doctor and hospital costs are covered. But if employees seek medical treatment from a health-care provider not on the PPO list, they must foot a large portion of the bill themselves.

The one exception to this rule: emergency care. Employees who require emergency treatment while out of town or who are unable to go to a participating hospital have their medical bills paid regardless.

The PPO concept got its start in 1978, when the Motion Picture Health and Welfare Fund struck a deal with a group of Canoga Park, California, chiropractors. The plan called for the chiropractors to provide services to fund members at a cut rate.

Today, PPOs take a variety of forms. Some operate like insurance carriers and charge participants a flat monthly fee. Others are simply groups of health-care professionals who agree to provide medical services to a company's employees. They're paid by the corporation solely on a fee-for-service basis. As a rule, PPOs can be set up by health-care providers, purchasers of health-care services, or combinations of the two.

In some respects, PPOs work like HMOs. But there are differences between the two types of organizations. An HMO takes care of all your medical problems for a fixed fee, and it accepts individual members. A PPO usually provides treatment only on a fee-for-service basis at discounted rates, and it serves groups of employees only. Also, PPOs generally offer a larger choice of doctors.

Proponents of PPOs tout the organizations as the best way so far to cap health-care expenditures. Whether that is the case, no one knows. The idea is simply too new.

And there are drawbacks to consider. For example, it's difficult to know if the prices PPOs quote are really less expensive. If a doctor's charges are already high, the discounted price may still be higher than rates charged by other physicians in your area.

How Much Insurance Do You Need?

Obviously, you want to transfer to an insurance carrier the risk for huge losses that can result from an illness or accident. And, as with all insurance, you want to obtain the most coverage for the least amount of money and to purchase no more insurance than you need.

But how much health insurance is enough?

One rule of thumb has it that you should purchase enough insurance to cover 75 percent of any medical expenses you may encounter. But would you want to run the risk of having to pay 25 percent of a million-dollar medical bill?

You should find out how much you would be out of pocket if medical disaster strikes. What is your deductible? Is it a reasonable amount that you can handle comfortably?

Does your policy include coinsurance? Say, for example, that your plan requires you to pay 20 percent of the bills, while the insurance carrier covers 80 percent. Figure out at what point that 20 percent would put you into serious financial trouble.

And, to protect yourself adequately, make sure your plan includes stop-loss coverage.

Stop-loss provisions require the insurance carrier to pick up the entire tab once your out-of-pocket medical expenses (also called out-of-pocket maximums) exceed a preset amount—$5,000, say. Without stop-loss coverage, you continue to foot as much as 20 percent of the bill—and 20 percent of an enormous sum can add up to more than you can afford.

Caution: Stop-loss goes only so far. Many policies clamp a ceiling— usually, $250,000—on benefits paid by the plan over your lifetime.

If you pay your own premiums, seek a policy that includes no such limit or a very high limit—$1 million to $2 million, say. The difference in the premium should amount to no more than $1 or $2 a month.

If you're enrolled in an employer-paid group plan, you may want to purchase a supplemental policy. But be prepared to pay for it. Since demand for the policies is small, these plans cost upward of $300 a year. But the extra coverage is important.

These days, with the escalating cost of health care, $1 million in major medical coverage is not unusual. Nor is it too much. We have all read about children who require multiple organ transplants or victims of AIDS. With these and other catastrophic situations, you can easily run up medical bills of $1 million or more. So you want enough insurance to ensure that you will never go medically bankrupt.

You should apply the general rules of insurance to medical coverage. Just remember these points: Always transfer the risk of infrequent catastrophic losses—the cost of treating major illnesses. Never transfer the risk of frequent small losses, such as the cost of a tooth extraction.

Money Matters

Investigate carefully the policies available from commercial insurance companies. Pay attention to deductibles, exclusions, and payment limits.

Also, as a rule, stick to financially strong, reputable insurance companies. And shop around. Compare the policies of at least three carriers before you buy one.

Another idea: Ask your doctor's office manager—or your doctor—which companies he or she likes to deal with and which ones have been troublesome.

Although you can—and should—do your own comparison shopping, ask your insurance agent for help. He or she can find out about costs and help identify the best companies in your area. Most good agents will recommend only those companies that have treated their clients well at claim time.

You should base your decision to purchase a policy as much on benefits as on price. Often, you pay only a little more for a lot more coverage.

Tips: One way to cut back on your health insurance premiums is to boost your deductible. Another way is to purchase a policy that includes a coinsurance provision.

Watch Your Step

Some pitfalls to avoid: the absence or limited coverage of psychiatric care and such costly but critical services as kidney dialysis.

When it comes to psychiatric coverage, you may be willing to accept limits on the amount of your insurance coverage for outpatient services, such as group therapy. But should you need inpatient psychiatric service, the coverage should be identical to hospitalization for any other illness. Here's an example to illustrate why.

Some years ago the sixteen-year-old daughter of a man we know went to a party. Someone dropped a hallucinogenic drug into her drink.

A few hours later, she was in the psychiatric ward of a nearby hospital. Before his daughter's treatment was finished, the man had exhausted the $20,000 of coverage provided by his insurance plan and spent $60,000 of his own money.

And be warned that some states regulate how much the insurance company must pay for psychiatric outpatient treatment. Check out your policy for such limitations.

Another potentially troublesome area: alcoholism. Despite the widespread consensus that alcoholism is a treatable disease, many insurance companies still balk at paying benefits for treatment. Again, check your policy.

Finally, take note: If you change jobs, pay attention to when your old policy ends and your new one begins. For example, company-provided health insurance may not become effective until thirty days after you begin your new job. So you may want to hedge your bets against medical disaster and extend your existing plan to cover you and your family during this interim period. The cost is usually the amount of the monthly premium for your coverage, plus 2 percent.

If you're self-employed and purchase the policy yourself, you can sign up for a plan that takes effect at once.

You Choose

Health insurance is a standard fringe benefit. But many employers, as part of cafeteria benefit plans, now offer a choice. (See Chapter 28 for more on cafeteria plans.) The choice may be between a traditional health insurance plan and an HMO.

Or you may simply have options in designing your plan. For example, a corporation may allow employees to choose health insurance with either a $100 or a $300 deductible. If you select the higher deductible, your own contribution is less.

To Be Continued

When Congress adopted the Comprehensive Omnibus Budget Reconciliation Act of 1986 (COBRA), it did widows and dependents of active workers a big favor. This law requires companies that employ more than twenty people to continue to provide group health insurance for up to three years to widows, divorced or separated spouses, and dependents of active employees.

In the case of terminated employees and their dependents—or employees who lose coverage because their hours are reduced—companies must continue to offer coverage for up to eighteen months.

The coverage, however, isn't free. The law allows companies to collect a monthly premium equal to 102 percent of the amount the company actually pays for each employee. (The 2 percent—an amount, incidentally, which many companies say is inadequate—goes to cover the company's administrative costs.) And the cost of many group health insurance plans tops $100 a month.

Caution: A conversion policy—that is, a plan that allows you to convert a group health insurance policy to an individual one—costs the same or more than a group plan. And the coverage is not as comprehensive.

For example, a conversion policy caps the amount the insurer pays for hospital care at $100 to $200 a day—at a time when semiprivate hospital rooms in the United States average more than $400 a day.

What Will Medicare Do for You?

Medicare, the federal government program initiated in the 1960s, pays for health care for people who are sixty-five years of age or older or disabled. Medicare is financed by the contributions of employees and employers through Social Security taxes.

Medicare benefits aren't paid automatically. You must apply to receive them.

Uncle Sam divides Medicare into two parts: A and B. Part A covers hospital expenses, nursing home care, and some outpatient medical expenses. Part B is a voluntary program. It is financed partly by the federal government and partly by monthly payments from people who sign up.

A supplementary insurance program, Part B covers costs not included in Part A, such as physicians' services and medical supplies. Part B, which in 1989 cost $24.80 a month, pays 80 percent of covered medical and surgical charges above an annual $75 deductible amount.

Apply for Part B about three months before you turn sixty-five. That way, the paperwork will be completed by the time you are eligible for coverage.

Write Now

If you're interested in understanding—and perhaps supplementing—your health-care coverage, here's a suggestion. Send copies of your current health-care policies to your independent insurance agent along with this letter.* Just insert the correct address, and it's ready to go.

J. Q. Professional
Executive Insurance Inc.

Dear Insurance Professional:

I am evaluating my medical insurance, and I would appreciate your assistance. I have listed below the specific information I need about my current coverage. Please feel free to fill in the answers on this letter and return it to me.

1. Maximum lifetime limit on total benefit payments:

_____.

2. Individual deductible amount:

_____.

3. Limit on deductible for a family:

_____.

*For the concept of the insurance letters in this section, we are indebted to Ben Baldwin.

4. Coinsurance provision:
   I pay: _____.
   Insurance company pays: _____.
5. Stop-loss provision (At what point is my share of coinsurance no longer required?):
   Per person: _____.
   Per family: _____.
6. Duration of stop-loss (At what point will I be required to make additional coinsurance payments?):
   _____.
7. Any other limits I should be aware of:
   _____.

I would appreciate your recommendations or comments on my medical insurance coverage.

I thank you in advance for your help.

Sincerely,

20 *A Matter of Policy*

How to Keep Your Income
Coming If You're Disabled

*I*f you're like most people, you're hard pressed to describe what kind of disability coverage you have. That's unfortunate, because what you don't know can hurt you.

The Health Insurance Association of America estimates that people between the ages of thirty-five and sixty-five are six times more likely to become disabled than to die.

Other troubling statistics:

- A forty-year-old executive has a one in six chance of becoming disabled before retirement.
- Of the people who have disability policies, only one out of six has a plan that pays benefits for a disability lasting longer than two years.
- The average duration of a disability that lasts more than ninety days is five years.

Blame it on modern medicine: What used to be the four major killers of adult Americans—hypertension, heart disease, cerebrovascular diseases, and diabetes—are now the four major disablers. So, while you're no longer as likely to die from these diseases, there's a very good chance they could keep you out of work for an extended period.

Here's what you need to know to protect yourself should you become disabled.

Your Disability Coverage

Disability coverage is vital—its lack constitutes an unacceptable risk for most people. So you should identify how much you need and make sure you have enough.

Insurance carriers limit the amount of coverage you can buy, usually to 60 to 70 percent of your gross earnings. Insurance companies want you to have an incentive to return to work. If you can collect as much on disability as on the job, why go back to the daily grind?

But high-earning executives and professionals may be subject to greater restrictions. The maximum amount of disability coverage now available is about $20,000 a month. The cost of disability insurance is based on your age, sex, smoking habits, and occupation. Insurance companies assume that some occupations—construction worker, say—are more hazardous to your health than others.

Another variable in the cost of your policy: the *waiting period* you select. This waiting period is the length of time you must be disabled before your policy begins to pay.

For example, a twenty-five-year-old female banker whose policy has a 60-day waiting period will pay $240 a year to receive disability benefits of $500 a month. For a policy with a 120-day waiting period, she will pay about $50 less a year.

If you own your own business, the best way to plan for disability is to make sure you're not indispensable. Your company should be able to carry on in your absence.

If it does, you should be able to take most or all of your salary from your business. In this case, disability payments supplement—instead of replace—your income.

When you shop for disability coverage, ask questions—lots of questions. Here's a checklist to follow, plus some advice on how to cut costs.

When do benefits start?

Most insurance companies will issue your first disability check 30 to 60 days after the so-called *elimination period* ends. This ominous-sounding term is insurance jargon for the time you must be off the job before your disability policy starts to pay benefits.

Let's say you take a nasty tumble on the ski slopes on February 15, and the doctor informs you that you'll be laid up—in, heaven forbid, a body cast—for three months. You immediately inform your employer of your accident. Two weeks later, on March 1, you collect your final paycheck, and your disability insurance takes effect.

If the elimination period in your policy is 30 days, expect to receive your first check one month from the end of this period—in this case, May 1. That means that you will not have been paid for two months. Is this a risk you can afford?

If you can afford the risk, you may be able to reduce your disability insurance premiums by as much as 15 to 20 percent by purchasing a policy with a 60- to 90-day elimination period. (Beyond 90 days, premiums go down, but only slightly.)

Some employers allow employees to choose among several disability insurance policies as part of a cafeteria benefit plan. The longer you wait for benefits to begin, the lower your cost. If you choose a lower-priced plan, make sure you're willing to accept the trade-off. (See Chapter 28 for more information on cafeteria plans.)

You must balance the amount you save on insurance premiums against the loss of income for 90, 120, or even 180 days should you become disabled. And, of course, a lower-cost plan may make sense only if you have enough cash in your emergency reserve to see you through until the insurance carrier pays.

Does it matter who pays my disability premiums?

Under the tax law, if you pay your own disability insurance premiums and become disabled, the benefits you receive aren't subject to taxation. But if your employer covers the premiums and you're laid up, the amount you receive from the insurance carrier is taxed like your salary or any other income.

For this reason, it may pay to foot the bill yourself.

If your employer provides disability coverage as part of a fringe benefits package, you should—under most circumstances—accept the benefit. The exception: If you can trade the coverage for cash to buy your own policy. But usually you don't have a choice. So calculate whether your company-provided coverage is enough. If not, supplement the policy with insurance you purchase yourself.

If you participate in a cafeteria plan, you may want to choose a benefit other than disability insurance and purchase a disability policy on your own.

When do benefits stop?

What you want is lifetime coverage. That way, you receive benefits no matter how long you're disabled. Lifetime policies, however, generally cost more and are not offered by insurance companies to all occupational groups. If you can get this coverage, do so.

If you can't, buy a plan that pays benefits as long as possible. Try to purchase a plan that pays benefits until you reach an age when pension plans and Social Security fill the gap, which can be anywhere between fifty-five and sixty-five.

What if I can't return to work in my own occupation?

Disability insurance policies typically contain clauses that call for a reduction in benefits if you go to work in "any occupation." These policies may not be in your best interest.

Say, for example, that you're a consultant and are constantly on the road. One Saturday night a drunk driver slams into you. You're confined to a wheelchair following the accident and are unable to travel with the frequency your chosen profession requires. But you can teach at a local university during your recuperation, though your teaching income is only a fraction of what you would earn as a consultant.

In this situation, you may not collect any benefits—or, at best, you'll collect only reduced benefits—if your disability policy calls for benefits to stop if you engage in "any occupation." However, with a plan that specifies your "own occupation," your full disability benefits continue, even though you have income from your teaching position.

So, if you have an "any occupation" plan and can afford the additional expense of an "own occupation" policy, buy it.

How much should I arrange to receive each month?

Refer to the cash-flow work sheet you prepared in Appendix III to figure out how much money you need each month. And apply for a policy that replaces as much of your income as the insurance company will allow.

Also, consider other sources of income that might come into play if you are disabled. If, for instance, you have investment income that can be applied to your cost of living, or if you have a working spouse, you may want to reduce the amount you need in benefits.

Tip: Many companies base coverage for employees on base salary, not, for example, compensation plus commissions or bonuses. Again, if your company plan doesn't provide maximum coverage, think about buying supplemental disability insurance.

Will I receive benefits when I'm recovering?

In the eyes of most insurance carriers, you're either sick or well. And that's the end of it. In real life, though, there's often a period of time when you can return to work, but only part time.

Under a typical all-or-nothing policy, benefits stop as soon as you set foot in your office. You receive no payments while you're recovering.

With a so-called *residual rider,* you continue to receive a portion of your benefits while you work your way back to a full-time schedule. If you return to work and collect, say, 60 percent of your salary, then you'd receive 40 percent of your disability benefits. Expect your premiums to jump 15 to 20 percent if you add this extra.

One final note: The Social Security Administration is not overly generous with disability assistance, so, if you're under age sixty-five, don't count heavily on the agency for help.

Will benefits increase over time?

If you want to increase your personal coverage or supplement your company plan, you must take a physical examination—unless your group or individual disability insurance policy is marked "guaranteed future insurability."

With guaranteed policies, your coverage increases every time you get a raise. If you are paying your own premiums, you can expect premium hikes of 5 to 10 percent for each boost; but you won't have to take a physical.

Your individual or group policy may include a cost of living, or COLA, rider. With this rider, you may boost your coverage as the cost of living increases—again, with no medical questions asked.

Can the insurance company cancel the policy?

The answer is yes—if you have a policy not marked "guaranteed renewable." With guaranteed policies, the only cause for cancellation is nonpayment of premiums.

Another tip: Your policy should also be stamped "noncancelable." That one word guarantees that your insurance premiums are set for the life of the policy. The insurance carrier may not charge you more—or less—than the amount stated in the policy.

How much is the premium?

If you're buying your own coverage or supplementing company coverage, talk to a number of insurance agents—or one agent who represents a number of companies—to get quotes. Find out which insurers provide coverage. Then ask about restrictions: Do you have to stop smoking? Must you go on a diet?

Also ask about step-rate premiums. With a step-rate arrangement, you can pay lower premiums now and higher premiums as you get older.

Does my disability coverage extend to my spouse?

You can add a rider to your disability policy that will pay a monthly benefit if your spouse becomes totally disabled. But this rider covers homemakers only.

Benefits are provided for a period of fifteen months. And they equal 50 percent of the amount you pay a housekeeper for performing your spouse's regular duties. One catch: The housekeeper can't be a relative.

What death benefits are payable?

You should see if your policy contains *transition benefits*—that is, benefits that extend to your spouse or dependents in case you die. If your plan does include these benefits, check to see how long they last. Also find out whether or not your survivors receive a policy premium refund should you die.

Write Now

A fast way to find out what your current disability insurance covers—or to shop for supplemental coverage—is to telephone or write your insurance agent.

Here's a sample letter to use.

J. Q. Professional
Executive Insurance Inc.

Dear Insurance Professional:

I am evaluating my disability insurance, and I would appreciate your assistance. I have enclosed copies of my current policy and have listed below the specific information I need about my current coverage. Please feel free to fill in the answers on this letter and return it to me.

1. If I become disabled, how much will my disability insurance benefits add up to each month?

_____.

2. How long must I wait after I become disabled before I receive my first benefits check?

_____.

3. Will my policy continue to pay benefits for my lifetime?

_____.

4. If my coverage is limited, how long will my policy continue to pay benefits?

_____.

5. Does my policy provide for "any occupation" or "own occupation" coverage?

_____.

6. Will I receive benefits if I'm able to return to work part time?

_____.

7. Do my benefits increase with my salary?

_____.

8. Is my policy "guaranteed renewable" and "noncancelable," or can

the insurance company cancel the policy or change the cost of the policy at its discretion?

_____.

9. Are my premiums fixed or step rate?

_____.

10. Does my coverage extend to my family?

_____.

11. Does my coverage contain transition benefits?

_____.

I would appreciate your recommendations or comments on my disability insurance and advice on whether I should supplement it.

I thank you in advance for your help.

Sincerely,

21 *From Here to Eternity*

Getting the Life Insurance You Need

*L*ife insurance is—or ought to be—an important part of almost every personal financial plan. It helps you meet your risk management and estate planning goals. And some people even use life insurance as an investment vehicle.

The challenge: Life insurance policies now come in so many varieties that finding the right one has gotten terribly complicated. Don't despair. Just read on.

We're going to help you find your way through the insurance maze. We'll help you figure out whether you need life insurance, and, if so, how much and what kind.

First, though, a few general comments.

The Choice of Your Life

Fact: Most Americans own some type of life insurance.

The American Council of Life Insurance reports that nearly 80 percent of all men and 65 percent of all women are covered by life insurance. And among families with children under age eighteen, the percentages are even higher. In nine out of ten of these families, at least one member has a life insurance policy.

But just because most people buy life insurance doesn't mean that they own the right policy—or that they are paying what they should for the protection they require.

Your need for life insurance changes as your circumstances change. There are times when you need large amounts of coverage. And there are times when you need little or none.

How Much Is Enough?

An individual with no dependents and sufficient resources to cover funeral expenses probably doesn't need any life insurance at all. Practically everyone else, though, does.

If funeral expenses are your only concern, look into a "burial policy," in an amount large enough to cover no more than your burial costs.

If you have dependents—and not enough resources to adequately provide for them after your death—you most likely need insurance to maintain your family's standard of living. You may, for instance, have children to be educated and a spouse who does not work outside the home.

How much insurance do you need at any given time? We've provided a work sheet in Appendix VI for you to fill out. The work sheet also helps you determine if your current life insurance coverage is adequate.

It asks you to calculate how much money your family needs to live on each year. Most financial planners think this figure should come to around 75 percent of your current annual take-home pay.

You must consider expenses—such as funeral and burial costs—and funds to provide for your children's education and your spouse's retirement. That very soon begins to sound like quite a lot of money, but bear in mind that you don't always have to provide for all of these contingencies with insurance alone. Families often have other sources of income to draw upon.

For example, you can subtract the amount of Social Security survivor benefits that would be available to your surviving spouse while your children are in school.

Also deduct any income your family would realize from company pension and profit-sharing plans or from personal savings and investments.

And consider the possibility that your spouse might land a well-paying job. If so, you'll need less insurance than you otherwise might.

Finally, remember this good news: Life insurance proceeds are not taxed as income to your beneficiary. (See Chapter 38 for more on how estates are taxed.)

Time After Time

So far we've covered just the simple issues—whether you need insurance and, if so, how much at any given time. It's from this point on that people start finding the insurance issue a confusing one.

But while the types of policies available have proliferated—thereby complicating choices—insurance buyers also now have a better shot at getting what they need at the least cost.

Moreover, despite the growing variety of policies on the market, they all fall into one of two categories or some combination of the two. We'll begin with the first broad category: term insurance.

Term insurance—which agents refer to as "no-frills" insurance— provides coverage for a fixed period, usually a year. The insurance company pays only if you die during that time.

Term comes in two varieties: nonrenewable and renewable. Despite the name, *nonrenewable term insurance* can be renewed, but only by requalifying when the policy expires. This usually means filling out a health questionnaire or taking a physical examination.

Nonrenewable term is less expensive than renewable—by 25 cents to 50 cents per $1,000 of coverage. But there's another cost—the possibility that you may be left with no insurance at all just when you most need it.

Say you purchase a nonrenewable policy, then become severely ill or disabled. Your insurance carrier declines to continue your policy, because you are now a great risk. You are left with no coverage, and your ill health may discourage other carriers from selling you a policy.

With *renewable term insurance*, on the other hand, you qualify for renewal automatically—no questions, no physicals. The insurance carrier must renew the policy at your request. The only permissible reason for cancellation: your failure to pay premiums.

Despite its higher cost, renewable term is usually preferable to the nonrenewable variety, because you are assured that you can continue your coverage.

But which kind of renewable? There are two: decreasing face-value policies and fixed face-value policies.

With a *decreasing face-value policy*, you pay the same premium from year to year, but the death benefit decreases as you grow older. With a *fixed face-value policy*, you pay higher premiums as you age, but the death benefit remains the same.

In most cases, fixed face-value policies are the right choice. As always, however, there are exceptions to the rule. Among them: policies that cover full-time homemakers.

Here's an example. You buy a life insurance policy covering your wife, who does not work outside the home. The amount of the policy is enough to cover the cost of hiring someone to care for your children and manage your household—a sensible precaution.

As your children grow older, however, your need for child care declines. You no longer require a full-time baby-sitter, for instance, once your children reach school age. So opting for a decreasing face-value policy makes sense, since its value goes down as your child-care costs decline.

The price of term insurance? Term is the least expensive type of life insurance, because it includes only death benefits.

For term insurance, you should expect to pay between $1 and $6 a year for each $1,000 of coverage, depending on your age, sex, and health.

A thirty-year-old nonsmoking man, for example, will pay $200 to $300 a year for a policy with a death benefit of $100,000. Nonsmoking women under the age of twenty-five pay the least, about $150 for the same $100,000 policy.

Another feature of term insurance: flexibility. Unlike other kinds of policies, you can easily reduce the amount of your coverage as your needs change without additional costs.

The primary disadvantage of term insurance: increasing premiums. Your insurance carrier raises your premiums every time you renew your policy. The carrier assumes—with some validity—that the older you get, the more likely you are to die.

The same $100,000 term policy that costs a thirty-year-old man $200 a year may cost a fifty-five-year-old man $530 a year. And by the time he reaches age seventy, his premiums may climb to $2,900.

Be aware that some term insurance policies are "convertible"—you may trade them in for another type of insurance, such as whole life (discussed next).

A final word on term: Frequently it is the best insurance buy, but that's not always true. Recently, for instance, many people have been cashing in their old whole life policies and buying term instead on the assumption that the term coverage is cheaper.

It may be. But it's also possible, depending on your age and other factors, that the old whole life policy you had been paying on for years is now the better buy. That's because premium rates for most whole life policies remain level over time.

The Whole Story

Whole life insurance dates back to the 1800s and is the second big category of life insurance. It is simply term insurance with an investment feature built in.

Whole life works like this.

You give your insurance carrier money in the form of premium payments. The company takes a chunk of your cash to pay for the insurance portion of the policy.

The remainder of your premium—with the exception of certain insurance company administrative expenses—is invested by the insurance company on your behalf.

Most whole life premiums go into the insurance company's general investment portfolio, which is loaded with bonds, mortgages, and equity securities.

But the cash value that accumulates in a whole life policy—that is, the capital and interest—belong to you. You can take it out in the form of policy loans, or you can cash the policy in. If you die while the policy is in force, your beneficiary receives the face value of the policy.

There is one advantage to investing money through a whole life plan rather than through other investment vehicles. Interest you earn on the investment portion of an insurance policy accumulates tax free until you withdraw it.

Another plus of traditional whole life insurance: level premiums. You pay the same amount for coverage each year regardless of your age or health.

But this advantage has its cost: high premiums. A fifty-year-old man in good health, for example, pays at least $2,000 a year for a $100,000 whole life policy, whereas term insurance costs him about $400 a year. In addition, there are commissions for insurance salespeople attached to these policies.

Why the higher premium? Because you are paying for investment features, as well as death benefits. Also, because of high commissions, the cash value builds up slowly during your initial years of ownership, because most of your premium dollars go to cover commissions and processing costs. So this type of policy is generally not recommended if you're planning to hold on to it for less than five years.

Many financial planners say that traditional whole life insurance may not be your best investment. Here's why: As we've seen, premium dollars go into the insurance company's general investment portfolio, which is packed with bonds, mortgages, and equity securities. And even though you get a guaranteed return, the dividend rates are usually low.

So what should you do if you already have a traditional whole life policy? Check the policy. If it's paying competitive dividends, you may be wise to keep it, unless you can find a better alternative.

Universal Life Insurance

Universal life insurance—a variation on whole life—was introduced in 1979. With this type of policy, the investment portion of your premium goes into the insurance company's general investment account for these policies.

Unlike the cash value of a traditional whole life policy, a universal life policy's cash value grows at a variable rate. The rate generally depends on the interest that's currently paid in the money markets. Most insurance companies will notify you at least annually of the interest rate your policy will earn in the coming year.

One advantage of universal life policies: They offer protection along with a competitive yield on the investment component after sales charges.

Another advantage of universal over traditional whole life: You may vary your annual death benefit and your annual premium. While whole life premiums are usually fixed, with universal life you can decide, within limits, what you can afford each year.

In good years, financially speaking, you may decide to put more money in the policy and get a greater buildup of your cash value.

In leaner years, you may skip paying the premium altogether. When you skip payments, the carrier simply deducts the cost of maintaining the life insurance portion of your plan plus administrative expenses from the accumulated cash value.

A definite plus for universal policies: You know what you pay for. You get an annual report showing exactly what happened with your policy for the year.

The report shows the amount of your insurance, the cash value of your account, the cost of your insurance, company fees, any premium payments that have been deducted from your savings, and your rate of return.

Because universal life policies separate insurance protection from company fees and profits, it is easy to compare policies among carriers. When you do, you may be surprised at the variations in charges and credits.

Variable Life Insurance

Variable life insurance is not as new as universal life, and it is available from more and more insurance companies.

As with traditional whole life, a portion of the variable life premium goes to cover the cost of insurance, and the rest is invested. Whereas whole life premiums are generally invested in long-term bonds and mortgages, variable life premiums are invested according to the policyholder's—meaning your—wishes.

So the carrier will invest your premium dollars in an array of investment vehicles, from common stocks and mutual funds to zero-coupon bond funds and fixed-income instruments. Note, though, that carriers manage the specific funds your money is invested in. So you can't choose an investment vehicle that's not in your insurance company's portfolio.

Several times a year, you may switch among investment vehicles without penalty. It's up to you, for instance, to decide when to move funds in or out of a stock mutual fund, and you're the one making the calls on market turns.

If you're comfortable with investment decisions, variable life offers a hands-on alternative to whole life policies, while also meeting your basic life insurance needs.

On the down side, the cash value of variable life policies is uncertain. The pure insurance portion of the policy, though, never falls below a certain floor.

Keep in mind that variable life can be expensive. The sales commission and the service fees cut considerably into the amount available for investment.

Like whole life policies and universal life, variable life policies may not be for those concerned with short-term insurance needs. Rather, variable life is better used by those who can predict their future insurance needs with reasonable certainty.

Flexible-Premiums Variable Life Insurance

These plans combine features of universal and variable life. As with universal life, you may change the premiums and death benefits.

But, as with variable life policies, you specify how you want the savings portion of the policy invested. You may also shift your money from one investment vehicle to another during the year. The insurance carrier, however, may charge you a fee to make the switch.

Flexible-premiums variable life is another type of whole life policy. And, as with other whole life policies, you pay no taxes on earnings until you withdraw the money.

Single-Premium Life Insurance

Here's how a single-premium life insurance policy works. You put up a large lump sum (usually no less than $5,000) to pay for your death benefits, and you earn a competitive tax-deferred interest rate.

You may obtain cash from the policy at any time through a policy loan that charges interest of about 6 to 8 percent. Insurance companies offer attractive interest rates, and they may offer guarantees to hold a steady rate over three to five years if you direct them to.

But beware: The company may impose a back-end load—that is, charge you a percentage of your cash value when you take your money out.

For example, one insurance company's early cancellation penalty comes to 7 percent of premiums in the first or second year and drops by 1 percent a year after that time. In other words, you must keep your money in the policy for nine years before you can withdraw it without penalty.

Another caveat: Make sure the company offering this type of policy is sound: Single-premium and other investment-oriented policies attract a fickle pool of policyholders, quick to bail out with changes in market conditions. So a large run on a particular type of policy may seriously undermine the insurance company's ability to return your money.

One good source of information on insurance companies: A. M. Best, which publishes a directory of insurance carriers and rates them according to their financial strength.

Deferred Annuities

What about deferred annuities? Investment in deferred annuities through the vehicle of insurance policies is on the rise. The reason: Thanks to the 1986 Tax Reform Act, annuities remain one of the few tax-deferred savings vehicles left.

A deferred annuity is similar to an individual retirement account (IRA) in one respect: Earnings on the money set aside in a deferred annuity accumulate tax deferred until withdrawn.

But unlike an IRA, contributions to deferred annuities are not limited to $2,000 a year. You may set aside any amount at any time.

Another important difference between annuities and IRAs: Contributions to deferred annuities are not tax deductible, while contributions to IRAs are for certain taxpayers. (See Chapter 32 for more on IRAs.)

There are two types of annuity payment methods available (when your deferred annuity is calculated): fixed and variable.

With a *fixed annuity*, the amount you receive is paid out in regular installments. The only variable: You decide how frequently you want to receive payments. For example, you may decide to receive payments monthly or quarterly. Your neighbor may want annual payments.

With a *variable annuity*, the amount of the payout fluctuates with the type of account you have. The reason: You decide how the dollars you set aside are invested, so the amount you receive depends on the value of your underlying portfolio.

You may opt for stocks, bonds, money-market securities, or mutual funds. And you may switch investments as often as you like.

While annuities certainly offer advantages, they—like any investment—have drawbacks as well. For example, insurance companies typically require annual minimum deposits (usually $300 to $1,000) to maintain the policy.

Also, insurance carriers impose penalties for early withdrawal of funds from annuities—usually 6 to 7 percent of the amount you take out.

As we've mentioned, one key consideration when buying an annuity or any insurance policy is the financial soundness of the insurance company. You should also look at the returns a carrier has paid in the past.

To Buy or Not to Buy

Some personal financial planners argue that the best time to buy life insurance is when you're young. That way—if you're starting a whole life policy—you lock in a lower premium.

True enough, but you pay that premium over a much longer period of time. And, as a result, you pay about the same amount to the insurance carrier in the end as you would if you had waited to buy life insurance until you really needed it.

Remember, no matter what they call the policy you own, you are paying fees each year to maintain your policy and provide life insurance protection. The cost of maintaining the policy goes down as you grow older, but the charges for life insurance coverage go up. So the trick is to figure out how much insurance you need, what kind you need, and when you need it.

Write Now

Here's a sample letter for inquiring about your life insurance coverage.

J. Q. Professional
Executive Insurance Inc.

Dear Insurance Professional:

I am evaluating my life insurance, and I would appreciate your assistance.

My principal objective is to own enough life insurance to provide adequate security for my survivors at a mimimum cost.

I have not decided whether I need or want any additional life insurance. However, I would like you to send me a statement showing the cost of yearly renewable and convertible term and whole life insurance for a *male/female, nonsmoker/smoker*, age _____.

If you have alternative policies, such as variable life, that you would recommend, please send me information on them.

I require complete disclosure on any alternatives you present, including itemized expenses, commissions, mortality charges, amounts earning a return, and details regarding the return. I also need to understand any penalties I might have should I cancel the policy at any time.

I have enclosed copies of the declaration pages from all my life insurance policies. These should adequately describe my current coverage.

I would appreciate your recommendations or comments, including ways in which I may improve my coverage.

I thank you in advance for your help.

Sincerely,

22 Don't Spin Your Wheels

What You Need to Know About Automobile Insurance

*I*f you've moved from one state to another, you know that consistency is not a word that applies to car insurance. Premiums vary by hundreds of dollars, depending on where you live. And so do the minimum requirements for liability coverage.

Still, there are some rules about buying automobile insurance that apply no matter where you live or where you drive your car. We review them in this chapter.

Driver, Get Insured!

Driving without insurance is sheer foolishness.

In today's litigious society, you expose yourself to a potentially devastating lawsuit from which you may never recover financially.

But what kind of insurance is right for you?

If you're like most people, you need a comprehensive personal auto policy plan that includes six different types of coverage: bodily injury liability, property damage liability, medical payments, uninsured motorists protection, collision, and comprehensive physical damage.

Here's a rundown of each type of coverage.

Bodily Injury Liability

You're driving down the street. The road is slick. And the signal light ahead of you changes from yellow to red. You slam on the brakes—just a little too late.

You smash into the car in front of you, and the driver strikes his head on the windshield. He suffers a slight concussion.

Naturally, you're worried about what happens if he sues. Bodily injury liability coverage protects you in this situation.

This insurance pays when someone else is injured or dies as a result of an accident that is your fault. It also covers injuries or deaths from accidents caused by members of your family and by people who drive your car with your permission.

Say, for example, that you lend your car to your best friend. While looking for a parking spot in the local mall, he knocks a pedestrian to the ground.

Bodily injury liability covers the damages. It pays the pedestrian's medical bills and covers the cost of your defense if the pedestrian sues. And, if the court rules that you're liable for the injury, it pays the damages assessed against you—up to the limit of your policy.

In the case of death, the insurance carrier may pay a lump sum to the beneficiaries of the accident victim—but, again, only up to the limit of the policy. If your policy is relatively new, a single limit is probably posted—typically, $100,000 or more. It's the maximum the policy will pay for any accident.

Many older policies state the maximum amount the insurance carrier pays for any *one* person injured in a *single* accident. They also note the total amount they will pay if more than one person is injured or killed in an accident you cause.

Let's say your insurance policy lists your bodily injury liability coverage as "100/300." That means your policy would pay, at most, $100,000 for a single injury or death and a maximum of $300,000 if more than one person is hurt or killed.

Caution: Most states require drivers to purchase minimum bodily injury coverage of $10,000 per person and $20,000 per accident. But don't use state law as your guide. Many of these regulations are woefully outdated and don't reflect the true cost of medical care—not to mention court costs and jury awards. They're in place only to impose a rock-bottom standard.

Buy at least $100,000 of coverage per person and $300,000 per accident. Anything less, and you're underinsured.

Besides, bodily injury liability coverage is not expensive. The cost of increasing your liability limits is less than the proportional increase in the coverage provided.

Here's a typical example. Say you want to beef up your bodily injury coverage from $10,000 per person and $20,000 per accident to $100,000 per person and $300,000 per accident. Your current coverage costs you $225 a year. So, you figure, you'll pay more than ten times as much if you boost your coverage. Wrong: The greater protection would probably cost you about $450 a year—or only twice the cost for more than ten times the coverage per person.

Property Damage Liability

Your son heads for the basketball court in your station wagon. But there's a problem—he forgot the basketball.

So he pulls back into the driveway, puts the car in neutral, and dashes into the house for his ball. The car starts to roll downhill.

It stops—when it hits your neighbor's fence. The damage is covered by the property damage liability portion of your policy. This insurance also covers any legal bills that may mount up for your son's defense if your neighbor sues.

Property damage liability covers damages caused by you—the owner of the car—and for damages caused by members of your family and people who drive your car with your permission.

This coverage is sometimes coupled with bodily injury liability protection. A 100/300/50 liability policy, then, would provide $100,000 of bodily injury liability coverage per person, $300,000 per accident, and $50,000 of property damage liability.

In most states, the amount of property damage liability you may buy is tied to the level of bodily injury liability protection. For example, if you're covered for $100,000 per person and $300,000 per accident, you'll be required to purchase $50,000 of property damage liability protection.

The ratio of bodily injury liability coverage to property liability insurance—on a per person basis—is two to one in most states. On a per accident basis, it is six to one. Check with your insurance agent for the requirements that apply in your state.

Medical Payments

If you're injured in a car accident, medical payments insurance pays your medical expenses. It also covers the medical costs of other people injured in the same accident.

So how does medical payments insurance differ from bodily injury liability? You don't have to be judged at fault for this coverage to become effective.

The advantage of this coverage: If someone else caused the accident, your medical payments insurance pays your medical bills immediately. Then your carrier recoups its costs from the other person's insurance company.

Insurance companies sell medical payments insurance in amounts ranging from $500 to $10,000.

What happens if you exhaust the limits of medical payments coverage? Your health insurance policy would pick up where your medical payments plan leaves off. (Your health insurance, however, covers only *your* medical expenses, not your passengers'.)

Uninsured Motorists

As its name implies, uninsured motorists insurance protects you if you're involved in an accident with an uninsured driver. The protection covers you and anyone else riding in your car at the time of the accident. It also covers you and members of your family if you're injured while riding in someone else's car or if you're hit by a car while walking or riding a bike.

Not all states require uninsured motorists coverage, but you should consider purchasing it anyway. Here's why: Even if your state law requires automobile insurance, there will always be people who break the law and drive without it. And the driver who hits you may be one of those people.

Many states have laws specifying the minimum amount of uninsured motorists coverage you must purchase. But, again, you shouldn't use this minimum as a guideline. Many of these laws have been on the books a long time and, consequently, are outdated. You can purchase coverage of up to $100,000 per person and $300,000 per accident from most insurers.

You should consider purchasing *under*insured motorists coverage, too. It covers you for injuries you receive in an accident involving an underinsured auto and is sometimes offered in conjuction with universal motorist coverage. Underinsured motorists property damage coverage is also available in some states.

Collision

One foggy night, you drive your new sports car into the rear of the parked car ahead of you. Your grill now looks like your nephew's accordion.

But rest easy. Your collision insurance covers the cost of repairs. And you don't have to worry about who is at fault.

If you get into an accident with another car and the driver of the other car is to blame, your carrier seeks reimbursement from that person's insurance company. If you are to blame or live in a state that has no-fault laws, such as New Jersey or Michigan, your insurance carrier foots the bill anyway. (We discuss no-fault laws later in this chapter.)

But insurers don't want to repair every little scratch. So, to prevent people from filing claims for minor damages, most collision insurance is sold with a deductible of $100 or more—$250 is the norm.

Many people buy this coverage with high deductibles. The reason: Collision insurance can be expensive—$1,000 a year or more—and raising the deductible lowers the premium. The amount of premiums you save varies by location.

Another consideration when you buy collision coverage: the year, make, and model of your car. The newer and more expensive your car, the more costly your collision coverage.

Also, the cost of collision insurance in most states depends on your driving record, age, sex, and location. A person living in Chicago, for example, will shell out a lot more than someone from a small city like Paintsville, Kentucky, because accidents are more common in Chicago than in Paintsville.

When you purchase collision insurance, you have to think carefully about how much your car is worth and how much you can afford to pay for accidental damage. You should weigh the cost of the coverage and high and low deductibles against the likelihood of an accident and the value of your car.

If you're driving a brand-new Mercedes, you may want to consider full coverage. If your car is a ten-year-old Chevy, you may decide to pass up collision coverage altogether: It could cost more to provide the insurance than the car is worth.

Comprehensive Physical Damage

You park your car on a quiet side street and stroll to your favorite restaurant. Your dinner is delightful, but when you return to your automobile, your evening is ruined. All four of your tires have been slashed.

Comprehensive physical damage protection pays for the cost of replacing them. In general, this insurance covers damage that results from causes other than automobile accidents—a fire, say, or vandalism or theft.

The cost of this insurance varies widely and depends, in large measure, on the area of the country in which you live. For example, car theft is more common in Massachusetts than in Kansas. So the amount you pay for such coverage is greater in Massachusetts.

Comprehensive protection covers the cost of the car itself as well as the damage or loss of personal possessions inside the car. But you need an endorsement to your policy to cover special audio equipment such as cassette tapes, custom-installed tape decks, and CB radios.

Comprehensive physical damage coverage may include a deductible of $50 to $100 or more. Again you can lower your annual premium by raising your deductible.

It's Not Your Fault

Many states have enacted no-fault car insurance laws.

With no-fault, also known as "personal injury protection," you bypass the complicated and often expensive task of finding out who's to blame for automobile accidents. Your insurance carrier covers the cost of property damages and personal injuries you suffer in an automobile accident, regardless of who is at fault.

But even in no-fault states, suits by injured parties are possible. State laws dictate when a person has the right to sue. Most states, for instance, allow you to take your case to court when death or permanent injury results from an automobile accident or when costs from the accident top a certain threshold.

One problem with no-fault: In some states, the mandatory coverage is not enough to pay for the actual expense of an accident. So even if you are protected by no-fault insurance, you should make sure the other auto coverages you buy are adequate to meet your needs.

Are You Covered?

Let's say you've forgotten to tell your insurance carrier that, on special occasions, you let your sixteen-year-old son drive your car.

Unfortunately, on one of these occasions, the young man gets into a fender bender. Your insurance carrier will probably cover the repair bill this first time. But after that, you're on your own.

If you don't now include your offspring in the policy—and he gets into another smash-up—the insurance company most likely will refuse to pay.

And suppose your son's first accident is more serious. Instead of a fender, he hits a young medical intern. Because of the accident, the intern is unable to practice medicine for the rest of his life. In this case, your insurance company may choose to refuse you coverage.

Our advice: Remember to report additional drivers, changes in drivers, and changes in covered vehicles to your insurance carrier.

You Get What You Pay For

When it comes to automobile insurance premiums, it's almost impossible to generalize. As we've noted, premiums vary by location, age, sex, and type of car. Carriers also consider your driving record—and the driving record of your peers. For example, in many states, young unmarried men pay higher automobile insurance rates than any other category of driver. The reason: They are statistically more likely to have accidents.

As a rule, rates decline as drivers reach age twenty-five to thirty or get married. Eventually, married men pay about the same amount for car insurance as married women do. Likewise, drivers with clean records pay less for insurance than those with a history of accidents or traffic violations.

The best way to buy automobile insurance is to shop around. The insurance industry is extremely competitive, and rates vary widely in most states. For example, a study by the New York State Insurance Department shows that premiums quoted by car insurance companies in Manhattan vary by as much as 83 percent.

Under certain conditions, discounts are also available. For instance, if you own more than one car, you may receive a 10 to 20 percent break on your premiums. And a 5 percent discount may apply if your children have completed a driver education or defensive driving course.

Many companies also offer price breaks for students with a grade average of B or above. In addition, insurers give discounts to parents whose college-age children are away from home—and away from the family car. Finally, most carriers offer discounts on cars equipped with special safety equipment or antitheft devices.

There are two major factors—other than price—to keep in mind when you shop for insurance: service and reliability.

You should try to give your business to an agent who'll provide you with fair and efficient service. Word of mouth is often the best way to find a good insurance agent; ask your friends and coworkers for recommendations. Then talk to your prospective agent about the procedures you would follow in case of an accident, including notification, estimating damages, and renting a substitute car.

You should also purchase coverage from a carrier who will be around to pay any losses you may have. Be wary of fly-by-night, bargain-basement companies that advertise they will insure anyone, regardless of his or her driving record. Your local library and state insurance department should have publications that give information—number of years of operation, financial strength, and industry ratings—about specific insurance companies.

Write Now

Use the following letter to help you get what you need from your automobile insurance carrier. Just fill in the blanks, and it's ready to go.

J. Q. Professional
Executive Insurance Inc.

Dear Insurance Professional:

I am evaluating my automobile insurance, and I would appreciate your assistance. I have listed below the specific information I need about my current coverage. Please feel free to fill in the answers on this letter and return it to me.

The make of my primary car is a _____. The model is a _____. The primary driver is _____. My present coverage on the car is as follows:

1. Bodily Injury Liability:
Amount: _____ Cost: _____
2. Property Damage Liability:
Amount: _____ Cost: _____
3. Medical Payments:
Amount: _____ Cost: _____
4. Uninsured Motorists Protection:
Amount: _____ Cost: _____
5. Underinsured Motorists Protection:
Amount: _____ Cost: _____
6. Collision:
Amount: _____ Cost: _____
7. Comprehensive Physical Damage:
Amount: _____ Cost: _____
8. Special Riders:
Amount: _____ Cost: _____
9. Total Cost:
Quarterly: _____ Annual: _____

The make of my second car is a _____. The model is a _____. The primary driver is _____. My present coverage on the car is as follows:

1. Bodily Injury Liability:
Amount: _____ Cost: _____
2. Property Damage Liability:

Amount: _____ Cost: _____
3. Medical Payments:
Amount: _____ Cost: _____
4. Uninsured Motorists Protection:
Amount: _____ Cost: _____
5. Underinsured Motorists Protection:
Amount: _____ Cost: _____
6. Collision:
Amount: _____ Cost: _____
7. Comprehensive Physical Damage:
Amount: _____ Cost: _____
8. Special Riders:
Amount: _____ Cost: _____
9. Total Cost:
Quarterly: _____ Annual: _____

I want to know the cost of the maximum available uninsured motorists coverage, underinsured motorists coverage, and medical payments coverage.

In addition, I want to know the difference in premiums for collision and comprehensive coverage if deductibles were increased to _____. I would also like to know the savings produced by eliminating collision coverage on my automobiles once their replacement value falls below _____.

Finally, I want to know the cost of increasing my liability coverage to the maximum available limit and to find out how to coordinate it with a personal umbrella liability policy.*

What changes would you recommend to bring my insurance into line with these objectives? Please list below the amount and cost of coverage for each of my cars.

MY PRIMARY CAR
_____

1. Bodily Injury Liability:
Amount: _____ Cost: _____
2. Property Damage Liability:
Amount: _____ Cost: _____

*We'll cover umbrella liability policies in Chapter 24.

3. Medical Payments:
Amount: _____ Cost: _____
4. Uninsured Motorists Protection:
Amount: _____ Cost: _____
5. Underinsured Motorists Protection:
Amount: _____ Cost: _____
6. Collision:
Amount: _____ Cost: _____
7. Comprehensive Physical Damage:
Amount: _____ Cost: _____
8. Special Riders:
Amount: _____ Cost: _____
9. Total Cost:
Quarterly: _____ Annual: _____

MY SECOND CAR _____

1. Bodily Injury Liability:
Amount: _____ Cost: _____
2. Property Damage Liability:
Amount: _____ Cost: _____
3. Medical Payments:
Amount: _____ Cost: _____
4. Uninsured Motorists Protection:
Amount: _____ Cost: _____
5. Underinsured Motorists Protection:
Amount: _____ Cost: _____
6. Collision:
Amount: _____ Cost: _____
7. Comprehensive Physical Damage:
Amount: _____ Cost: _____
8. Special Riders:
Amount: _____ Cost: _____
9. Total Cost:
Quarterly: _____ Annual: _____

We have _____ drivers in our family. Their names and license numbers are as follows:

Name: _____ License Number: _____
Name: _____ License Number: _____
Name: _____ License Number: _____
Name: _____ License Number: _____

I thank you in advance for your help.

Sincerely,

23 *Home Sweet Home*

How to Find the Right Homeowner's Policy

*R*eading insurance policies is no fun. But you're asking for trouble if you don't take the time to study your homeowner's plan.

The fact is, whether you own your home or rent it, you must protect yourself from potentially devastating losses. And knowing what is—and isn't—covered in your present policy is the only way to make sure you have the protection you need.

Take heart: You don't need the training of an insurance broker to understand your policy. This chapter provides the necessary information.

It Takes All Kinds

Let's start with a rundown of the plans available.

Most insurance carriers offer six different types of homeowner's insurance. (It's called *homeowner's* regardless of whether you own the roof over your head or rent it.)

The first four types are for people who own their homes. The remaining two are for those who rent their houses or apartments or live in condominiums or co-ops.

The policies cover the loss of the house itself—if you own it—and the loss of your personal belongings, such as furniture and appliances.

The policies for people who own their houses are known as Forms One, Two, Three, and Five.

Form One

Form One—sometimes called Homeowner's 1 or HO-1—is the least expensive of the policies, and, as you might expect, provides only limited protection.

Form One spells out the specific disasters it covers. If a "peril"— jargon for the direct cause of a loss—isn't listed, you aren't insured for it.

These policies typically cover damage to your home and personal possessions from ten sources:

- Fire and lightning
- Windstorms and hail
- Explosions
- Riots and civil commotion
- Vehicles
- Aircraft
- Smoke
- Vandalism and malicious mischief
- Breakage of glass
- Theft

Form Two

Form Two is also called Homeowner's 2 or HO-2. Form Two—like Form One—lists the specific disasters covered. If your house or possessions suffer damages from a cause not named in your policy, you—not the insurance carrier—foot the repair bill.

The difference between Form Two and Form One policies is the number of perils covered. In all, Form Two policies cover damage caused by seventeen sources—the ten perils listed under Form One plus damage from

- Falling objects
- The weight of ice, snow, or sleet
- The collapse of buildings
- Accidental discharge or overflow of water or steam
- The explosion of steam or hot-water systems
- Frozen plumbing, heating units, air-conditioning systems, and domestic appliances
- Power surges

Form Three

Form Three—also known as Homeowner's 3 or HO-3—is the most popular type of plan sold. While Forms One and Two cover only the specific disasters listed in the policy, Form Three provides "all-risk" coverage for your house and any other structures on your property.

So you're protected against every possible calamity, except those specifically excluded in the policy: earthquakes, floods, termites, landslides, wars, tidal waves, and nuclear accidents.

Form Three covers personal belongings, but only under Form Two's seventeen named conditions.

Form Five

For arcane insurance reasons, we temporarily skip over Form Four and go straight to Form Five.

Form Five is another all-risk policy. (Plans that are labeled Comprehensive Form, Homeowner's 5, and HO-5 are Form Five policies.) It protects your house from the same disasters as Form Three, and includes the same exceptions.

But Form Five differs from Form Three in one key respect. It extends all-risk coverage to your personal belongings.

Form Five costs about 30 percent more than Form Three, so it's not as popular. But, in most cases, you're better off to spring for the additional premium.

Warning: Some insurance companies don't sell Form Five policies. Instead, they offer Form Three policies with riders to boost coverage of personal possessions. These plans provide more comprehensive coverage than a typical Form Three policy, but the coverage is not as good as you'd get with Form Five.

The policies for people who rent or own condominiums and co-ops are known as Form Four and Form Six.

Form Four

Form Four is designed for renters. When you buy Form Four, you protect your possessions only from those causes specified in your policy—the same causes specified in an HO-3 policy. Other names for Form Four insurance: Tenants Form, Contents Form, Homeowner's 4, and HO-4.

Form Six

Form Six is similar to renter's insurance but is for people who own condominiums or live in co-op apartments. Form Six provides coverage only for your belongings and only under the circumstances listed in your policy, which are the same as in Form Four.

If you own a condominium, your condominium association usually buys a master property insurance policy that covers the building itself. The same holds true for co-ops. It's a good idea to take a look at this master policy to make sure your building is adequately covered.

You can—and we suggest that you do—purchase a separate Form Six policy to protect your furniture, jewelry, electronic gear, and other personal possessions. We also recommend that you add a rider to your policy that calls for the insurer to pay if your condo association assesses you a fee for its uninsured losses.

Form Six is also known as Condominium Unit Owners Form, Homeowner's 6, and HO-6.

What Kind of Policy Is Right for You?

No matter what kind of coverage you purchase, your insurance carrier is required to pay no more than the total amount stated in the policy. So if your policy specifies $100,000 of coverage and damages total $130,000, the $30,000 difference comes out of your own pocket.

We recommend policies that pay benefits of 80 to 100 percent of the replacement value of your house or belongings. Otherwise, you won't collect nearly enough to cover your damages.

Say your house is worth $200,000, and it is destroyed in a fire. An 80 percent actual cash-value plan would pay you no more than $160,000.

Actual cash-value policies provide adequate coverage for the house itself—but not for the contents. If you're covered by an actual cash-value policy and suffer a loss, an insurance adjuster will decide how much your possessions have depreciated since you bought them. So if your house is destroyed, you don't receive the full replacement value of your personal property. You receive the replacement value minus depreciation.

One of our financial planners tells the story of a man, John, whose home was gutted by fire. John lost his house and everything in it.

Soon after the fire, an insurance adjuster was dispatched to survey the damage. The adjuster asked for an inventory of household items. Luckily, John kept one in his safe-deposit box.

Then the adjuster set about to decide how much the company should pay for each item in John's house—from the living-room sofa to the books in his den. John had purchased his sofa eight years before for $1,500. Replacing it would cost $2,000.

But here's the rub: Under the terms of the policy, the adjuster had to take into account the effects of wear and tear, or depreciation.

A sofa, by insurance standards, has a useful life of fifteen years. So the adjuster subtracted $800—$100 for each year since John purchased his sofa—from its replacement value. John wound up with $1,200 for his couch—or a full $800 less than it would cost him to replace it.

The adjuster applied the same principle to every single item in John's house—from the grandfather clock in the upstairs hallway to the linens on his bed.

The lesson: If you want your insurance carrier to pay you the actual replacement cost if your house and your belongings are damaged or destroyed, you need a "replacement cost endorsement."

This endorsement is a rider added to your policy. It prevents your insurance carrier from deducting for depreciation.

Be prepared for an increase in insurance premiums if you tack on the replacement cost endorsement to your homeowner's policy. But we recommend the endorsement despite this added cost.

Homeowners should expect premiums to jump 10 percent with a replacement cost endorsement. Condominium owners should expect a 25 to 30 percent increase, renters and residents of co-ops a 50 percent increase.

The reason rates jump so much for condominium and co-op owners and renters: Their policies cover the contents of their homes, not the structures themselves. So the basic premium is much less than that of a policy that covers both a house and personal possessions.

Another point: Always check your policy for exclusions from coverage. Many plans omit certain items—such as animals, sale samples, business property, and collector's items. You will need to purchase special riders to cover these items.

You can purchase riders that cover different categories of merchandise—jewelry, for example, and artwork and antiques. But insurance companies require that some items be insured separately—specifically, those that are valued in excess of $5,000.

In most cases, the insurer issues you a check to cover the cost of damage to your property. But be warned that the insurance company may insist on repairing the damage or replacing the property itself. The reason: It wants to safeguard itself against unreasonable cash claims.

How Do You Calculate Replacement Value?

If you don't know what it would cost to replace your house, ask a real-estate agent, broker, or local contractor for an appraisal.

Most professionals in the appraisal business are members of the American Institute of Real Estate Appraisers and the American Society of Appraisers. These organizations will provide you with names of their members. Call their local chapters or their offices in Washington, D.C.

Your insurance agent or company may also be of help. If your house is valued at $200,000 or more, most insurance companies will send an appraiser to your home after you sign up for a policy. He or she will not only appraise your house but make suggestions on how to improve safety and security.

Expect to pay a fee if you ask a real-estate agent or building contractor to make an appraisal. These professionals may either charge a flat fee or may base the fee on a percentage of your house's appraisal value. The former method is usually more advantageous to you. Insurance agents generally don't charge if you purchase a policy from them.

Also, many large insurance companies provide do-it-yourself kits for appraising houses and their contents. These kits contain a household inventory and instructions on how to prepare a video inventory. You may find these kits helpful.

In any case, be sure to get an estimate of the replacement value, not the market value. The *replacement value* is the amount it would cost to build a house comparable to yours. The *market value* is the amount for which you could sell your house.

Even if your house burns to the ground, the land still retains its value. So it's possible, in areas where land is expensive—cities such as Boston, New York, and San Francisco—for the replacement cost to be substantially less than the market value. The opposite is true, however, for homes that are replete with marble fireplaces, ornate wood paneling, and other expensive special features.

Note that many homeowner's policies include an "inflation guard." This clause automatically boosts your coverage—and your premiums— each time you renew your policy, thus taking into account the effects of inflation.

Inflation guard is a handy feature, but don't rely on it forever. At least every five years, get your house appraised to make sure your coverage is in line with current costs.

Also, notify your insurance carrier at once if you make improvements to your home that cost 3 percent or more of its replacement value. And increase your coverage to reflect the changes.

On Shaky Ground

Although earthquakes are most frequent in California, they can occur without warning in any part of the country. And few people are insured for earthquake damage. While damage from earthquakes is excluded from almost all homeowner's insurance policies, it can be purchased separately.

Ask your insurance agent for quotes on several policies. In most areas of the country, the cost of this coverage is low—often less than $100 a year. The added protection is worth it.

While insurers do protect you against earthquake damage—for an additional price—they won't cover flood damage at all. They consider such policies too risky.

So Uncle Sam has gotten into the act. In certain areas of the country, flood insurance is available from the U.S. Department of Housing and Urban Development. If you live in an area where flooding is likely, check with your insurance agent and purchase this added protection.

Premiums generally run about $35 per $15,000 of coverage. To sign up for federal flood insurance, simply write or telephone your insurance agent. He or she will make all the arrangements required for you to purchase the policy.

Easy Riders

Also, if you ever purchase a mobile home, you should know that insurance carriers do offer coverage for these structures. There's just one restriction: The mobile home must be at least 10 feet wide and 40 feet long. Coverage is the same as that provided under Forms One and Two—that is, you're insured for named disasters only.

Premiums for these policies generally add up to more than those for a homeowner's plan, because the possibility of damage, particularly by wind and snowstorms, is greater. But you should, nonetheless, avail yourself of whatever protection you can afford.

Another word to the wise: Many homeowner's plans automatically limit coverage of personal property to 50 percent of the value of your house. If you want your coverage to exceed that amount, you must purchase a special rider.

The cost of these riders varies. For example, a person in Atlanta, Georgia, would pay more than a person in Fairborn, Ohio, because the cost of living is higher in Atlanta. But expect to pay at least $1 per $100 of appraised value of personal property.

What Is Covered?

Your homeowner's policy covers not only the house itself but any "appurtenant structures"—meaning garages, storage sheds, and other separate buildings.

Moreover, homeowner's policies reimburse you for living expenses if your home is damaged and you're forced to seek shelter elsewhere, in a hotel or motel, say. A policy typically pays your hotel bill, plus the difference between your normal food costs and the expense of eating out.

Don't expect payment if you stay with a friend. The policies are designed to cover your actual out-of-pocket costs.

This coverage is standard, and you get it automatically regardless of whether you own or rent. But there are usually dollar limits to the coverage. Check your policy to see how much it will pay.

Something else you may not know: Your homeowner's policy covers damages to family gravestones and markers. If vandals tip over a family member's stone, your policy pays to have it repaired—as long as the deceased was once a member of your household.

Are You Liable?

Homeowner's policies also automatically include some liability protection and extend coverage to members of your household, including your pets. So if your schnauzer takes a chunk out of the mailman's leg, rest easy. Your insurance will pay any claims.

Standard liability protection also covers medical payments to others and damage to other people's property that is caused by you or your family. For example, your children are playing baseball in your backyard, and your daughter hits a home run. The ball ends up in your neighbor's living room. Your homeowner's policy pays for replacing your neighbor's window.

Homeowner's insurance also includes personal liability protection. If someone slips on the ice on your sidewalk and sues you for negligence, your policy covers the cost of your defense. What's more, it pays any judgments against you.

Warning: Some renter's insurance policies do not cover liability. If you are a renter and want protection from liability, you might want to purchase an additional or "Special Form Liability for Renters" policy.

This protection is inexpensive, and it's an absolute necessity in this litigious age. (See Chapter 24 for more on liability policies.)

Tip: If you have household help, you may want to buy a rider that protects you from liability claims by domestic workers.

What Is Not Covered?

Not everything in your house is covered by your homeowner's insurance, even if you purchase a replacement value plan.

Among the items not protected—or protected only to a certain dollar amount—are the following: antiques, silver, and furs. If you want these valuables and others protected over the dollar amount listed on your policy, you must insure them separately.

Baubles, Bangles, and Beads

You own several pieces of expensive jewelry, which you want to make sure are properly insured. What kind of coverage should you look for?

The most sensible way to insure these valuables is through an addition to your homeowner's policy called a *personal articles floater*.

With a floater, your coverage goes wherever you do. If the item is in your house, it is protected. Likewise, if you take the item away from home, it's covered. So if you're away on business and your gold bracelet is stolen from your hotel room, you're protected by your floater.

Standard homeowner's coverage caps the amount you may collect for certain categories of items. The following limits are typical for homeowners' policies. (They may be lower on renters' policies.)

DOLLAR LIMITS ON PERSONAL PROPERTY

ITEM	CEILING
Money	$ 200
Bank notes	200
Bullion	200
Coins	200

ITEM	CEILING
Medals	$ 200
Securities	1,000
Manuscripts	1,000
Stamp collections	1,000
Valuable papers	1,000
Watercraft (including their trailers, motors, and equipment)	1,000
Other trailers	1,000
Grave markers	1,000
Jewelry	1,000
Watches	1,000
Furs	1,000
Precious and semiprecious stones by theft	1,000
Firearms by theft	2,000
Silverware, silver-plated ware, or pewterware by theft	2,500
Property on the residence premises used for business purposes	2,500
Electronic data-processing equipment	5,000
Rugs and tapestries	10,000

The floater covers your loss as long as you provide proof of the item's value. A sales slip is acceptable. So is a professional appraisal. (But every couple of years, you should reappraise items of substantial or increasing value.)

A typical floater will cover all risks except those specifically excluded in the policy—typically, wear and tear, war, and nuclear accidents.

Premiums are based on the value of the items you insure, usually $1 to $2 per $100 of value. So a $10,000 painting might run you $100 to $200 a year in premiums.

But not all floaters are the same. Most floaters usually state the maximum amount they will pay. That means a company can—and will—pay you less than the declared value if you suffer a loss.

Say you purchased a fur coat five years ago for $10,000, and you've been paying premiums based on a declared value of exactly $10,000. While you're away on vacation, someone breaks into your house and steals the fur. You report the loss to the insurance company.

But you collect only $8,000. Fur coats, the insurance company tells you, decrease in value over time. Since your coat is five years old, you're entitled to only 80 percent of the amount you paid.

If you want to receive the full amount an item is worth, make sure your policy pays *replacement value* and not actual cash or depreciated value. Ask for a *valued form* or *valued form contract policy*.

Expect to pay more, though, for this type of protection. Rates typically run 20 to 40 cents more per $100 of assessed value.

Write Now

A fast way to shop for homeowner's insurance—and find out what your current policy covers—is to telephone or write your insurance agent.

Here's a sample letter to use.

J. Q. Professional
Executive Insurance Inc.

Dear Insurance Professional:

I am evaluating my homeowner's insurance, and I would appreciate your assistance. I have listed below the specific information I need about my current coverage. Please feel free to fill in the answers on this letter and return it to me.

    1. Does my present policy provide all-risk coverage on my house?

_____.

    2. Does my present policy provide all-risk coverage on the contents of my house?

_____.

    3. Does my present policy limit coverage on my personal possessions to an amount equal to 50 percent of the value of my house?

_____.

    4. Does my present policy pay actual cash value or replacement value?

_____.

    5. Does my coverage automatically increase each time I renew my policy to take into account the effects of inflation?

_____.

    6. What are the limits of my liability protection?

_____.

    7. Does my policy cover the computer I have at home and use for business?

_____.

    8. If so, is the software covered as well as the hardware?

_____.

    I want to know the cost of increasing my liability coverage to a minimum of $300,000 and of purchasing an umbrella policy to provide additional protection.

    I also want to make sure that I have comprehensive all-risk protection to cover all personal property losses. These loss payments are to be made on a replacement cost basis, rather than an actual cash value or depreciated basis.

    Please let me know if there are any discounts available for the following: smoke detectors, fire extinguishers, dead bolt locks, or other protective devices. I presently have _____.

    Also, please let me know the cost of including earthquake coverage in the policy and recommend ways to use deductibles to cut my premium payments.

Listed below are special items that should be included on a rider and insured for their replacement value:

Item:
_____

Value:
_____

Appraisal Method:
_____

Item:
_____

Value:
_____

Appraisal Method:
_____

Item:
_____

Value:
_____

Appraisal Method:
_____

Item:
_____

Value:
_____

Appraisal Method:
_____

I have enclosed copies of the declaration pages from all my property insurance policies. These, and the information below, should adequately describe the properties. However, if you have any questions, please feel free to telephone me. My telephone number is _____.

Address:
Property 1: _____ Property 2: _____
Square Footage:
Property 1: _____ Property 2: _____
Construction Type (Brick, Frame):
Property 1: _____ Property 2: _____
Number of Stories:
Property 1: _____ Property 2: _____
Finished Basement:
Property 1: _____ Property 2: _____
Number of Fireplaces:
Property 1: _____ Property 2: _____
Central Air Conditioning:
Property 1: _____ Property 2: _____
Number of Bathrooms:
Property 1: _____ Property 2: _____
Estimated Replacement Cost of Primary Structure:
Property 1: _____ Property 2: _____
Estimated Replacement Cost of Other Structures:
Property 1: _____ Property 2: _____
Estimated Replacement Cost of Personal Property:
Property 1: _____ Property 2: _____
Liability:
Property 1: _____ Property 2: _____
Medical:
Property 1: _____ Property 2: _____
Deductibles:
Property 1: _____ Property 2: _____

I thank you in advance for your help.

Sincerely,

24 *Under the Umbrella*

Get Smart About
Liability Protection

*M*ost insurance carriers impose limits on how much your automobile and homeowner's insurance can pay in a case involving a liability claim.

And as large as that upper limit may sound, it can easily fail to cover your bills—which is why an umbrella or personal excess liability policy makes sense. An umbrella policy picks up where your automobile and homeowner's policies leave off.

Say you're involved in an automobile accident and are judged at fault. The court awards damages of $500,000 to the person you injured. But your car insurance caps your liability protection at $300,000. Without an umbrella policy, the remaining $200,000 would come out of your own pocket— not exactly a pleasant prospect.

You may buy umbrella liability coverage in the amount of $1 million to $5 million. Most people opt for the $1 million plan.

The cost for a person who owns a house and one car is about $125 to $150 a year for a $1 million policy. The price may be as low as $60 a year if you own no car, and $100 a year if you own no house. (You pay more if you own a car, because more liability claims stem from auto accidents.)

Since the advent of umbrella policies in the 1970s, it has made good sense to give all your insurance business to one company. That way, the company that writes your umbrella policy won't—in the case of an accident—be wrangling with the company that insures your automobile.

240

Write Now

Here's a sample letter for inquiring about your umbrella liability coverage.

J. Q. Professional
Executive Insurance Inc.

Dear Insurance Professional:

I am evaluating my liability insurance, and I would appreciate your assistance. Would you provide me with a quote on a comprehensive personal liability policy?

I have enclosed copies of the declaration pages from my property and car insurance policies and have listed below the specific information I need. Please feel free to fill in the answers on this letter and return it to me.

1. What would the cost be for $1 million of coverage?

_____.

2. What is the maximum amount of coverage I can purchase?

_____.

3. What is the cost of this maximum coverage?

_____.

4. Will this policy provide protection against liability exposures not covered in my other insurance policies?

_____.

I would appreciate your recommendations or comments on my liability insurance, including ways in which I may improve my coverage.

I thank you in advance for your help.

Sincerely,

Tax Planning in Changing Times

25 Taxing Matters

Mastering the Fundamentals

*T*axes have an enormous impact on your personal finances. In addition to reducing cash flow, they're an important influence on the kinds of investment decisions you make. They also affect the way you borrow, the type of life insurance you buy, and how you save for retirement. The fact is, taxes have a significant effect on virtually every aspect of your financial life.

We cover the relationship between taxes and other financial topics throughout this book. But here, in Part Five, we'll concentrate on strategies to slash your tax bill, so more money flows into your pocket—and less into Uncle Sam's.

First things first, though. To do effective tax planning, you need to understand some basic tax concepts. We'll run through them in this chapter. Then, in the next chapter, you'll learn more about specific tax-saving strategies.

Your Tax Rate

Before we begin, a word about the difference between your effective tax rate and your marginal tax rate.

Your *effective tax rate* is the rate at which you pay tax on all your taxable income. Say you're married and file jointly and your tax bill in

1990 adds up to $12,582 on your taxable income of $60,000. Your effective tax rate equals 21.0 percent ($12,582 divided by $60,000).

Your *marginal tax rate* is the rate you pay on the last dollar you earn. Using the previous example, let's say you also receive a $5,000 year-end bonus. Your marginal rate on the bonus is 28 percent, the rate you pay in 1990 on taxable income in the $60,000 to $65,000 range.

Knowing your marginal tax rate also helps you calculate how much a deduction is worth to you. If your marginal tax rate is 28 percent, a $1,000 deduction saves you $280 in tax.

Theoretically, there are now only two tax brackets. In practice, though, there's also a third bracket of 33 percent (more on this bracket later in this chapter).

For 1990, the 15 percent rate applies to income equal to or less than $32,450 for married individuals filing joint returns and surviving spouses, $26,050 for heads of household, $19,450 for single people, and $16,225 for married individuals filing separate returns.

Any income you make over these amounts is taxed at the rate of 28 percent. (These amounts are adjusted for inflation annually.)

Here's something else you should know for 1990: If you're a single filer with taxable income of more than $47,050 or a married joint filer with income exceeding $78,400, you'll pay a top marginal rate greater than 28 percent.

The reason: You are subject to a so-called *phase-out surtax*. You won't just pay 15 percent on part of your income and 28 percent on the rest (as less well-off taxpayers do).

Rather, you'll shell out an additional 5 percent tax on part of your earnings. The result: You'll eventually pay a flat tax of 28 percent on all your taxable income—not just the amount above a certain level.

So you pay an extra 5 percent tax—in addition to the 28 percent tax—on taxable income that falls within the following ranges. (Uncle Sam adjusts these ranges annually for inflation.)

- $78,400 to $162,770 for married couples filing joint returns and surviving spouses
- $67,200 to $134,930 for heads of household
- $47,050 to $97,620 for single people
- $39,200 to $123,570 for married individuals filing separate returns

With the surtax, the two-bracket system effectively becomes a four-bracket system—15 percent, 28 percent, 33 percent, and back to 28 percent. Here's how it works.

Let's say you file a joint return, and your taxable income in 1990 comes to $100,000. Of this amount, $21,600 is subject to the 5 percent surtax ($100,000 less $78,400). Your additional tax equals $1,080 (5 percent times $21,600).

So if you are married and file jointly, and your taxable income comes to $162,770 or more, the surtax gobbles up the benefit of the 15 percent rate on your first $32,450 of income.

Now for another wrinkle—a second phaseout.

What Congress giveth in the 1986 Tax Reform Act—a sizable increase in each taxpayer's personal exemptions—it also taketh away for high-income individuals.

The new law increased the personal deductions you may claim for yourself and each dependent to $2,000 in 1989, and $2,050 in 1990.

But high-income taxpayers begin to lose the tax benefits of these higher deductions as their incomes rise. This phaseout works much like the surtax we just discussed. Above the income levels indicated in the following list, you're hit with another 5 percent surtax. If your income is high enough, this surtax eliminates the entire tax benefit of all the personal exemption deductions you claim.

The personal exemption phase-out surtax is equal to 5 percent of taxable income exceeding these levels:

- Married individuals filing joint returns and surviving spouses, $162,770
- Heads of household, $134,930
- Single individuals, $97,620
- Married individuals filing separate returns, $123,570

Each personal deduction you claim is worth a maximum of $574 in tax benefits in 1990. Why? Well, multiply the $2,050 deduction by the 28 percent tax rate. It comes to $574. And that's what you would save in taxes if Congress hadn't imposed this 5 percent phase-out surtax.

You don't pay the 5 percent surtax on all income above the appropriate level, though—just until the $574 benefit has been eliminated. When is that? Figure it this way. How much income does Uncle Sam have to tax at 5 percent to get back his $574? The answer: $11,480 ($11,480 times 5 percent equals $574).

So, your income above the appropriate level is subject to the 5 percent tax in increments of $11,480—the number of increments corresponding to the number of personal exemptions you claim.

The income of a married couple with two children is subject to the surtax between $162,770 and $208,690 ($162,770 plus $45,920, which is 4 times $11,480).

Capital Gains: The Long and Short of It

As you remember, in the not-so-distant good old days, long-term capital gains received special—and very favorable—tax treatment. When you sold an investment that you had held for more than six months, you paid tax on only 40 percent of your profits.

No longer. You pay the same rates on long-term capital gains as you do on ordinary income, such as salaries, interest, and dividends. This means that, if you report income above certain amounts, your gains may even be taxed at 33 percent, due to the 5 percent surtax. (Short-term capital gains have always been taxed at the same rates as ordinary income.)

What happens if you have more losses than gains?

You may deduct from your ordinary income up to $3,000 in net capital losses a year—regardless of whether they are short or long term. If your losses top the $3,000 ceiling, you may carry them over to succeeding years—and use them to offset capital gains or write off $3,000 a year against ordinary income until the losses are used up.

Another point: Even though long-term capital gains no longer receive favorable tax treatment, you should keep track of them. Here's one reason. The law still requires you to categorize your gains into short and long term and report them on your tax return.

Another reason is that long-term gains might again be treated advantageously, especially if President Bush has his way.

And when you record your gains, keep this fact in mind. Unless Congress makes a change, you must hold assets for more than a year before they qualify for long-term treatment.

Kid Stuff

The 1986 Tax Reform Act spelled significant changes—most of them for the worse—in the way your children are taxed. Let's take a look.

In the past, any income your child received was taxed at your child's marginal tax rate, which, in most cases, was lower than your own. Now, any unearned income of more than $1,000 is taxed at your marginal rate (if it's higher) until your child reaches age fourteen. Once your child is fourteen or older, all earnings are taxed at his or her rate.

What if you are divorced? Income topping $1,000 is taxed at the marginal rate of the parent who has custody. If you and your spouse have joint custody—or if you are married but file separate returns—your child's income is taxed at the rate of the parent in the higher marginal bracket.

Note, though: These rules apply only to unearned income. If your child has a job, the money he or she pockets qualifies as earned income, and it is taxed at his or her marginal rate. This holds true even if your child is paying taxes at your marginal rate on unearned income.

No Alternative

Let's say that you make a lot of money, but your tax bill is really low. Lucky you, until you remember the alternative minimum tax (AMT).

This is the tax that says: "Take all the deductions, credits, and deferrals you have coming to you. But, in the end, you're still going to pay your fair share of tax."

As a concept, the AMT is simple enough. First, you figure your tax in the regular way. Then you take your regular taxable income and add back some of the deductions that you took out and some other so-called *preference items*.

You subtract the exemption the law allows you—$40,000 for married taxpayers filing jointly, $30,000 for single filers—and multiply the total by a flat rate of 21 percent. Finally, you compare the result with your regular tax. You owe the government the larger amount.

Of course, the calculation isn't really that simple. For example, special phase-out rules eliminate the exemption for higher-income individuals. This and other technicalities make the AMT a nightmare of complexity.

Which taxpayers are most likely to be subject to the AMT? Those who

- Deducted losses from passive investments, such as limited partnerships
- Claimed large amounts of miscellaneous deductions
- Invested in oil and gas partnerships
- Paid high state and local taxes
- Deducted investment interest that topped their investment income
- Deducted substantial consumer interest
- Exercised incentive stock options
- Refinanced their home after June 30, 1982
- Donated appreciated property to charity
- Acquired real-estate investments before 1987 that they continue to hold
- Reported accelerated depreciation write-offs that exceeded straight-line deductions for the same property (see Chapter 11 for a discussion of depreciation)
- Received interest from certain tax-exempt bonds

Don't panic. If just one of these items applies to you—and the amount involved is small—it's unlikely you'll trigger the AMT.

But if your tax calculations reveal a combination of these items—or a substantial amount in any one category—you might be a likely AMT candidate.

One last word about the minimum tax: The AMT will affect many more taxpayers than in the past. Why?

First, the AMT rate of 21 percent is 75 percent of the top regular tax rate of 28 percent. In the past, the ratio was only 40 percent (a 20 percent AMT and a 50 percent top regular rate). As the ratio goes higher, it is more likely the AMT rate will apply.

And there are adjustments and preference items to add back in. These include passive losses you may claim during the law's phase-in period, the excess of fair market value over the cost of property you donate to charity, and home mortgage interest on refinanced debt that tops old debt.

State of the Art

Forty-three states—the exceptions are Alaska, Florida, Nevada, South Dakota, Texas, Washington, and Wyoming—levy some type of personal income tax. And the rates imposed run as high as 10 to 15 percent.

Don't make the mistake some taxpayers do and overlook state and local taxes when it comes time to adopt tax-saving strategies.

Making the Best of It

Now you know the basics of the tax law. But how do you use this knowledge to your best advantage? Read on to find out.

26 *Winning Ways*

How to Make the
Tax Law Work for You

What tactics can you use to slash your personal tax liability? Here's a checklist of some basic strategies.

Beat the Floor on Deductibility

Under the current law, you may write off miscellaneous itemized deductions only to the extent that they exceed 2 percent of your adjusted gross income (AGI).

What qualifies as a miscellaneous itemized deduction? Annual subscriptions to professional journals, continuing education courses that relate to your job, union and professional dues, job-hunting expenses, investment adviser and management fees, and tax preparation and advisory fees—just to name a few.

Here's an example of how the floor works. Your AGI totals $50,000, and your miscellaneous deductions come to $1,000. Since $1,000 is exactly 2 percent of $50,000, you may not write off a single cent. If however, your miscellaneous deductions totaled $1,050, you could deduct $50—the amount that exceeds 2 percent of your AGI.

In order to get at least a partial write-off under the new rules, you should attempt to bunch as many of these expenses as possible into a single year. Here's how.

Toward the end of the year, take a hard look at your bills in these "miscellaneous" categories. If you see that by paying for, say, a continuing education course you took this year, you will exceed the 2 percent floor, go ahead and write the check by December 31.

But if your calculations show you'll fall below the floor, wait until January before paying these bills. You may be able to beat the floor next year.

Similarly, your medical expenses must exceed 7.5 percent of your AGI before you may deduct any of them. So if these expenses are already high, pay as many of them as you can this year in order to beat the floor.

Restructure Your Debt So You Can Deduct Interest

Uncle Sam won't wholly subsidize interest payments on your automobile or sound system anymore. The deduction for personal interest is phased out gradually through 1990. In 1990, you may write off only 10 percent of consumer interest. By 1991, you may write off none. How do you adjust your strategies for this change?

One tack to take is to restructure your debt by tapping the equity in your home. You may either refinance the mortgage on your first or second home, take out a second mortgage, or apply for a home-equity loan. And the interest is deductible in full as long as: the loan is secured by your principal residence or your second home; the amount of the loan does not top the cost of your house; and you meet the qualifications we discussed previously. (See Chapter 16 for the rules on home-equity debt.)

But be careful. As we've seen in Chapter 16, you should never let the tax tail wag the interest deduction dog. In other words, don't ever put yourself in financial jeopardy—or in a position to lose your house. Before taking any action, carefully think through whether you can pay back a loan secured by your home.

Remember, too: Refinancing costs money. You have to worry about points, appraisal fees, and title costs, among other expenses.

Moreover, when it comes time to calculate your alternative minimum tax liability, you may not deduct interest on that portion of a refinanced mortgage that is greater than your mortgage balance before refinancing.

Keep an Eye on Changes in Tax Rates

This much is certain about tax rates: Eventually, they're going to go up, or they're going to go down. And you must adjust your tax planning tactics as the rates change.

Here's why: One set of strategies applies if tax rates are going up; another if tax rates are coming down. For example, it might make sense to defer income when tax rates are high—and falling—but not when tax rates are going up.

Take Advantage of Income-Shifting Opportunities

The current tax law reduces the benefits of transferring income-producing assets to a minor child. In the past, you could give cash or property to your child. And any income these assets earned would have been taxed at your child's marginal tax rate, which, in most cases, was lower than your own.

Now, you still may give your children cash or property. But any income of more than $1,000 from these assets is taxed at your marginal rate—until your child reaches age fourteen. Once your child is fourteen or older, all earnings are taxed at his or her rate.

But the income-shifting game is not entirely over. Remember: Of the first $1,000 of your younger child's income, $500 is tax free and $500 is taxed at the child's lower rates. You should invest your child's money to take advantage of this rate structure.

And shifting income to children age fourteen or older still makes good sense. Indeed, whatever tactics you used with your older offspring still apply—with one major exception: short-term trusts.

These trusts, you may recall, were extremely useful for shifting income from a high-bracket taxpayer—you, the parent—to a low-bracket taxpayer—your child. Clifford trusts, named for the defendant in the Supreme Court case that legitimized their use, were the most popular of these short-term trusts.

Now, income and deductions generated by Clifford or other short-term trusts will be included directly in the grantor's—that is, your—taxable income. However, Clifford trusts that were in existence on March 1, 1986, escape the new rule.

You may still build college funds or other savings for your kids by giving assets outright. Be careful, though. The money now belongs to your child. And losing control of your assets—or taking a chance that little Janie will use her funds to buy a Mercedes rather than pay for a college education—are risks you must weigh carefully before making a big gift. (We'll cover income-shifting strategies for college financing in Chapter 27.)

Pay Attention to Withholding and Estimated Taxes

In order to win the withholding game, you don't want to be either over-withheld—and make an interest-free loan to the government—or under-withheld—and end up paying penalties to Uncle Sam.

If you are a salaried employee, make sure when you fill out your W-4 or W-4A form that you take all the exemptions to which you're entitled. You should know that the IRS will scrutinize your form W-4 if you take more than ten exemptions. But if you're entitled to them, go ahead and take them.

If you work for yourself—or have substantial income beyond your wages and salaries—plan your estimated taxes early on. Estimated tax payments are due to the IRS quarterly: April 15, June 15, September 15, and January 15.

The total amount of your quarterly installments plus withholding taxes must at least equal the lesser of

- 90 percent of the tax for the current year; or
- 100 percent of the tax on your previous year's return

Suppose that you estimate your current year's tax liability at $50,000. Last year, your taxes totaled $44,000. You could make estimated payments based on 90 percent of your current year's liability, which comes to $45,000 ($50,000 times 90 percent). Or you could make the payments based on the full amount of last year's tax, or $44,000. Naturally, you would base your quarterly estimated payments on $44,000.

What if you underpay your taxes? You pay a penalty on the amount your payments fall short. The penalty you owe depends upon the amount of your underpayment and current penalty rates, which are based on interest rates.

You can't deduct the amount you pay in penalties. So all the more reason to plan ahead.

Keep Track of Carryforwards

Uncle Sam allows you to carry forward some unclaimed deductions—unused passive losses and investment interest, say, that exceed investment income. These items roll forward to succeeding years until they are used up. But you can carry them forward only if you remember them from year to year. So keep track of these unused write-offs.

Plan Ahead to Work with the Alternative Minimum Tax

Start early in the year to project your income and expenses to see whether you may be subject to the alternative minimum tax (AMT).

If you are, it isn't the end of the world. But since the AMT is a completely separate tax system, you must learn to live within its rules and plan accordingly.

Here's one idea: If you discover you are subject to the AMT, you may want to accelerate receiving income. It may be better to pay tax on that income at the AMT rate of 21 percent than risk paying tax at a higher rate the following year. You may also want to defer deductions to the following year, when they may yield a higher tax benefit.

You may want to weigh carefully whether or not to exercise incentive stock options. (For information on options, see Chapter 29.)

By using a minimum tax credit, you may often recoup in future years AMT you pay this year. So it's difficult to apply a standard rule of thumb for tax planning if you find yourself in an AMT situation. The best advice: Check with your tax adviser and plan for more than your current-year tax situation.

Put Your Money into PIGs

Another strategy to consider: If you post losses from passive investments, consider putting your money into PIGs. No, we don't mean hog farming.

We're referring to passive investments that generate income—*passive income generators*, as they're known, or PIGs. Some examples of PIGs: nonleveraged real-estate investments and investments in S corporations.

When you invest in PIGs, you can use your passive losses to offset your passive income. Evaluate PIGs as you would any other investment. In other words: Invest in them because they make economic sense—not because they make tax sense.

Give Appreciated Property to Charity

One way to boost your deductions for charitable contributions is to donate appreciated property, such as common stocks. Here's how.

Say that you plan to donate $2,000 to your favorite charity. You can write a check for that amount, or you can donate property valued at $2,000.

You opt to donate property. So you sign over to the charity 100 shares of XYZ Corporation stock valued at $20 a share that you bought ten years ago for $1 a share. And you claim a deduction of $2,000.

The beauty of this maneuver: You get a tax deduction equal to the market value of the stock—even though you paid a paltry $1 a share for it.

Caution: The stock or other property you donate must be long-term property. In other words, you must have held it for more than one year.

Also, remember that the appreciation is subject to the alternative minimum tax. Appreciation must be added back to your income when you calculate your AMT liability. Our advice: Check with your tax adviser before making a gift of appreciated property.

PART SIX

Family Matters

27 *Bright Ideas*

The Right Way to Finance Your Child's Education

*I*f you think college costs are high now, today's price for a college education will look like pocket change in a few years.

University administrators estimate that the average cost of a four-year college education will zoom from $20,000 today to more than $51,000 by the year 2000. And what if Junior opts for a private school? Expect to pay about twice as much.

Obviously, unless you are extremely wealthy, you should plan ahead. For some people, though, it may already be too late.

In this chapter we tell you how best to save for your children's education. Then we outline ways to pay if time has run out.

ABCs

Before getting down to dollars and cents, ask yourself this key question: What do you and your children really want when it comes to college?

Think first about your family's attitude toward college. Do you consider attendance a must for your son or daughter? What about your child's own wishes? Have you openly discussed the subject with your youngster?

If college is a priority, evaluate whether your child is more likely to attend a private or public institution. As we've seen, it makes a big difference when it comes to toting up the final bill.

And speaking of that bill, who will have primary responsibility for paying it? In some families, the parents fully shoulder college costs. In others, the children work during the summer—or during the school year—to help pay the bills.

Another important question: Is your child likely to qualify for scholarships, fellowships, or loans? (These programs are discussed at the end of this chapter.)

Once you've answered these questions, you'll have a better idea of how much money it will take to educate each of your children. And you can adopt a game plan to get you the dollars you need.

What's Your (Bottom) Line?

You know your child is college bound. What amount must you salt away each year to meet your target? Fill out the college funding work sheet that you'll find in Appendix VII and you'll have the rough answer.

The work sheet and the filled-in sample in Appendix VIII give you an idea of the approximate amounts you need. Attempting to be more precise—particularly if the children are very young—is probably a waste of time. Why? There are too many unknowable factors—for instance, the rate of inflation ten to twenty years from now, the rate of return your investment will earn, the amount of money a particular college will cost, and the type of degree your youngster will want.

Getting There

The investment strategies you use to build your education funds must take the tax law into account. You'll use one set of strategies if your children are under age fourteen and an entirely different set if your children are age fourteen or older.

Strategies for Younger Children

Let's consider children under fourteen first.

From a tax perspective, you could invest money for these offspring just as you would your own funds. The reason: The tax considerations are the same—generally your child's net unearned income of more than $1,000 is taxed at your rates.

But it may be a better idea to slant the investments on behalf of your under-fourteen-year-old children toward those on which tax is deferred. At least it's a good idea to do so until they reach age fourteen—and pay tax at their own rates. Here are some good choices for these college funds.

Series EE United States Savings Bonds

The law says you don't have to pay taxes on the interest these bonds earn until they mature unless you choose to report the interest annually on your return. So buy Series EE bonds—in your child's name—that mature after your child's fourteenth birthday. That way, income from the bonds is deferred and ultimately taxed at the child's lower rate.

You may purchase a Series EE bond for as little as $25 or as much as $5,000. (The face value equals twice the amount of the purchase price.) The government caps your total investment in EEs at $15,000 per person. So you may buy up to $15,000 worth of bonds (with a face value of $30,000) for each of your children.

When you buy a Series EE bond, you pay no sales commission. If you hold the bond until it matures, you can cash it in and receive—at a minimum—its full face value.

The key phrase here is *at a minimum.* Although you are guaranteed to receive at least twice what you paid for the bonds, the actual interest rate is variable. But there's no risk. Rates on current Series EEs vary only upward. If interest rates fall, you still collect the minimum rate stated at the time you purchased the bonds. And if interest rates go up, you receive more than the face value of the bond at maturity. So Series EE bonds are a hedge against inflation.

Tip: Beginning in January 1990, the interest from these bonds is tax-free if you use them to defray college costs. However, you must meet certain conditions:

- The bond must have been issued after December 31, 1989.
- You must be 24 years old or older.

- You must use the bond proceeds for qualified education expenses incurred by you, your spouse, or dependents.

You will pay tax on some of the interest, however, if you are married and are filing jointly and your AGI falls between $60,000 and $90,000 (between $40,000 and $55,000 for single taxpayers).

Annuities

Investors in annuity insurance policies benefit in the same way as investors in U.S. savings bonds: Their income isn't taxed until it is actually paid out.

You may purchase an annuity for your minor child. And the IRS won't tax the appreciation until the annuity payments begin—presumably, after age fourteen.

Any number of annuity insurance policies work for this purpose. But remember, you are paying for some insurance coverage as well as making an investment.

Tax-Exempt Bonds

By definition, you pay no federal taxes on these bonds. You may also escape state and local taxes. But be warned: Most state and local governments tax income from bonds issued in another state. For example, if you live in Boston and purchase a municipal bond issued by the city of New York, income from that bond is subject to both state and local tax. But you pay no tax if you purchase a bond issued in Massachusetts.

Buy bonds with a maturity date that coincides with your child's first year of college. Another alternative: Buy tax-free bonds that mature when your child reaches age fourteen, then switch to taxable bonds with a higher yield. You may put the tax-free bonds in your name or your child's name. It makes no difference from a tax standpoint. And there are advantages to both.

Putting them in your child's name forces you to keep them reserved for your offspring's college fund. You're less tempted to dip into these funds for your own use.

The plus of keeping them in your own name? If interest rates rise—and your bonds decrease in value—you can sell them and, most likely, make better use of the capital loss deduction than your child could. (See Chapter 7 for more information on bonds.)

Tip: You may be better off buying shares in a municipal bond mutual fund than buying individual bonds. The reason: The fund gives you diversification.

Zero-Coupon Bonds

Invest in zero-coupon bonds that mature the year your child starts school. You buy zero-coupon bonds for much less than their face value. You receive no interest from year to year, but the bonds appreciate considerably by maturity.

These bonds are attractive, because the interest rate on reinvested earnings is fixed. The only catch: Even though no interest is actually paid each year, the IRS "imputes"—or counts—the interest as income. So you pay taxes on the amount even though you don't receive it until maturity. You avoid this problem altogether, of course, if you buy tax-exempt zero-coupon bonds.

(See Chapter 7 for more on zero-coupon bonds.)

Nondividend-Paying Growth Stocks

Buy nondividend-paying growth stocks in your child's name. Then hold the stocks until after the child reaches age fourteen.

The IRS won't tax the appreciation until the shares are sold. If the sale takes place after your child turns fourteen, the gain will be taxed at his or her lower rate.

Another strategy: Put the shares in your name, and transfer them to your child when he or she reaches age fourteen. You receive few or no taxable dividends. Meanwhile, if your stock goes down while your child is under fourteen, you can make good use of the capital losses. And, until your child's fourteenth birthday, you maintain control over your assets.

Obviously, as with all investments, you must evaluate the risk. With growth stocks, there is the possibility you could lose all or a portion of your principal.

In Trust

Another idea for squirreling away college funds: Set up a *minor's trust*. You can put in a sum of money all at once or make smaller gifts each year for a period of years. The trust terms: Income accumulates for your child unless distributed at the discretion of the trustee. But all principal and income must be distributed to the child by the time he or she reaches age twenty-one.

The trust pays tax at the rate of 15 percent on its taxable income up to $5,450 in 1990 (and 28 percent on income above $5,450). And you may give up to $10,000 a year to each child—$20,000 if your spouse joins you in making the gift—with no gift tax consequences. Gifts to the trust qualify for the annual gift tax exclusion.

Here's an example: When your child is eight, you and your husband put $20,000 into a minor's trust. Assuming the funds are invested at 8 percent (and 15 percent tax is paid each year), the trust will build to $38,600 by the time your child turns eighteen and needs money for college. If you had paid tax at your 28 percent tax rate each year, the $20,000 would have grown to only $35,000. So, combining interest earned and taxes saved, you're $3,600 better off.

A minor's trust also works well for children age fourteen or older. Be aware, though: You will have to pay administrative costs.

A Penny Earned

Now, a word about earned income.

As you recall from Chapter 25, if your child has a job, the money he or she makes is earned income and is taxed at his or her rate. That means if you're a business owner, you still have a good opportunity to shift some income to your lower-rate child—even when the child is younger than fourteen.

Say you need some part-time help in your hardware store and decide that daughter Jane, age eleven, is old enough to tackle the job. For three hours a day, four days a week, Jane keeps tabs on inventory. You pay her the going rate for this type of work—$4 an hour.

Jane's annual earnings of $2,400 ($48 a week for 50 weeks) are taxable to her. She files a tax return, but pays no taxes. Why? The standard deduction for dependents is the greater of $500 or earned income up to the regular standard deduction. And the regular standard deduction comes to $3,250 in 1990. (After 1988, the standard deduction is annually adjusted for inflation.)

And you benefit as well. You may write off the $2,400 you paid Jane as a business expense, which reduces your taxable income by that amount.

One word of warning, though: Don't pay your children more for a job than it is worth. Uncle Sam frowns on a stock person making, say, $20 an hour, particularly if the young worker is the business owner's minor child.

Another idea: Encourage your children to get an outside job and set aside some of their earnings in a college fund. The same tax rules apply.

Strategies for Older Children

And if your child is age fourteen or older?

Let Uncle Sam help you out with accumulating capital for future college costs. It's easy. Just shift some of your income from your tax bracket to your child's bracket and invest it.

Remember, if you establish a savings account or stock portfolio in your child's name to help build savings for a college education, the money you give is taxed at that child's rate—as long as the child is fourteen years of age or older. (See Chapter 25.) You may give up to $10,000 a year to each child—$20,000 if your spouse joins you in making the gift—with no tax consequences.

The least complicated way you can achieve this end is under the Uniform Gifts to Minors Act (UGMA) or the Uniform Transfers to Minors Act (UTMA). These acts allow parents—or any individual, for that matter—to give money to a child but keep it under the control of a custodian.

The custodian may be a family member, a legal guardian, or any trusted adult you choose. But the person who gives the money—known as the *donor*—should probably not act as custodian. Why?

If the donor is the custodian and he or she dies before your child reaches majority, the money will be subject to estate tax in the custodian's estate. (If your estate is small—or covered by the unlimited marital deduction—the custodian issue isn't as important. See Chapter 38 for more on the rules governing estates.)

Banks, mutual-fund companies, and brokerage firms can provide all necessary forms for setting up an UGMA or UTMA account. And there are no legal fees involved in establishing one.

The only drawback to the accounts: The money belongs to your child once he or she reaches majority, so you can't force him or her to use it for college. Generally, the custodian controls the money until your child reaches twenty-one, even if the majority age in your state is younger.

Of course, your older child can also get a job or work for you in a family business. Earned income—like unearned income—is taxed at his or her lower tax rates. And, like younger siblings, he or she pays no tax at all on this income until it exceeds the standard deduction.

Early Payments

Finally, a note about prepaid tuition plans. They come in two varieties. We talk about one type here—and one type later on.

The newest kind—set up by some colleges and even some states—works like this: You pay four years' tuition at a substantial discount when your child is young. Then, when your child reaches college age, his or her education is already paid for. And it's guaranteed, no matter how much tuition costs have shot up.

These plans may sound like the answer to parental prayers, but we recommend that you approach them with caution.

Here's why. What happens if your prospective scholar nixes that particular school (or vice versa)? You may get back only the amount you paid in or you may lose your money entirely.

To prevent this grim scenario from unfolding, some colleges are joining together and allowing prepaid tuition to apply to several schools. This move reduces the risk—but it doesn't eliminate it.

Another problem: You may have to pay gift tax on the amount you pay into the plan—the $10,000 annual gift tax exclusion does not apply to tuition prepayment plans. And, once your child begins college, he or she will be liable for tax on the difference between the amount paid and the tuition value actually received—what Uncle Sam refers to as the "accretion in value."

How to Pay for College When It's Too Late to Save

If you're the parent of a high school junior or senior, you're down to the wire as far as college funds are concerned.

What's your best bet? Actually, there are three best bets: You can dip into savings—either yours or your children's. You or your college-bound child can borrow money. Or you can apply for financial aid from schools or government sources.

Dipping into Savings

Say you own some stock, and it has appreciated nicely. You're in the top 28 percent tax bracket. Now, you need cash to pay for your son's education.

Why not transfer the stock to your child and let him use the proceeds for school? With this strategy, he pays taxes on the appreciation at his rate. If the stock was in your name when you sold it, you would pay taxes at your higher rate.

Here's an example. Let's assume you purchased $5,000 worth of stock when your son, Kevin, was just a tot. Now, with Kevin ready to enter college, your nest egg is worth $25,000. You sell your stock and make a handsome $20,000 profit. But you have to pay taxes of $5,600, leaving only $19,400 available to pay tuition.

If, however, Kevin sells the stock, which you've now put in his name, he owes only $3,072 in taxes. And $21,929—or an additional $2,529—is available to pay his college bills.

Be careful, though. It's okay to transfer assets to your son or daughter. But you can't insist that he or she sell the assets to fund college costs. The law mandates that anyone selling securities must act out of his or her own free will.

Another word of caution: Don't forget about gift taxes. See our discussion of this subject in Chapter 38.

On Loan

What about borrowing for your children's education? Here's one of the best ways: Tapping the equity in your house.

As you know, the tax law won't allow you to deduct the interest you pay on a student loan. But you may still write off your mortgage interest. So consider using a home-equity loan to fund your child's education. (See Chapter 16 for more details.)

Uncle Sam also offers several attractive loan programs. Among them: Guaranteed Student Loans, Parental Loans for Undergraduate Students, and National Direct Student Loans. And some states have educational loan programs as well. Check with the college or your state office of financial aid to find out more.

Here's another idea: Loan your child money for school. Then set up a plan that allows your youngster to repay you principal plus interest once he or she graduates.

But if you adopt this strategy, bear in mind the tax ramifications: This maneuver results in additional income to the higher-bracket taxpayer—you—and a deduction for the lower-bracket taxpayer—your son or daughter.

And, while we're on the subject, a word about interest-free loans. You may no longer use these loans as income-shifting devices for tax purposes. The reason: The IRS may impute income to the parent and a deduction to the child. Of course, you might still want to use interest-free loans to help your child finance his or her education—just make sure you understand the tax consequences.

The Best Things in Life Are Free

Because there are so many scholarship sources, getting a handle on all of them isn't easy for the beleaguered parent. You needn't be overwhelmed, though, if you follow this plan of attack:

- Find out what the college itself can do for you.
- Investigate the traditional aid sources, mostly governmental.
- Get creative with some nontraditional sources.
- When you think you've exhausted everything else, go back to the school one last time.

Schools themselves frequently can help students that they especially want to attract. They'll use installment plans, loans, merit scholarships, athletic scholarships, and discounts for more than one family member attending the institution.

Many of the most competitive schools, including Ivy League colleges, offer financial aid strictly on the basis of need. In fact, a group of these schools meets every year to ensure that students get the same aid package from each.

That way, they reason, qualified students will not have to forgo their first choices for financial reasons. Often, the more expensive the college, the more aid available.

Applications, Please

Public and private colleges have devised almost standard procedures for calculating the amount and kind of aid available to prospective students and their parents.

Along with their application materials, most colleges send you one of two different computerized financial aid forms. You need only complete each form once, even if your child is applying to more than one school.

There are two forms because colleges usually appoint one of two agencies—the College Scholarship Service (CSS) or the American College Testing (ACT) program—to analyze a family's financial needs.

Both agencies use a complicated formula to evaluate your family's assets and to calculate a "reasonable" family contribution toward the annual college cost. Then they subtract this contribution from the yearly cost of attending the school. The balance is what you hope financial aid will cover.

The agencies also send your financial-need information form to the federal government's Pell Grant program. An official in that office automatically assigns an "aid index" and notifies you if your child is eligible.

When you do apply for aid, pay special attention to these points. Observe all deadlines for the financial aid forms that come with school applications. They count. Also, complete your taxes early. Questions on the forms are based on income tax returns. You may estimate if you must, but be as accurate as possible. You'll have to correct any errors later, which may delay the process and jeopardize your child's chances for aid.

Many colleges, especially the most selective ones, will give your child 100 percent of the financial need calculated by the agency. Some colleges, however, provide just a portion of that help. In either case, you may still have to look elsewhere for more assistance.

The first place you should look is to the traditional college aid sources—direct and campus-based state and federal government aid programs.

The college's student aid office will help you identify and apply for government programs. But the aid itself comes from the federal and state governments.

Bright College Days

If you still need help, take a look at subsidized jobs at the school of your child's choice. In college work-study (CWS) programs, students find a job with an approved employer—a nonprofit organization, say, or a professor—on or off campus. The college then draws on government-provided funds to subsidize a portion of the paycheck, usually about two-thirds.

Hup, Two, Three, Four

If your children don't mind trading some of their time for money, and don't object to military service, they can get help paying for their educations through various military programs.

The Army, Navy, Air Force, and Marine Reserve Officers Training Corps (ROTC) programs provide scholarships that pay all tuition, fees, and book charges. They also cough up a tax-free stipend.

In return, students must attend weekly ROTC classes for two years. And, once they graduate, they must serve in the military for six years.

The National Guard in each state will provide up to $15,000 in tuition aid for guard members after they have served for two years.

And veteran's benefits are available to students who have served in the military or who are spouses or children of deceased or disabled veterans.

Get Creative

Scholarships and tuition aid programs turn up in the most unlikely places—social and civic clubs, alumni organizations, churches, and employers, for example.

Unfortunately, there is no systematic approach you can follow to ensure that you haven't overlooked one of these. Some aid programs are based on merit; some on athletic or other skills; some on need; and some are there practically for the asking—provided you know to ask.

The first place to check: a school's guidance counselor or librarian. When you think you've looked everywhere and applied for every conceivable aid program, make one final visit to the school your offspring is intent on attending. See if there isn't one last thing the administrators there can suggest.

Pay Out

Assuming that you don't find an aid program or combination of programs that covers all the costs, the day will come when you have to pay the bill. But even at this point, you have choices.

Remember, schools have devised payment options that can minimize shock to the parental checkbook. Sometimes these options even reduce the total costs.

For instance, more and more schools offer tuition prepayment—the forebear of the prepaid plan we discussed earlier. When your child first enters the school, you pay all four years of tuition and expenses at the freshman year price, thereby hedging against future tuition increases.

Since your child has already made his or her college choice, these plans—unlike the long-range programs—may make sense. But what if your student decides to transfer in his or her junior year? Is the tuition refundable? And consider the size of the lump sum you need to make the payment. The bottom line? You'd better analyze this option thoroughly before you pay.

The monthly payment plan, another option many schools offer, lets you spread the financial damage of the annual charges over an entire year.

Other schools have other payment options. Ask the financial officers at the schools of your choice to tell you about them.

PART SEVEN

What Your Company Is Doing for You

28 *Hidden Assets*

How to Get the Most from Your Company Benefits

*I*f you're like most people, you don't think much about the fringe benefits that come with your job. You simply accept them as your due.

But not scrutinizing these perks is a big mistake. Unless you know your benefits inside out, you can't make the most of them.

And these are not goodies to overlook.

As the U.S. Chamber of Commerce points out in a recent survey, the value of fringe benefits adds up to a third of a typical employee's annual salary.

In this chapter, we tell you how to get the most out of the fringe benefits your company provides. And we cover the important tax consequences of these fringes.

Uncle Sam Wants You

Most people, of course, don't get to choose their benefits. You take what you're offered. But don't count yourself among those employees who don't even know what they have.

The first thing you must do: Analyze the fringes provided to you and see how they meet your goals and objectives. For example, one of your goals is protecting yourself from risk. To accomplish this end, you need life insurance. Does your company provide it? If so, how much and what kind? You may find you have adequate coverage, or you might discover you need supplemental coverage.

Understanding the benefits your employer provides is especially important if you're on your way up. The fact is, as your pay increases, so does your choice and scope of benefits. Among the most common perks offered to people at or near the top: stock options, company cars, health club and country club memberships, and personal financial planning.

Taxes are another reason to learn more about your fringes. Many of the benefits your employer provides are taxable to you.

Say you're the chief executive of a small bank, and the bank pays $2,000 a year for you to belong to a local country club. Under the law, the bank—as your employer—must report the value of that annual membership as income to you on your W-2 form. And this amount is taxed the same way as your wages.

Remember, though, that taxable fringes are better than no fringes at all. The annual cost of your country club membership to you is $560— that is, 28 percent (your tax bracket) times the annual membership fee— not the full $2,000 your employer pays.

The Menu, Please

Understanding your fringe benefits is also critical if your company offers a cafeteria—or flexible benefits—program.

With a cafeteria plan, you design your own benefits package from the options available. Your employer gives you a flat dollar amount to spend. Then you choose the fringes you want from a preset "menu."

Among the benefits that cafeteria plans typically offer: medical insurance, dental insurance, life insurance, accidental death and dismemberment coverage, disability benefits, and contributions to a 401(k) plan.

Cafeteria plans date back to the 1970s, when personnel consultants and employers first took note of the growing diversity of the work force.

Many employees wanted—and needed—to shape their own benefits plans. For example, they didn't want health insurance coverage if their spouses' employers were already providing it. They wanted to put the value of that particular fringe to better use.

Tip: Cafeteria plans let you accept cash at the beginning of the year rather than a particular benefit. For instance, you could choose $100,000 in life insurance coverage, or you could accept $50,000 in coverage and receive $250 in cash—an amount that otherwise would have covered the premium on the additional $50,000 in insurance.

When selecting your fringes, though, be careful to sign up only for the level of benefits that you think you'll actually use. Here's why: Say you opt for $2,000 worth of child care as one of your fringes. And you use just $1,000. The law prevents your employer from refunding you the value of the unused benefit—the extra $1,000—at the end of the year. So if you sign up for excessive benefits at the beginning of the year, you could end up a loser.

All There Is

The summary that follows tells you about benefits your company might offer. And it explains which are tax free and which are reported as income to you. Use this rundown to review the fringes you receive.

As we've seen, some benefits—health, disability, and life insurance, among them—are critical to your overall financial security. So, with these fringes, ask yourself if you need to supplement your employer-provided coverage with policies you purchase yourself.

Now, for our summary, in alphabetical order.

Athletic Facilities

Use of any company-operated athletic facility—a gym, pool, tennis court, golf course, or skating rink, say—is not taxable to you. And this rule applies even if your company sets aside a facility exclusively for the use of its executives—or any other group. The only restriction: The facilities must be owned or leased by the company—either alone or with other employers.

But keep in mind that Uncle Sam treats company-paid memberships in outside health clubs as compensation. So the amounts paid for them are taxable to you.

Child Care

Many companies operate child-care facilities on their premises or contract with nearby child-care centers for such services.

And that's good news for employees. Up to $5,000 in child-care assistance is not taxable to you—as long as the service is available on a nondiscriminatory basis.

Company Airplanes

It is a wise policy to avoid flying on company airplanes for any but business purposes. The reason is simple: The value of personal flights you take on company-owned aircraft is reported as income to you, and you pay tax on the amount.

The law provides complicated guidelines to calculate the value of such flights. We won't run through the calculations here, but you should know that the value approximates expensive charter flight rates. So personal travel on a company plane can prove quite costly—especially for a company's directors, officers, and top executives.

Company Cafeterias

If your company provides a cafeteria and subsidizes the cost of food to its employees, this service must be nondiscriminatory. As long as access to the facility isn't restricted to the company's executives and, on an annual basis, the revenue from the cafeteria equals or exceeds direct operating costs, you aren't taxed on the benefit—so eat up. If it is restricted, though, executives are taxed on the benefit.

Company Cars

In the old days, Uncle Sam left it up to you to report on your tax return the dollar value of driving company cars during off hours. But the 1984 Tax Reform Act shifted the burden to your employer. Now, your company must list the value of so-called *personal usage* on your W-2 form.

How do employers compute the value of personal usage? One method is the annual lease value. In a complex set of regulations, the IRS ties this value to the annual cost of leasing an automobile. Uncle Sam even provides a table listing lease values for automobiles costing up to $60,000. This table is updated annually. A copy of the 1990 table follows.

ANNUAL LEASE VALUE

FAIR MARKET VALUE	LEASE VALUE
$ 0 to 999	$ 600
1,000 to 1,999	850
2,000 to 2,999	1,100
3,000 to 3,999	1,350
4,000 to 4,999	1,600
5,000 to 5,999	1,850
6,000 to 6,999	2,100
7,000 to 7,999	2,350
8,000 to 8,999	2,600
9,000 to 9,999	2,850
10,000 to 10,999	3,100
11,000 to 11,999	3,350

FAIR MARKET VALUE	LEASE VALUE
$12,000 to 12,999	$ 3,600
13,000 to 13,999	3,850
14,000 to 14,999	4,100
15,000 to 15,999	4,350
16,000 to 16,999	4,600
17,000 to 17,999	4,850
18,000 to 18,999	5,100
19,000 to 19,999	5,350
20,000 to 20,999	5,600
21,000 to 21,999	5,850
22,000 to 22,999	6,100
23,000 to 23,999	6,350
24,000 to 24,999	6,600
25,000 to 25,999	6,850
26,000 to 27,999	7,250
28,000 to 29,999	7,750
30,000 to 31,999	8,250
32,000 to 33,999	8,750
34,000 to 35,999	9,250
36,000 to 37,999	9,750
38,000 to 39,999	10,250
40,000 to 41,999	10,750

FAIR MARKET VALUE	LEASE VALUE
$42,000 to 43,999	$11,250
44,000 to 45,999	11,750
46,000 to 47,999	12,250
48,000 to 49,999	12,750
50,000 to 51,999	13,250
52,000 to 53,999	13,750
54,000 to 55,999	14,250
56,000 to 57,999	14,750
58,000 to 60,000	15,250

Here's an example of how the rules work. Say the fair market value of your company automobile is $15,000. For 1989, the IRS sets the annual lease value of that car at $4,350.

Say, too, that a quarter of the miles you rack up on your company car are for personal reasons. You report your personal usage to your employer. That means you will have taxable income equal to 25 percent of the lease value—$1,087.50. And this amount must be included on your 1989 W-2 form.

What happens if your only personal use of the company automobile is for commuting? Another batch of rules applies. Commuting is not considered business use—even if you install a telephone and transact business while you're driving.

Commuting, in the eyes of Uncle Sam, is always personal use—with one exception. Here's an example to illustrate.

Let's say your employer provides you with a car for bona fide business reasons—that is, you do not receive the automobile as part of a compensation package. Also, you are not an officer, director, or top executive of your company. You actually need the car to perform your job properly, and you do not use the automobile for personal reasons—except on a *de minimis* basis, meaning rarely. In this case, the IRS assumes that your use of the car for driving to and from work is worth $3 a day to you in extra taxable income.

But if your use doesn't meet the limited conditions we just described, you can't use the flat dollar amount for reporting income. Instead, you add up the mileage to and from work for the year and use the result to compute what portion of the car's value must be reported as income to you.

Suppose, for example, that you log 14,000 miles this year in your company car, and your only personal use is driving to and from work. To calculate your personal usage, you divide the number of miles you rack up commuting—3,000, say—by the total miles—14,000.

The result—21 percent—is the percentage of the car's annual lease value that your employer must report as income to you. So if your company car has an annual lease value of $4,350, the amount listed on your W-2 form is $914—that is, 21 percent times $4,350.

Death Benefits

Your company may pay death benefits—meant to cover funeral expenses—of up to $5,000 to your beneficiaries without reporting that amount as income to them. Any benefit of more than $5,000 will be treated as taxable income to your beneficiaries.

Your company may also provide accidental death and dismemberment insurance for accidents suffered on or off the job. Benefits paid to you or your beneficiaries are not treated as income and therefore are not taxable.

Dental Insurance

There was a time when employers rarely provided dental insurance. Today, this coverage is one of the hottest fringe benefits available. And, because it is tax deductible for the employer and not taxable to the employee, it is included in many cafeteria plans.

Dental programs are primarily preventive. For example, they pay for cleaning; but, if you break a tooth, you may have to foot part of the bill.

Typical dental policies provide coverage for as much as 80 percent of your total annual dental expenses, up to an annual maximum limit—usually $1,000 per person. But be warned: Policies usually cap coverage for orthodontia and other cosmetic dental services. In fact, some policies exclude orthodontia altogether.

(See Chapter 19 for more on dental insurance.)

Disability Insurance

When it comes to disability insurance, our advice is simple: If your employer doesn't offer disability coverage, purchase it yourself.

If your employer does provide insurance, don't assume that the basic coverage provided will protect you and your family for any prolonged period of disability. You may need to buy supplemental coverage.

If you participate in a cafeteria plan, you may want to opt for a benefit other than disability insurance, then pay for disability coverage out of your own pocket.

Here's why: If your employer covers the cost of your disability insurance policy, payments you receive from the policy are taxable to you. However, if you pay for the disability insurance policy yourself, the benefits you receive later on aren't treated as taxable income to you.

(For more on disability insurance, see Chapter 20.)

Discounts for Employees

Many employers sell company products and services to their employees at a discount. But strict tax rules apply to these price-reduction programs.

The law states that a company—on a nondiscriminatory basis—must limit any discount on its services to 20 percent in order for the discount to be nontaxable. Discounts on products are limited to the gross profit—that is, the selling price minus the cost of goods sold—an employer would make if it were to sell the product.

Nondiscriminatory discounts, however, are usually available not only to you, but also to your spouse and dependents. In addition, they may be provided to retired and disabled employees.

Caution: The IRS does not allow employers to offer tax-free discounts on items that have the potential to appreciate significantly over time. In other words, if you make discounted investments—in real estate, commodities, securities, coins, and so on—through your company, you'll pay income tax on the discount.

Education Programs

Seminars and training programs paid for or sponsored by your employer are still tax free to you. But general tuition assistance is another story.

Through September 30, 1990, tuition assistance to you—up to a ceiling of $5,250—is tax free, even if the courses you take are not job related. But certain restrictions apply.

General tuition plans are tax free only if you receive them at a college or university that employs you.

Otherwise, tuition assistance is reported as income to you. The result: If you earn your college or graduate degree at the expense of your employer, the amount will be included by your employer as income on your W-2 form.

You may be able to treat the amount as a miscellaneous deduction on your tax return. But, remember, you may deduct only that portion of these costs that tops the new 2-percent-of-adjusted-gross-income floor on miscellaneous itemized deductions. (See Chapter 26 for more on this new rule.)

Exercise Classes

Exercise classes at the company aren't taxable to you—as long as they are open to all employees on a nondiscriminatory basis. Some companies pay for the instructor; others don't. But many businesses gladly provide space for the classes.

Financial Planning Services

Growing numbers of companies are providing personal financial planning services as a perquisite to middle managers and executives.

These services may cover income tax planning and preparation, investment advice, guidance on making the most of compensation and employee benefits, retirement counseling, and estate planning. Computerized financial plans are also popular.

In most cases, the IRS treats the value of financial planning services as compensation. In turn, virtually the entire amount qualifies as a miscellaneous deduction on your return. So, if you itemize your deductions and this amount, combined with other miscellaneous deductions, exceeds 2 percent of your adjusted gross income, you will be able to write it off.

Still, in the worst case, paying tax on the services is always better than paying for the services yourself.

Life Insurance

The cost of your employer-paid life insurance is reported as income to you, unless the insurance is provided under a group term policy.

But even under group term plans, the benefit is tax free only up to $50,000 of coverage. If your employer pays for additional coverage, the cost is considered taxable income.

The cost of additional insurance that is reported as income to you isn't what your employer actually pays under a nondiscriminatory plan for the coverage. Rather, it is an amount based on an IRS table of average or "uniform premiums." And, as with other fringes, your cost is the tax—not the full amount.

Here's an example to illustrate how the table works.

Let's say you get promoted and your new title means that your insurance coverage is hiked from $50,000 to $200,000. The first $50,000 of coverage is tax free to you. But the value of the remaining $150,000 in coverage must be reported to you as income.

Your corporation computes this amount by using the following IRS table. You are thirty-seven years old. So the monthly value of each $1,000 of additional life insurance protection is—in the eyes of the IRS—11 cents.

Your company divides the amount of additional coverage it provides to you—$150,000—by $1,000. It then multiplies the monthly cost—11 cents—times the number of thousands of dollars of additional coverage—150. The result—$16.50—is reported to you as additional monthly income.

The total of $198 for the year is listed on your W-2. The total cost to you for this extra benefit is only the tax on the $198 of income.

IRS UNIFORM PREMIUMS FOR TAXING GROUP TERM LIFE INSURANCE COSTS

AGE	MONTHLY COST PER $1,000 OF PROTECTION
Under 30	$0.08
30 to 34	0.09
35 to 39	0.11
40 to 44	0.17
45 to 49	0.29
50 to 54	0.48
55 to 59	0.75
60 to 64	1.17
64 to 69	2.10
70 or older	3.76

Low-Interest or No-Interest Loans

In the old days, companies were free to make low-interest or no-interest loans in any amount to their employees. And there were no tax consequences for either the borrower or the lender. Then Congress adopted the 1984 Tax Reform Act.

Now, loans of $10,000 and less are considered *de minimis*—too small to really matter. But loans of more than $10,000 are subject to strict regulations. Today, if you borrow more than $10,000 from your employer, you must report as taxable income the difference between the "applicable federal rate" (based on a rate the federal government pays on its borrowing) and the interest your employer charges on your loans.

Say you borrow $50,000 at 4 percent from your company for one year. The interest amounts to $2,000 (4 percent of $50,000).

If you had borrowed the money at a time when the federal rate was 10 percent, you would have to report income of $3,000, which is the difference between the $2,000 you actually paid and $5,000—the amount your interest would have totaled under the federal rate.

But here's where you get a break. The law allows you to claim a deduction for the amount of "imputed" interest—that is, the $5,000—you would have paid under the federal rate. You may write off $3,000 more than your actual interest expense.

Whether you get full benefit—or any benefit—for this write-off depends on the rules governing interest deductions. For example, assume that you use the money you borrowed to pay off consumer debt. After 1990, your write-off will not produce any tax benefit. (See Chapter 16 for more on interest deductions.)

Medical Insurance

More than 90 percent of the people who are employed full time in this country are covered by employer-provided medical insurance.

Most companies cover employees' medical expenses in one of two ways—through an insurance policy or through a self-funded plan. With either method, sums that are paid to reimburse you for medical expenses are not reported as taxable income to you.

Uncle Sam allows your employer to cover your doctor, hospital, and nursing bills, as well as the cost of diagnosing and treating your illnesses and diseases. Your employer may also cover a wide range of special medical expenses, including

- Annual physical examinations
- Eyeglasses
- Hearing aids
- Artificial limbs
- Artificial teeth
- Dental care
- Guide dogs
- Transportation, including to and from medical appointments and in medical emergencies
- Rental of medical equipment

(See Chapter 19 for more on medical insurance.)

Mental Health Services

More companies are discovering the advantages of providing counseling services for employees. These services boost morale. And they often help employers cut expenses due to absenteeism and loss of employee productivity.

One New York insurance company, for example, reports in a recent study that fewer employees take leaves of absence or go on disability when counseling programs are in place. These programs may take the form of group therapy, marital counseling, and stress management, as well as personal crisis intervention.

And counseling is not a taxable fringe.

No-Additional-Cost Services

Services your employer provides to you at no additional cost to the company need not be reported as income to you. For the most part, no-additional-cost services are those that are ordinarily offered for sale to the public by a company but, because of excess capacity, are available to employees.

Falling into this category are such goodies as empty hotel rooms and standby airline tickets. Another example: A moving company allows its employees to use its vans during off hours to move furniture and other large items.

A company may treat no-additional-cost services as nontaxable fringe benefits only if they are made available to a broad category of employees—not just top executives.

Parking

A free parking place is still available as a tax-free perquisite as long as it is on or near the company's premises. This is one perk that may be provided on a discriminatory basis.

Pension and Profit-Sharing Plans

These plans are discussed in Part Eight.

Retirement Planning

Growing numbers of businesses are offering counseling to employees who are nearing retirement or taking early retirement. The counseling may consist of advice on personal money management, or it may be designed to help workers cope with the idea of being permanently off the job.

Sometimes it is provided along with personal financial planning. Other times—for example, as part of an early retirement program—it is offered separately. Retirement planning is taxable to employees only if it takes the form of individual counseling. Company-sponsored seminars are tax free as long as they are nondiscriminatory—that is, they're open to a range of employees, not just top executives. (See Part Eight for more on retirement planning.)

Social Security

Social Security pays benefits when you retire or become disabled. And both you and your employer pay Social Security taxes. (For more on Social Security, see Chapter 31.)

Stop-Smoking Programs

Under the rules, your employer need not report the cost of a stop-smoking program as income to you. However, the program must be open to rank-and-file employees and not favor key executives or shareholders.

Unemployment Compensation

Say you're in an industry that has fallen on hard times, and you're laid off. You're entitled to collect unemployment compensation benefits from your state. Unemployment benefits—which apply to anyone who is laid off—are funded by payments made by your employer.

Weight-Loss Programs

The law does not require you to report the value of a weight-loss program as income. Again, there is one sticky point: The program must be open to rank-and-file employees and not discriminate in favor of top executives.

Workers' Compensation

The primary aim of workers' compensation is the economic security of injured workers and their families. Workers' compensation laws are administered by the various states.

Workers' compensation is financed by insurance. Your employer pays premiums based on your salary (so much per $100 of compensation). Then, if you are injured or die in a work-related accident, you or your survivors are entitled to cash payments and medical benefits.

Working-Condition Fringe Benefits

Working-condition fringes are items that relate to your particular job. They may be provided tax free by companies on a discriminatory basis. For example, your company may pay for special training or magazine subscriptions for you without extending similar benefits to other employees.

Your employer may also write off the cost of a bodyguard, a bulletproof vest, bulletproof glass for your car, a briefcase fitted with alarms, or karate classes—all tax free—if it can prove to Uncle Sam that your job puts you in danger.

29

It's Your Option

All the News About Stock Options

*T*here's no more popular fringe for luring new employees and keeping old ones than stock options—and for good reason.

Stock options give you the opportunity to profit from appreciation in your company's stock. And, unlike buying options on the open market, you pay nothing for this right. You receive it free of charge as a benefit from your employer.

Let's take a look at how stock options can pay.

What Is an Option?

Stock options work like this. Your company grants you the right—or option—to purchase a specified number of shares of company stock at a specified price within a specified time period.

You may exercise the option—that is, purchase the shares—at once. Or you may wait until a later time when the price of the shares is higher.

But whenever you exercise your options, you purchase the stock at the *option price*—generally, the price for which it was selling on the date the option was granted.

Here's an example. On January 1, your company grants you the option to buy 1,000 shares of its stock at the current market price of $10 a share. A year later, when your company's stock jumps to $12 a share, you exercise your option. You purchase 1,000 shares at your $10-a-share option price. So you pay $10,000 for stock that's now worth $12,000.

Who Gets Options?

In some companies, stock options are restricted to a handful of top executives. In other companies, they're extended to middle managers and line-level employees.

Suffice it to say that if you are a senior or middle manager and you are eyeing another job, you should learn what you can about your new employer's policy on options.

Many people are bargaining for stock options when they join new companies, and many are getting them as part of a total compensation package. In any case, you can't be a savvy businessman or businesswoman and not be aware of the ins and outs of this benefit.

Playing by the Rules

Stock options come in two forms—*incentive stock options* (ISOs) and *nonqualified stock options* (NQOs). What's the difference between them?

With ISOs, you pay no income tax until you sell the stock. But with NQOs, you pay income tax when you exercise the option, and you also pay tax when you sell the stock—that is, if you sell the stock at a gain.

Let's return to our previous example. If your option is of the ISO variety, you pay no tax when your option is granted, because, in the eyes of Uncle Sam, you haven't profited—at least not yet.

If you are not subject to the AMT, you also pay no income tax when you exercise your option, even though, in this case, you post an immediate paper profit of $2,000 (the difference between the $10,000 you paid for the stock by exercising your option and the current market value of $12,000). But you will have to shell out a few dollars to the IRS a little more than a year later, when the stock zooms to $20 a share and you decide to sell.

You pay income tax on the difference between the selling price—$20 a share, or $20,000—and the amount you paid under the option—$10 a share, or $10,000.

With NQOs, different rules apply. You pay tax on the *spread*—that is, the difference between the original option price and the market price—at the time you exercise the option.

Again, let's go back to our example.

If your options are NQOs, you pay income tax when you exercise on the difference between the $10,000 you paid for the stock and the current value of $12,000.

You also pay tax a year later, when you sell the stock at $20 a share, or $20,000. Tax is levied on a gain of $8,000, which is the difference between the selling price and your cost basis—in this case, the market price at the time you exercised your options.

By definition, NQOs are options that don't meet the requirements of ISOs. So if you or your employer violate any of the ISO rules, your ISOs become NQOs.

Here is a checklist of the ISO requirements.

From the date the option is granted until three months before the date the option is exercised, you must be an employee of the company granting the option.

That means if you are on a company's list of optionees, you can actually leave the company and exercise the option within three months of your departure. And you still obtain the tax advantages. If you don't exercise your options within the required time period, though, the options become NQOs by default.

If you leave a company due to disability, you have the same rights as other former employees—that is, you may exercise your stock options within three months after you leave and still get the tax advantages. However, if you leave the company because of permanent or total disability—and your employer's plan allows it—you have up to one year to excercise your ISOs.

What happens if you go on sick leave—or some other company-approved leave? As long as you're still employed by the company, you may exercise your ISOs. Should you die, your options go to your beneficiaries.

The option period may not exceed ten years.

And the company must grant ISOs within ten years of the date the shareholders formally approve a stock option plan.

Gains from the sale of shares qualify for long-term capital gain tax treatment only if you hold the shares for more than two years from the date the option was granted and for more than one year from the date the option was exercised.

Say you were granted an option on January 15, 1990, and purchased the shares three months later—on April 15. The law requires you to hold the shares until January 16, 1992—two years after the option was granted.

Since the 1986 Tax Reform Act eliminated the benefits of long-term gains, this rule is not as important as it once was. But as we saw in Chapter 25, you still need to keep track of long-term and short-term gains.

The option period may not exceed ten years.

And the company must grant ISOs within ten years of the date the shareholders formally approve a stock option plan.

No more than $100,000 in ISOs may become first exercisable in any one year.

Companies may grant stock options in any amount they choose—$100,000, $500,000, or even $1 million or more. There is just one catch. In the case of ISOs, no more than $100,000 in options may "become first exercisable in any one year."

Say, for example, that your company grants you $200,000 in options. The company must specify that no more than $100,000 in options are exercisable this year.

You may exercise your post-1986 ISOs in any order.

Say you hold an option to purchase 1,000 shares at $20 a share, another to buy 1,000 at $15 a share, and still another to purchase 1,000 at $10 each. You received the $20-per-share option in 1985, the $15-per-share option in 1987, and the $10-per-share option in 1988.

You may exercise the post-1986 option that carries the lowest price tag—the $10-per-share option issued in 1988—even if you hold options granted before 1987.

But be warned: Options issued before 1987 must be exercised in the order they were granted. So if you were also granted options in 1983 through 1986, you must exercise the 1983 option before the 1984 option, and so on.

And Still More Rules

Some rules, however, apply to both NQOs and ISOs.

For example, both NQOs and ISOs may be exercised only by you or your heirs. That means you may not contribute your options to an IRA or other retirement plan. (Uncle Sam wants to prevent your IRA from pocketing tax-deferred gains.)

Nor may you assign your spouse the right to exercise ISOs during your lifetime. You may not even assign ISOs in a divorce settlement.

For this reason, options frequently become a touchy issue during negotiations in a separation or divorce agreement. Lawyers for both sides must come up with a formula to compensate for the fact that you may have a considerable part of your wealth tied up in stock options.

Also, you may not sell your right to exercise an option or pledge it for a loan at a bank. But you may exercise the option, then pledge the shares.

Special rules apply, as well, to corporate "insiders"—officers and directors of public companies—when it comes to stock options. For one, if you sell any stock at a gain six months before or six months after you exercise your option, you may have to forfeit the profit to your company.

Because of the complicated insider regulations that apply to any purchase of stock, you must plan carefully when to exercise your options—both to minimize your tax liability and to maximize your gains. If you fall into the corporate insider category, consult with an attorney and tax adviser as soon as you are granted options.

Pros and Cons of Options

The pluses of options: their leverage. With options, you still receive—at no cost and no risk—the right to profit from appreciation in your company's stock.

The minuses: Gains from the sale of stock acquired through options will be taxed at the same rate as salaries and other types of ordinary income.

Also, the bargain element on the exercise of ISOs is still an adjustment item for alternative minimum tax purposes. (See Chapters 25 and 26 for more about the AMT.) So you have to be careful in the timing of ISOs.

ISOs Versus NQOs

Why ISOs rather than NQOs?

Incentive stock options continue to provide tax deferral, since you report no gain for regular tax purposes until you sell the stock.

Also, the capital gains income that is more likely to be generated by ISOs may still be useful as an offset to capital losses. Without the gain, you may be limited by the $3,000 cap on deductibility of capital losses against ordinary income.

Why NQOs rather than ISOs?

There are few rules and restrictions on NQOs. For example, NQOs can be granted at less than the current market price of the stock. In addition, there is no AMT preference to worry about. And you may exercise NQOs or sell stock you acquire through an NQO at any time.

Using Stock to Buy More Stock

Here's a potent strategy you won't want to overlook.

The law says that you can use company stock you already own to pay for the exercise of a stock option. And this rule could spell hidden treasure.

An illustration: You join XYZ Corporation in Silicon Valley. You're a specialist in computer management and planning and start out at a salary of $80,000 a year.

When you're hired, you agree that you will buy 5,000 shares of XYZ at $1 per share. And you do exactly that. You also receive ISOs for 25,000 shares at $1 per share. You wait three years, until the stock of XYZ is up to $5 a share.

You exercise your option, paying with the 5,000 shares you already hold. You now have 25,000 shares worth—at the current price—$125,000.

And you parted with only $5,000 in cash to get them.

Moreover, you carry out this purchase as a tax-free transaction. You owe no tax at all until the day you sell the shares.

No Risk

A word about a variation on options, known as *stock appreciation rights,* or SARs. With SARs, you receive the right to profit from the appreciation in your company's stock without having to buy the stock itself. You get the appreciation in cash.

For example, your company grants you a SAR on 1,000 shares. The SAR gives you the right to receive a payment equal to the amount those shares appreciate over the next year. The stock goes up $1 a share. You get a $1,000 check.

Stock appreciation rights are even more attractive these days.

Why? With elimination of the favorable tax treatment of long-term capital gains, profits from stock options are taxed the same way as gains from SARs—as ordinary income. But with SARs you get an added advantage over options: You don't have to buy the stock to profit from appreciation in its price.

Explore All Options

Now that you have a clearer understanding of the rules governing options, you're poised to take full advantage of any ISOs, NQOs, or SARs your company has to offer. Remember, doing so can boost considerably the money you'll have on hand to fund your goals and objectives.

PART EIGHT

Your Retirement Nest Egg

30 Searching for the Bottom Line

How Much Do You Need for Retirement?

*A*h, retirement.

A daily golf game, a yacht, exotic travel, a place in the sun, afternoons at the track—it can be whatever you want it to be. Or it can be much less.

What makes the difference is a retirement plan.

Retirement plan? When did you last look at yours?

Don't panic. Retirement is something you should begin planning for early in your career. But a plan started later in life is far better than no plan at all.

So, what better time to start planning than now?

And, even if you think you've already laid out a pretty good strategy for funding your postemployment years, periodic updates can only improve it. Shifts in the investment climate and changes in the tax law affecting retirement investments can make a once sensible plan woefully inadequate.

This chapter and others in this section provide you with the tools you'll need to build and upgrade your retirement plan.

One Step at a Time

"The thing I should wish to obtain from money would be leisure with security," once remarked the English mathematician and philosopher Bertrand Russell.

Leisure and security.

These two words neatly sum up most people's definition of a perfect retirement. But to achieve this enviable end, you must begin at the beginning. You must ask yourself what you want. And you must calculate how much money you'll need when you are no longer employed.

But, before you get started, a word about inflation.

What Goes Up Must Come Down—Maybe

Although inflation is now much lower than it was in the 1970s and early 1980s, you still have to take it into account when you plan for retirement.

To be safe, you should probably assume a 4 to 6 percent annual inflation rate. Most economists feel this level is a reasonable estimate for the next ten to twenty years.

Many sources of your future retirement income are automatically adjusted for inflation. Social Security benefits, for example, are indexed to changes in the cost of living. And many pension plans make regular cost-of-living adjustments.

Also, if your investments are fairly flexible, you can shift funds to benefit from rising interest rates. And if you work after you retire, the income you earn will reflect the inflation rate. For example, a job that pays $10 an hour today may pay $16 an hour ten years from now.

Of course, during your retirement years inflation may run higher than 4 percent at some times and lower at others. No one can predict inflation rates with total accuracy.

Our advice: Aim for a rate of return on your investments that is 4 to 6 percent higher than the current inflation rate. You can usually get this rate without investing in vehicles that are exceptionally risky. For example, say inflation today is running around 4 percent. You'd want your retirement investments to return about 9 percent.

Remember: The rate of return on your investments must exceed the inflation rate. If it doesn't, you're getting no return at all—or worse, a negative return.

How Much Is Enough?

Now, let's look at how much it takes to live during retirement. Or—more accurately—what will it cost each year to maintain the standard of living you crave for those golden years?

First, turn back to Chapter 4.

Take another look at the "Can I Afford to Retire?" illustration. You'll see examples of the steps you should take to build your retirement planning strategy.

Then take out pencil and paper and get ready to build a cash-flow forecast. By estimating how much you'll require each year after you retire, you'll see how much you should accumulate by the time you leave your job. The retirement cash-flow work sheet you'll find in Appendix IX will help you with this analysis.

Most of us want—at a minimum—to maintain our present standard of living. So start there. Construct a cash-flow forecast based on your current spending patterns. But keep in mind that some costs will decline after retirement, while others will rise.

For example, medical costs may increase dramatically. So you should be careful not to underestimate these expenses. However, if you now live in a cool climate but retire to a warm one, your heating costs will be less. And if you continue to live in your old family home, chances are your mortgage will be paid off.

Moreover, many of the expenses formerly associated with your job—from eating lunch in restaurants to commuting—will be sharply reduced or eliminated. On the other hand, with more leisure time, you may want to increase your spending on travel, entertainment, and hobbies.

Also, by the time you retire, your life insurance policy may be paid up. Or, if it is not, you may find that you need less protection than you have been carrying. So you may safely reduce your premium costs. The high cost of raising and educating your children may be behind you, too.

Obviously—no matter what your style of living—you must be coldly realistic in estimating your own needs and expenses. You should also aim to have adequate savings—two to three months' income—always on hand to take care of unforeseeable emergencies.

What about an inflation cushion?

Unfortunately, as we've seen, there's no accurate way to factor in the effects of inflation. Any results will at best be a guesstimate. So we advise that you use the present value of money when you fill out your work sheet.

Ultimately, the amount you need for retirement depends on two factors—your longevity and your life-style.

To do a reasonably accurate forecast, you must estimate how long you'll be retired—twenty years, thirty years, or maybe even more.

Also, you must decide on the life-style you want—in housing, dining, clothing, transportation, vacations, and charitable giving—indeed, every aspect of your life.

What Do You Have?—Your Home

Selling a house and moving to smaller quarters is a big step—one you need to consider carefully and discuss with your family. But some people do use the equity in their homes to provide extra retirement income. Let's run through how you'd project income from selling your house.

Let's say that you just turned sixty-two, and you've decided to sell your home and move into an apartment near a golf course. Your home is worth $300,000 today. The cost basis of your house—that is, its cost plus improvements—totals $80,000.

But Uncle Sam gives homeowners age fifty-five and older a big one-time tax break when they sell their principal residence. You may exclude from your taxable income the first $125,000 in capital gains that you realize from the sale.

Now let's assume neither you nor your spouse, if you're married, has used this tax benefit before. When we factor in the capital gains exclusion, the sale of your home looks like this:

Selling price	$ 300,000
Minus cost basis	(80,000)
Minus selling costs	(20,000)
Capital gain	$ 200,000

Now we figure in the one-time capital gains exclusion.

Capital gain	$ 200,000
Minus exclusion	(125,000)
Taxable gain on sale	75,000
Tax rate on gain	28%
Tax liability	$ 21,000

So after paying off your mortgage and giving Uncle Sam his due, you have these funds left to invest:

Selling price	$ 300,000
Minus mortgage	0
Minus tax liability	(21,000)
Minus selling costs	(20,000)
Funds available	$ 259,000

If you invest the $259,000 and receive a return of 6 percent after tax, you'd add about $15,540 a year to your income. Not bad, you say, and you're right.

Of course, this amount wouldn't simply be gravy. You'd still have housing costs. But you would eliminate taxes and maintenance costs on your old house.

So, as you near retirement age—and if you're not wedded to your house—you may want to evaluate the costs of other housing options.

What Do You Have?—
Your Other Retirement Income

How you collect your retirement income is an important factor in retirement planning. It influences the amount of income you receive and the taxes you'll have to pay.

And usually you get to decide how to collect this income only once. So exercise care in making your decision. And make sure you understand all the alternatives. We'll talk more about methods of collecting retirement income in the chapters that follow.

Here, though, let's tackle the important topic of annuities. Any retirement plan that makes payments on a so-called *annuity basis* guarantees fixed payments for your lifetime or for the lifetime of you and your spouse.

If you choose a *single life* annuity, you get payments only during your lifetime. If you opt for a *joint and survivor* annuity, you get retirement income for as long as either you or your spouse lives.

The joint and survivor option has several variations. Two that are frequently offered by pension plans: the 100 percent joint and survivor (JS100) and 50 percent joint and survivor (JS50).

The 100 percent option may provide lower monthly payments. But if the spouse who earned the pension—known as the *annuitant*—dies first, payments remain the same.

In contrast, the 50 percent option makes higher payments if both the annuitant and the spouse are living. But the payments change if the annuitant dies.

If, for example, your wife should die before you, payments from her pension are cut in half. You receive only half as much as you did before her death.

One point is clear. If you're married, you may want to opt for one of the joint and survivor options. A single life annuity provides a higher monthly payment than either of the joint and survivor options. But if you, the annuitant, were to die early on, your spouse would be cut off totally.

So the single life annuity rarely makes sense, unless, say, you carry enough life insurance throughout your retirement years to replace the pension income that is lost or you have other assets.

Another situation when a single life annuity might make sense: if your spouse's pension is large enough to compensate for the loss of your pension income.

In any case, the law now requires your spouse's explicit approval before you may select a single life annuity instead of a joint and survivor benefit. The reason: Uncle Sam wants to make sure that both parties are fully aware of the risks involved.

Prevention Is the Best Medicine

Fact: Today's fifty-year-olds can expect to spend more than twenty years— or about a third of their adult lives—in retirement. Here's our prescription for ensuring that you will spend that time in reasonable comfort.

Save before you spend.

Why do many people end up with too little retirement income? The answer is simple and has little to do with return on investment. Usually, those whose income falls short when retirement time rolls around just didn't save enough.

Of course, most of us spend first and plan to put away whatever money we have left. There's only one problem with this strategy. Just as work expands to fill the time allotted, our expenses increase to match the money we have available.

The result: no funds left to salt away.

A better idea: Save first and spend later. You've heard it before, but it bears repeating: Pay yourself first.

You can set up a savings program painlessly through a payroll savings plan or by asking your bank to transfer automatically an amount to your investment account each month. Or train yourself to write a check to your own account on a set date every month. A good time to begin is when you receive a raise.

Another idea: If you regularly receive an annual bonus, sock that money away, too.

Let Uncle Sam help you save for retirement.
To build your retirement savings faster, make full use of so-called *tax-favored plans,* such as IRAs, 401(k)s, and Keoghs. The amount you set aside in these plans accumulates tax deferred until it is withdrawn. And that fact can mean many thousands of dollars in extra savings. (See Chapters 32, 33, and 35 for more on these plans.)

Become familiar with your employer's retirement plans.
Make sure you factor in your employer's contributions to pension plans, 401(k) programs, thrift plans, or any other programs in place. And carefully evaluate the many investment vehicle choices you have within these plans.

Finally, coordinate the investment strategies of your qualified plan with your other investment strategies. (See Part Two for more on investment strategies.)

Reassess your financial profile.
You should be very clear about both your circumstances and your attitude when it comes time to invest for retirement.

Ask yourself these key questions: Do I think I'll take on another job after I retire, thereby reducing my reliance on investment income? What about my tax bracket—will it fall immediately after retirement or not until later?

How do I want to use my leisure time—managing my investments, or pursuing other interests? Am I fairly knowledgeable about investments? If not, do I want to learn? Am I willing—and can I afford—to take risks? Or is safety of principal my primary concern?

And finally: Am I comfortable with investments that tie up my funds for a long time? Or, do I prefer greater liquidity—especially during a time when I may make big changes in my habits and plans?

Only when you answer these critical questions, can you begin to develop an asset-allocation plan that fits your own needs.

(See Chapter 5 for more on asset allocation.)

Start early.
For many people—especially those in their twenties and thirties—putting aside money for retirement is near the bottom on their list of priorities.

After all, it's hard to envision yourself as sixty when you're a bouncy twenty-three.

But not starting early is a big mistake. The reason: The amount of money you'll have for retirement depends, in large measure, on when you begin your savings program. And the results may be surprising.

Here's an example. Say you set aside $1,000 a year starting at the age of twenty-five and ending at age sixty-five. You earn an average 5 percent after-tax annual return on your money.

At the end of those forty years, your investment of $40,000 will have grown to $127,000, thanks to the magic of compounding. Begin at age fifty-five, though, and you will accumulate no more than $13,207.

Finally, don't wait until next year to begin.

Every year you delay means substantially less money in your retirement nest egg. Say you are thirty years old. You decide that next year—at age thirty-one—you'll begin to squirrel away money for retirement.

You still have thirty-four years left to save, you figure, so what's the hurry? In fact, waiting that one year reduces substantially the amount you'll have at age sixty-five.

For instance, $2,000 per year earning 5 percent interest after tax grows to $189,673 in thirty-five years and to $178,641 in thirty-four years— about $11,000 less.

Staying Focused

As you read through the chapters that follow, keep in mind that money is only part of the retirement picture. Even more than with other areas of financial planning, retirement planning is life planning. You must carefully evaluate how you want to live after you retire.

31 *Security for the Future*

Adding Up Your Social Security Benefits

As should be clear by now, calculating the value of your retirement resources can be difficult. And one of the trickier areas is Social Security.

But it certainly pays to know what's coming to you. The reason: Despite the gloom-and-doom predictions, it is extremely unlikely that Congress will allow Social Security either to run out of money or to disappear. So these benefits are still likely to play a role in your retirement years.

In this chapter, we tell you what you need to know about Social Security.

Social Security benefits have two advantages. They are indexed to inflation, and they represent income you can count on month after month. Following are answers to some commonly asked questions about the system.

What is Social Security?
When Congress adopted the Social Security Act in 1935, its idea was to provide retirement benefits for wage earners. Since then, much has changed.

These days, the Social Security system provides monthly retirement benefits not only for wage earners but for their spouses and dependents as well. In addition, Social Security programs, such as Medicare, cover the cost of hospital stays and other required medical care for people who are sixty-five years of age or older.

Who's covered by Social Security?
Most employees in private industry, most self-employed people, and members of the U.S. armed services are covered by Social Security.

How is the system funded?

If you worked for a private employer, the company contributed 7.51 percent of your earnings—up to $48,000 in 1989—to Social Security in your behalf, and you contributed another 7.51 percent. The rate increases to 7.65 percent in 1990.

What if you were self-employed? Then you paid a self-employment tax of 13.02 percent—again on earnings up to $48,000 in 1989.

What is the Social Security Administration?

This is the governmental agency that oversees Social Security programs. The central office is in Baltimore, but there are district offices in all the principal cities of the fifty states, Puerto Rico, and the Virgin Islands.

How are records maintained?

The Office of Central Operations of the Social Security Administration maintains an earnings report on every person who has a Social Security number. The Administration receives reports of earnings of employees from employers and of self-employed people from the IRS.

Why are my earnings important?

Your benefits are based on your average earnings during your lifetime. So the more you earn, the more you collect.

How can I check my earnings record?

Use Form SSA-7004PC (request for earnings and benefit estimate statement, see Appendix X), available from your local Social Security Administration office or post office. (You may also photocopy the form that we've provided in the appendix.) After it receives your form, the Administration will forward a statement of total wages and self-employment income credited to you.

Tip: Even if you're years away from retirement, you should confirm your earnings history with the Social Security Administration every three years. Otherwise, you may bump up against the time limits on correcting earnings records. Also, if you discover that some of your earnings aren't credited to you, you should contact your local Social Security office at once.

Am I eligible for benefits?
You're entitled to Social Security benefits if you are—in the eyes of the government—"fully insured." Uncle Sam classifies you as fully insured if you've acquired a certain number of "calendar quarters of coverage."

What is a calendar quarter?
A *calendar quarter* is a period of three calendar months ending March 31, June 30, September 30, or December 31 of any single year.

How are quarters of coverage determined if I am an employee?
One rule applies to years before 1978. Another rule applies to years after 1977. Let's take a look at both.

For years before 1978, you receive one quarter of coverage for each quarter in which your earnings equal $50 or more. In addition, the Social Security Administration counts each quarter of the year as a quarter of coverage if your total earnings top the maximum Social Security earnings base for that year. This rule holds true even if you receive no wages during some of the quarters.

Here's an example. Say you were unemployed from January 1, 1977, to May 1, 1977. During the last eight months of the year, you held a job and earned more than $16,500, the maximum Social Security earnings base for 1977 (more about annual base wages later in this chapter). You're credited for four quarters of coverage.

For years after 1977, the amounts of earnings needed for one quarter of coverage are shown in this table:

YEAR	EARNINGS PER QUARTER
1990	$520
1989	500
1988	470
1987	460

YEAR	EARNINGS PER QUARTER
1986	440
1985	410
1984	390
1983	$370
1982	340
1981	310
1980	290
1979	260
1978	250

I'm self-employed. How are my quarters of coverage determined?
Again, two methods apply—one for years before 1978, another for years after 1977.

For years before 1978, you're credited with a quarter of coverage for each calendar quarter in which you receive $100 or more of self-employment income. However, you must also report at least $400 in net earnings from self-employment for the entire year.

For years after 1977, the amount of earnings needed for one quarter of coverage is the same as those listed in the preceding table.

Am I fully insured?
You're fully insured—meaning you're entitled to full Social Security benefits—if you have 40 quarters of coverage (a total of ten years' work). Once you've acquired 40 quarters, you're fully insured for life. Even if you don't work another day, you're still entitled to benefits.

How are my Social Security benefits calculated?

Congress adopted a new method for computing Social Security benefits in 1979. Known as *wage indexing,* this method bases the retirement benefit you receive on your "indexed" earnings over a fixed period of years after 1950.

The maximum earnings you can have credited for specific years are as follows.

YEAR	EARNINGS
1990	$51,300
1989	48,000
1988	45,000
1987	43,800
1986	42,000
1985	39,600
1984	37,800
1983	35,700
1982	32,400
1981	29,700
1980	25,900
1979	22,900
1978	17,700
1977	16,500
1976	15,300
1975	14,100

YEAR	EARNINGS
1974	13,200
1973	10,800
1972	9,000
1968 to 1971	7,800
1966 to 1967	6,600
1959 to 1965	4,800
1955 to 1958	4,200
1951 to 1954	3,600

Here's how to get a rough estimate of your retirement benefits. Use your earnings record to calculate your average annual earnings since 1951. Now turn to Appendix XI. You'll find a table there that lists average annual earnings and the benefits you can expect to receive based on those earnings.

Can I get an estimate of my benefits?
The Social Security Administration will—upon request—estimate your retirement benefits. Use Form SSA-7004PC—you'll find a copy in Appendix X.

How do I apply for benefits?
File an application with the office of the Social Security Administration nearest you.

When should I apply for retirement benefits?
Apply for Social Security two to three months before you expect to start collecting benefits. That way, you won't have to wait for your check.

What information does the government require?

The law says you must prove your age. So take along a copy of your birth certificate or hospital birth record. Baptismal certificates are also acceptable.

How often are benefits paid?

You receive a Social Security check once a month. The government mails the checks in time for you to receive them by the third day of the month.

When can I start collecting retirement benefits?

You're entitled to retirement benefits as long as you're fully insured and you've reached age sixty-two.

When should I start collecting Social Security? At age sixty-two? Or should I wait until I turn sixty-five?

When you file and start to collect Social Security benefits has an effect on how much you'll receive. For every month before age sixty-five that you begin receiving benefits, these benefits are reduced by approximately 0.5 percent.

So if you start collecting at age sixty-two, the youngest possible age, your check could be as low as 80 percent of the full benefit you would otherwise be entitled to receive (possibly as low as 70 percent of the full amount if you retire after 2021).

But for every month after you turn sixty-five that you postpone collecting Social Security, the benefits increase. Future Social Security benefits increase by 3 percent a year for those who reach age sixty-five between 1982 and 1989—but only until age seventy-two. Those who reach age sixty-five in 1990 or later may get an increased benefit of up to 8 percent a year, depending on how long after 1924 they were born.

Here's an example. Let's assume that your benefit at age sixty-five comes to $7,152. If you start collecting at age sixty-two, you get only $5,722, a 20 percent reduction.

But if you wait until age sixty-six to collect benefits, your payment climbs to $7,367; at age sixty-seven, $7,588; and so on until the ceiling is reached at age seventy-two.

Tip: The only people who collect more over the long haul by waiting until they're sixty-five to receive benefits are those who reach age seventy-nine, as you can see from the chart on the next page.

Does the full retirement age of sixty-five apply to everyone?

No, the law was changed in 1983 to gradually raise the age at which workers can retire to sixty-seven. This change is being phased in. And if you were born before 1938, you will not be affected by it. If you were born after 1937, however, your age of full retirement will rise as follows.

IF BORN IN	YOU WILL BE AGE 62 IN	YOUR AGE FOR FULL BENEFITS IS
1938	2000	65 years 2 months
1939	2001	65 years 4 months
1940	2002	65 years 6 months
1941	2003	65 years 8 months
1942	2004	65 years 10 months
1943 to 1954	2005 to 2016	66 years
1955	2017	66 years 2 months
1956	2018	66 years 4 months
1957	2019	66 years 6 months
1958	2020	66 years 8 months
1959	2021	66 years 10 months
1960 or later	2022 or later	67 years

Are my Social Security benefits taxed?

Since 1984, Uncle Sam has required that part of your Social Security benefits be included in your taxable income if your income tops a certain level. The ceilings: $32,000 for a married couple filing jointly and $25,000 for a single person.

If your adjusted gross income (AGI) plus one-half of your Social Security benefits tops these amounts, a portion of your benefits becomes taxable. (And for this purpose only, your tax-exempt interest income is included in your AGI.)

How much becomes taxable?

SOCIAL SECURITY
When to Apply

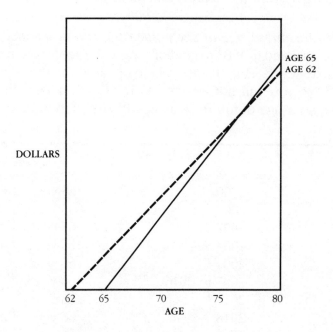

The taxable part is either one-half of your benefits or one-half of the difference between your AGI and the base amount—whichever is less. If your income is way above the threshold, chances are that one-half of your Social Security benefits are taxable.

Here's an example of how to do the calculation:

Adjusted gross income before Social Security benefits...................................... $60,000

One-half of Social Security benefits 4,524

Income for taxability test 64,524

This is more than the base amount of $32,000, so some part of your benefits is taxable.

Taxability test income $64,524

Minus base amount . . . . (32,000)

Difference 32,524

One-half of difference 16,262

In this case, half your benefits ($4,524) is less than half the difference ($16,262), so $4,524 becomes taxable to you.

Can I lose retirement benefits by working?

You can lose all or part of your monthly benefits by working if

- You are under age seventy but older than sixty-four, and your earnings from employment top $9,360 in 1990.
- You are under age sixty-five for the entire year, and your earnings from employment exceed $6,840 in 1990.

The amount you lose depends on the amount you earn in excess of these ceilings. Generally, $1 of each $2 in earnings above these limits is deducted from your benefits check. In 1990, $1 of each $3 in earnings are deducted from benefits for recipients who are ages sixty-five through sixty-nine.

But in the first year you become eligible for benefits, a monthly test also applies. The reason: so you lose no benefits in this first year. If, in 1990, you reach age sixty-five and retire, you will be paid full benefits for any month in which you earn less than $780 and are not self-employed. This rule holds true regardless of your total earnings for the year.

If you are between the ages of sixty-two and sixty-four, no benefits are lost during the initial year of retirement if your monthly earnings don't exceed $570 in 1990. This monthly test is available only once in the first year you're eligible. Again, this holds true regardless of your earnings for the year.

Can I receive retirement benefits regardless of my personal wealth?

You're entitled to retirement benefits no matter how well off you are. Also, the amount of retirement income you receive is immaterial. You lose all or part of your benefits only if earnings from services you provide exceed the limits noted previously.

Can my spouse and I both receive benefits?

If each of you is entitled to benefits because of your own earnings, you will receive benefits independently of each other. However, a spouse who is a full-time homemaker is entitled to receive one-half of your benefits as long as you live or 75 percent of your benefits after your death.

What benefits are paid to my survivors if I die?

A surviving spouse is entitled to survivor benefits if he or she is age sixty or older (age fifty or older if your spouse is disabled).

A surviving spouse who is younger than age sixty gets survivor benefits only if he or she is caring for a child who is under age sixteen.

Your surviving children are entitled to benefits, too, if they are under age eighteen (under age nineteen if they are full-time students).

Can I get benefits before reaching retirement age?

Yes, if you become disabled before reaching retirement age, you may be eligible for disability benefits. These benefits are figured much the same way as retirement benefits and are also payable to your dependents.

One big difference: You have to wait five months before benefits begin. Also, there is a special limit on family benefits.

To qualify, you must be fully insured.

Another requirement: You must have 20 quarters of coverage in the 40-quarter period ending with the quarter in which you become disabled.

If you are blind or under age thirty-one, special exceptions and rules apply, so you should contact your local Social Security office.

When am I considered disabled?

You are considered disabled if you cannot do any substantial gainful work. Also, the disability must last—or be expected to last—at least twelve months or result in death.

32 *All That Glitters*

IRAs Can Still Pay Off

*I*n this chapter, we take a look at individual retirement accounts (IRAs) to see what they will—and won't—do for you.

A Shadow of Its Former Self

When Congress adopted the Economic Recovery Tax Act in 1981, it voted to allow any working person to stash away as much as $2,000 a year in an IRA. But, alas, our legislators concluded that the 1981 rules were much too generous. So, in the 1986 Tax Reform Act, they decided to limit deductible IRA contributions to two categories of individuals:

- Those who do not participate in employer-sponsored retirement plans (or other types of retirement savings plans, which we'll describe in later chapters)
- Those who do participate in a retirement plan but whose income level falls below certain thresholds

If you belong in the first category, you may still write off IRA contributions of up to $2,000 per year—$2,250 if you have a nonworking spouse. But what happens if you or your spouse is covered by a company-sponsored retirement plan? You may still contribute up to $2,000 to your IRA. But the IRS may wholly, or partly, disallow any deduction. Here are the qualifying income levels.

Married couples filing jointly may still deduct their contributions in full if their adjusted gross income (AGI) is less than $40,000 a year. They will have the deductible amount of their contribution reduced if their AGI falls between $40,000 and $50,000—but no deduction is allowed if their AGI is greater than $50,000.

How much is your deductible? Let's run through the calculation. Subtract your AGI from the $50,000 ceiling and divide the result by $10,000. The answer equals the portion of your maximum IRA contribution you may deduct.

So if you and your spouse have an AGI of $45,000, you may still write off 50 percent of your maximum IRA contribution. The calculation looks like this: $50,000 minus $45,000 equals $5,000; $5,000 divided by $10,000 equals 50 percent.

Single people may deduct contributions in full if their AGI is below $25,000. But the amount they can deduct is reduced if their income is between $25,000 and $35,000 and none if their AGI tops $35,000.

The calculation is the same as for a married couple filing a joint return. You subtract your income—let's say it comes to $30,000—from the $35,000 ceiling and divide the result—$5,000—by $10,000. That's the percentage—in this case, 50 percent—you may still write off. To make it easier for yourself, just consult this table:

IRA DEDUCTION LIMITS

Income		Limit
SINGLE	MARRIED	
$25,000	$40,000	$2,000
26,000	41,000	1,800
27,000	42,000	1,600
28,000	43,000	1,400

Income		*Limit*
SINGLE	MARRIED	
29,000	44,000	1,200
$30,000	$45,000	$1,000
31,000	46,000	800
32,000	47,000	600
33,000	48,000	400
34,000	49,000	200
35,000 or more	50,000 or more	0

What if you file jointly and only one of you participates in a qualified plan? You're treated as if you both participated in the plan. So your ability to deduct an IRA contribution depends on your AGI for the year. And if you are married, live together, and file separate returns? The same rules apply, but the $2,000 deduction limit is completely phased out at an AGI of only $10,000. For example, say you report an AGI of $2,500 on a separate return. Your IRA deduction limit is $1,500. At an AGI of $5,000, the deduction limit is $1,000. At an AGI of $7,500, the limit is $500. And at an AGI of $10,000, the deduction disappears entirely.

But what if you are married, don't live together, and file separate returns? Each spouse is then treated as if he or she were single. The participation of either spouse in a plan doesn't affect the other spouse's ability to make a deductible contribution.

Whether or not the IRS considers you an active participant in an employer-sponsored plan depends on the type of plan. And you don't actually have to benefit from your company's plan to lose your ability to make tax-deductible contributions. You can be an active participant even if you are not vested in plan benefits.

The law considers you an active participant in a profit-sharing plan once your employer contributes to your account for the year. You are a participant in a 401(k) plan if either your company makes a contribution to the plan on your behalf or you defer part of your salary into the 401(k). Usually, you are an active participant in a pension plan if you are covered by the plan under its eligibility rules.

So if your company or organization provides any of the following retirement plans—and your income exceeds the thresholds—you probably aren't eligible to make tax-deductible IRA contributions:

- Qualified pension, profit-sharing, or stock bonus plans, including 401(k) plans and Keogh plans
- Qualified annuity plans
- Simplified employee pension plans (SEPs)
- Retirement plans for federal, state, or local government employees
- Certain union plans (so-called Section 501(c) (18) plans)
- Tax-sheltered annuities for public-school teachers and other employees of charitable organizations

Timing is important in determining whether you may deduct your IRA contribution.

Say you decide to leave Old Tie Inc. in December 1989 for a new position at Ascot Corp. You're not eligible for Ascot's pension plan in 1990, your first year there. So you may deduct an IRA contribution in calendar year 1990, right? Wrong.

Why? Old Tie's pension plan ends its fiscal year on January 31. And Uncle Sam determines your participation by looking at when a company-sponsored plan year ends.

You're out of luck in 1990, but you might be okay for a tax-deductible IRA contribution in 1991. That would be the case if the company-sponsored plan at Ascot, for which you become eligible in 1991, doesn't end its fiscal year until 1992.

As far as the IRS is concerned, you aren't participating in any plan in calendar 1991. So you may deduct away—up to the full $2,000.

For Better or Worse

If you do not participate in a company-sponsored retirement plan, your nonworking spouse may open a spousal IRA if the two of you file a joint tax return, and your spouse has income of $250 or less. Together, you may collectively contribute no more than $2,250 each year to these IRAs. But how you split the contribution between the two accounts is up to you.

There is, however, one exception: You may not allocate more than $2,000 to either account in any single year.

Here's an idea on splitting your contributions. If you plan to keep your money in the IRA as long as possible, the bulk of the account should be in the name of the younger spouse. If you want to get your money sooner, the older spouse should be allocated the larger part of the contribution.

What if your spouse has income of more than $250? Then your spouse may open his or her own IRA and deduct a contribution of up to 100 percent of his or her compensation ($2,000 maximum).

Hot Ticket

You may set up as many different IRAs as you wish—at as many different financial institutions as you'd like—as long as you qualify.

A word of warning on multiple accounts, though. Many IRAs charge flat annual maintenance fees that can run $50 or more. So if you have a lot of small accounts—all charging fees—your effective yield falls. You may deduct the annual fee for your account. But only if you pay it out of separate funds, not the IRA funds, and it and all other miscellaneous itemized deductions top 2 percent of your adjusted gross income.

You may accept as the manager of your IRA the institution where you place your account: the bank, savings and loan, insurance company, and so forth. Or you may manage your account yourself, investing as you see fit. In that case, you'd simply use a brokerage house, say, as custodian of your IRA.

You have the entire spectrum of regular investment vehicles at your disposal. So your IRA could be in the form of certificates of deposit (CDs), say, or mutual funds.

While the law permits almost complete freedom in investing IRA funds, it makes a few exceptions. You may not invest in art objects, antiques, gold or silver coins (except gold and silver coins minted in the United

States and coins issued by a state), stamps, or other collectibles. (The legislators wanted to keep taxpayers from using their IRAs to furnish their homes.)

If you use IRA dollars to invest in collectibles, the law treats the amount you invested as a withdrawal from your account. And you have to pay tax on that sum at your ordinary rates. Moreover, if you invested in the collectible before age fifty-nine and one-half, you have to pay an additional 10 percent penalty.

Clearly, some investments—namely those that are tax-free—do not make sense for an IRA. Here's why. If you buy municipal bonds, for example, the income the bonds produce is not subject to federal taxes— ever. But your earnings from an IRA are not tax-free; rather they're tax-deferred. When you finally withdraw the money, you pay tax on these earnings. So by purchasing tax-free investments for an IRA, you're converting tax-free income into taxable income.

Ready for a Change

The IRS imposes no penalty if you change investment vehicles. So, you may—depending on economic conditions—shift IRA dollars from a stock mutual fund to a bank CD or from a single stock to a money-market fund with no tax consequences whatsoever.

Let's say you have your IRA at a financial institution that offers a number of investment vehicles. In this case, you may transfer funds from one vehicle to another—within that institution—as many times as you like. However, you may switch your IRA dollars from one institution to another only once every twelve months.

Here's an example. Say you withdrew your IRA dollars from First Bank and, within sixty days, deposited them in a new IRA at Second Bank. No tax penalties apply. But then, within twelve months after you withdrew your funds from First Bank, you canceled the IRA at Second Bank and, again within sixty days, deposited the funds in an IRA with Third Bank. The rules say you will pay a penalty on your withdrawal from Second Bank. But if you wait at least twelve months before making the withdrawal from Second Bank, the transfer to Third Bank is tax-free.

Shifting funds even within the same institution does present one potential pitfall: You might get hit with a penalty imposed by your financial institution—the loss of interest for a three-month period, for example, for taking funds out of a CD before its due date.

In some cases, when you switch investments under an IRA plan, the interest rate on the entire account may drop to the lowest the financial institution is legally allowed to pay—usually passbook rates. That's because the bank or savings and loan wants to limit the transfer of funds from one vehicle to another.

One last point: You may switch your IRA account from one institution to another without penalty only once a year. But let's say you have your IRA at a financial institution that offers a number of investment vehicles. In this case, you may transfer funds from one vehicle to another—within that institution—as many times as you like. And you pay no penalty.

Should You?

A big question for most people since the rule changes: Should you or should you not make nondeductible contributions to an IRA?

As you recall, your deduction for contributions to an IRA may be limited, or totally eliminated, if you participate in an employer-sponsored retirement plan and your income tops certain levels. But nondeductible contributions are subject to no such restrictions.

The primary reason to make nondeductible contributions: Earnings on the funds you contribute to the account will build up at a much faster tax-deferred rate than earnings on regular taxable investments. In other words, you defer taxes on otherwise taxable income.

The primary reason not to make nondeductible contributions: penalties on withdrawals. Should you need your money before age fifty-nine and one-half, you'll generally pay a penalty on part of your withdrawal. If you're close to age fifty-nine and one-half, though, you may not need to worry about withdrawal restrictions. In that case, you may as well make nondeductible IRA contributions.

For many, though, investing in a tax-free bond is an attractive alternative to making nondeductible contributions to IRAs. Depending on your investment strategies, you can get similar results with your investment dollars—and face no restrictions—if you choose instead these tax-exempt vehicles.

However, the case for putting your money into IRAs grows with the spread (or anticipated spread) between interest rates on taxable and non-taxable investment vehicles. Also, the higher your tax bracket, the more sensible it is to make nondeductible contributions.

So when it comes to making nondeductible IRA contributions, then, go slow. There's no right answer. Analyze your personal situation carefully, and take a close look at your financial profile.

Remember, too, that the opportunity to set aside money in an IRA is limited. You make this year's contribution this year or up to April 15 of the next year. Otherwise, you're out of luck. You must decide from year to year whether an IRA contribution makes sense for you.

Getting It Out

You may generally begin withdrawing funds from an IRA without penalty only at age fifty-nine and one-half or if you become disabled. (Your designated beneficiaries have access to your IRA when you die.)

How you decide to withdraw the funds—in one lump sum or bit by bit over a period of years—will depend, in part, on your income needs after retirement. For example, you may want a lump sum so you can, say, pay off the mortgage on your house.

Unfortunately, this choice also involves tax consequences. An IRA is different from all other tax-deferred retirement plans in one significant respect. When you withdraw funds from an IRA in a single lump sum, the income is taxed to you at ordinary rates.

The government won't allow you to determine your income tax for the year by treating the IRA distribution as though it had been spread over five years—as you can with lump-sum payouts from other kinds of retirement plans. So you may want to steer clear of lump-sum withdrawals, at least as far as your IRA is concerned.

No matter how you take your IRA benefits—in a single sum or in smaller payments over several years—you're going to have to pay Uncle

Sam some of those taxes that you've deferred on deductible contributions and on all the earnings that have been accumulating tax deferred in the account.

The general rule that Congress applies to taxing IRA withdrawals is simple enough: If the money you withdraw has already been taxed once, it won't be taxed again.

So you won't have to pay taxes on withdrawals of nondeductible contributions from an IRA. But you'll have to shell out to the IRS on deductible contributions. You'll also pay taxes on all the earnings that have accumulated in the IRA.

And since these taxable and nontaxable funds will be mingled in your IRA, you'll need to know which are which. Some examples will help.

Let's say you make nondeductible IRA contributions of $2,000 each year for five years. By the time you've reached age sixty-five and decide to retire, those funds have earned $5,000.

If you withdraw the entire $15,000, you'll pay tax on the $5,000 of accumulated earnings. You'll owe no tax, however, on the $10,000 in contributions.

What if you want to withdraw only the $10,000 you put into the account, leaving the $5,000 in earnings? May you do that without paying tax? Sorry. Uncle Sam will treat any withdrawal as if part came from taxable funds and part from nontaxable.

Since two-thirds of the value of your IRA consists of nontaxable funds ($10,000 divided by $15,000), two-thirds of any withdrawal you make will be nontaxable. But on the other one-third, you'll have to ante up to Uncle Sam.

The same rule applies even if you use separate IRA accounts in an attempt to segregate your funds. The IRS aggregates all your IRAs for this purpose.

Getting It Out Early

To make sure people use their IRAs for retirement, not just as tax-deferred savings accounts, Congress imposes a 10 percent penalty for early withdrawal—before age fifty-nine and one-half or disability—of tax-deductible contributions to IRA funds and all accumulated earnings.

So, if you want to take a lump sum out at, say, age forty-five, you'll owe income tax on that amount, plus a penalty.

You may avoid the penalty, though, and still retire on your IRA before reaching age fifty-nine and one-half. Just have the custodian of your IRA make the distribution to you in the form of an annuity, or regular periodic payments.

The only catch: The payments have to be approximately equal and spread over your life or based on your life expectancy. (You may also avoid the penalty by having the payments made over the joint lives of you and your beneficiary or over the joint life expectancies of you and your beneficiary.)

Here's an example. You're fifty-five and can expect to live at least twenty more years. If you need the money, you may receive annual distributions from a $20,000 IRA of slightly more than $1,000 per year without paying any penalty.

Getting It Out Late

You'll also pay a penalty if you don't start taking distributions from your IRA soon enough. The law says you must begin not later than April 1 in the year that follows the year in which you turn seventy and one-half.

Getting On with It

Now that you're familiar with the rules on IRAs, let's turn to one of the newest—and best—tax-deferred plans available today: 401(k) plans.

33

Winning Proposition

What You Need to Know About 401(k) Plans

On behalf of Congress, we apologize for the name given 401(k) plans. The moniker 401(k) doesn't tell you anything but the number of the tax code section that describes these employer-sponsored savings plans. And—as you'll see—they're really quite terrific.

The Benefits

Why participate in your company's 401(k) plan? Actually, there are two reasons. One is the opportunity to capture additional dollars from your employer. The other is the chance to take advantage of favorable tax rules.

Many companies match all or a portion of the amount you set aside in these accounts. So it's worth contributing to the plan to garner these extra dollars from your employer.

The tax benefits: You may exclude from income your annual contribution of up to $7,627, and the income you earn in the plan is tax deferred until you take it out.

Say you sock away $7,000 per year for 25 years in a 401(k). Your contribution earns 10 percent annually. Actually, you're out of pocket only $5,040—that is, $7,000 minus the tax saving of $1,960 (28 percent times $7,000). At the end of 25 years—after pulling your money out in a lump sum and paying, say, 28 percent tax on it at that time—you net $545,236.

Now let's say you invest the same $5,040 each year for 25 years in nondividend-paying growth stocks. Your investment increases in value each

333

year by 10 percent. At the end of 25 years, you sell your holdings. After paying tax on your capital gain, you net $427,850—about $117,000 less than you have in the 401(k) plan.

Finally, say you invest your $5,040 each year in a security that earns 10 percent annually. Every year you pay taxes on your earnings. After 25 years, your contributions and after-tax earnings would come to only $351,699.

As you can see, a 401(k) plan is an excellent tool for helping you achieve your goal of a comfortable retirement. And if your employer makes a matching contribution, your return increases substantially. So how can you best take advantage of 401(k)s? Let's take a look.

Ground Rules

Although 401(k)s are established and managed by employers—and employers often contribute to them—they rely primarily on voluntary employee contributions.

You authorize your employer to deduct a set amount from your check each pay period and put it in a 401(k) account in your name.

The good deal is that the federal government excludes this deferred salary—plus any interest, dividends, and gains that accumulate on it—from current income taxation. Uncle Sam gets his due only when you withdraw the money from the plan, usually at retirement.

Sound familiar? It should, because 401(k)s are similar to IRAs.

What separates the two plans is the way the IRS treats the money deposited. You don't deduct your 401(k) contribution on your tax return. Instead, the money set aside in a 401(k) is treated as "deferred compensation" and isn't reported as income to you.

Say you earn $60,000 a year and deposit 5 percent, or $3,000, of your pay in a 401(k) plan. At the end of the year, you receive your W-2 form. It lists your income as $57,000—that is, your salary of $60,000 minus your $3,000 contribution to the 401(k).

The net result, of course, is the same with a 401(k) as with an IRA. You report less taxable income to Uncle Sam and, consequently, shell out less in taxes.

Contributions to 401(k) plans are still subject to Social Security (FICA) tax at the time you make them. But so are deductible IRA contributions.

That's not altogether bad news, though.

The reason: Your FICA wages are taken into account when Uncle Sam determines your eligibility for Social Security retirement benefits.

Another difference between 401(k)s and IRAs is the amount of money you may set aside. The maximum you may contribute to an IRA is $2,000 a year.

What's the limit on 401(k) contributions?

Actually, there are two. Congress set the annual ceiling for employee contributions at $7,627 in 1989. But the limit is adjusted for inflation in subsequent years. Ask your accountant—or the local IRS office—what the current limit is.

The second ceiling applies to how much your employer may contribute to your 401(k). Between the two of you—you and your employer— you may not put away more than $30,000 or 25 percent of your salary (after deducting your 401(k) contribution), whichever is less, each year.

Say, for example, that your salary adds up to $150,000 in 1989, and you decide you can get along on $143,000. So you set aside $7,000 in your 401(k) plan. That means your employer's contribution is limited to $23,000— the $30,000 ceiling minus your $7,000 contribution.

But the key phrase here is *whichever is less.*

Let's look at the reason. Assume your income in 1990 comes to $50,000. To calculate the ceiling on 401(k) contributions, you subtract $7,000 (your contribution) from $50,000 (your income), then multiply the result ($43,000) by 25 percent.

The answer—$10,750—is the maximum amount you and your employer may deposit on your behalf. Since you are setting aside $7,000, your employer may make an additional contribution of no more than $3,750 ($10,750 minus $7,000).

So, in this case, you might want to reduce your contribution to a 401(k), so your employer can increase its contribution.

Here's another wrinkle to keep in mind: Under some plans, the employer determines contributions on the basis of your annual compensation after deducting your 401(k) contribution. So, if your salary came to $50,000, and you contributed $7,000 to your plan, your compensation—

for the purposes of your employer's contribution—would total $43,000.

But if you also make 401(k) employee contributions of $7,000, the maximum amount your employer can contribute is reduced. Here's how the calculation works.

Assume your employer contributes 10 percent to the plan. This means that your employer's contribution will be $4,300—or 10 percent of $43,000. But here comes the kicker.

The sum of both contributions equals $11,300 ($7,000 plus $4,300). This amount goes over the maximum contribution limit of $10,750 by $550 ($50,000 minus $7,000 equals $43,000, and $43,000 times the limit of 25 percent equals $10,750). So your company contribution could be reduced to $3,750 ($4,300 minus $550) to avoid topping the legal limit.

A better solution: You should reduce your contributions, so your employer may contribute the full 10 percent in your behalf.

Say, for example, that you contribute $6,300 to your 401(k) plan. Your employer would then contribute $4,370 ($50,000 less $6,300 equals $43,700, times 10 percent equals $4,370). The total is $10,670, which is within the limitation.

Where Does the Money Go?

The government doesn't restrict the types of investments you may make with your 401(k) dollars. Your options depend on what your employer is willing to offer. Typically, these include

- Stock funds
- Money-market accounts
- Insurance products
- Government securities

Many plans offer participants at least three investment choices, although they are not required to do so. Some companies allow you to put money into any or all of the investment options the plan provides, while other companies limit your choices.

You should determine where to put your 401(k) money by looking at your overall asset-allocation strategy. In other words, 401(k) investments should be viewed as part of your total portfolio.

I Want My Money

When may you get your money out of a 401(k)? A plan may make distributions to you when you leave your job, reach age fifty-nine and one-half, become disabled, or suffer financial hardship. In addition, the plan may distribute funds to your beneficiary if you die. But in most cases, you'll be hit with a 10 percent penalty tax if you withdraw the money before reaching age fifty-nine and one-half or becoming disabled.

Another word of warning: Not all plans allow withdrawals for financial hardship, and the rules vary among those plans that do. Also, financial hardship withdrawals may be subject to a 10-percent tax penalty. However, if you make withdrawals for medical hardship the penalty will not apply to the extent your medical expenses are deductible.

Also, your plan may allow you to receive a lump-sum distribution. You pay no penalty as long as you roll the money over into another retirement plan—a corporate plan or an IRA—within sixty days. Any amount not rolled over is taxed as ordinary income unless it qualifies for special averaging treatment. And, unless you qualify for one of the exceptions described previously, you get hit with a 10 percent penalty as well.

Most 401(k) plans allow you to cash out your account when you leave your job. But even if you do not want to withdraw the money, you may have no choice. Your employer may cash out or distribute your account if the amount that you have credited to you under the plan is less than $3,500.

Neither a Borrower Nor a Lender Be

The good news?
   You may borrow from your 401(k) plan.
   The bad news?
   The law limits loans to the lesser of $50,000 or the greater of $10,000

or one-half of your 401(k) account balance. Also, Uncle Sam requires that you repay loans within five years, unless the money is used to purchase a principal residence. In that case, you have longer to pay it back.

One other point: Loans from 401(k) plans must carry a "reasonable" interest rate. But you may not deduct any interest payments you make—even if the IRS would otherwise allow the deduction. What's worse, even though the interest payment is not deductible, the amount you pay in interest to the plan is taxed when you finally get your 401(k) distribution.

There are other restrictions on loans from 401(k) plans—for example, the IRS severely limits loans made to business owners and other key employees. So see your accountant if you plan on borrowing money from your 401(k) plan.

What happens if you leave your present job with an outstanding 401(k) loan? Usually, you have to either pay the loan back immediately or treat it as a distribution. And, if you treat it as a distribution, you may have to pay early distribution penalties.

Better Safe Than Sorry

Most states and municipalities don't tax income when you put it aside in your employer-sponsored 401(k) plan, but there are some exceptions. Our advice: Check with your financial planner or tax adviser to determine whether or not your state or city taxes 401(k) contributions.

For Your Benefit

Many companies with 401(k) plans also have other pension plans that pay you retirement benefits based on your salary.

You may not know it, but your company may amend the definition of *compensation* in your retirement plan to include amounts you contribute to a 401(k) plan. That way, you won't lose out on extra benefits that you would have received had the 401(k) not been in place. Be advised, though: The IRS does not require a company to amend its pension plan in this way.

Also, your company may add in 401(k) plan contributions when it determines the level of other pay-related or pay-based employee benefits, such as life insurance, short- and long-term disability insurance, and survivor income. Otherwise, the benefits may be reduced.

Best Bet

What's the bottom line? Even with the restrictions, 401(k) plans are still one of the best retirement shelters around.

And if you work for a public institution, such as a university, you're not out in the cold. You may participate in something called a 403(b) plan.

These plans are similar to 401(k)s. If you participate in this type of tax-deferred plan, your taxable income is reduced by the amount of your contribution. And the amount you contribute—plus any earnings that accumulate—is tax deferred until you withdraw it.

Contributions to a 403(b) plan, though, are limited to $9,500 or 20 percent of your compensation, whichever is less. But if you also contribute to a 401(k) plan, you'll have to reduce your $9,500 by the amount of your 401(k) contribution.

Last Word

Now you know the ins and outs of these valuable company benefits. In the next chapter, we'll take a look at other employer-sponsored retirement and savings plans.

34 *In Good Company*

Get Smart About Company Retirement and Savings Plans

*P*ension plans aren't new.

In fact, in the United States, these programs date back to 1759, when a group of Presbyterian ministers adopted a plan to provide benefits for their widows and children.

What is new about company-sponsored retirement and savings plans is attitudes toward them. Today, we see these plans for what they really are—wealth-building tools.

What do you need to know to make the most of your company retirement and savings plan? You'll find out in this chapter.

First, though, a note about tax reform. Because of limitations imposed by the 1986 Tax Reform Act, fewer people will be able to make deductible contributions to IRAs. This means there will be more emphasis on employer-sponsored retirement plans.

But tax reform also had an impact on corporate plans: There will be lower limits on the number of dollars your employer may salt away for you.

Not a Question of Semantics

Many kinds of plans are given special treatment under the tax code. What's common to all of them? Contributions to the plans are "tax advantaged."

That means you pay no taxes on the contributions your employer makes in your name until you withdraw the money. Also, earnings on the amounts contributed accumulate tax deferred—again, until you begin to collect your pension, usually at retirement.

Employer-sponsored pension plans come in two varieties: defined-contribution and defined-benefit plans.

With a *defined-contribution plan*, your employer may put away a specific amount—say, 10 percent of your salary—every year. The contribution is credited to a separate account in your name. And the pension you receive when you retire is based on two factors: how much was set aside in your behalf, and how well that money was invested by your company's pension plan manager.

With a *defined-benefit plan*, you receive a specified sum every year after retirement—no matter what the contributions or how much they earned.

Strictly Voluntary

Some companies allow you to make voluntary after-tax contributions to your company-sponsored plan. Usually you make these contributions to a defined-contribution plan.

But some defined-benefit plans also allow contributions. While these contributions are not deductible, the earnings on the contributions—like earnings on your employer's contributions—accumulate tax deferred until you withdraw them.

But now—and this is a change from past law—every dollar you contribute to a plan reduces by a dollar the amount your employer may set aside in your behalf.

Say your salary is $40,000, and you sock away $4,000 in your company plan. That means your employer may contribute no more than $6,000 for you. Why?

The 1986 Tax Reform Act mandates that every dollar you contribute counts toward the maximum contribution limit—which is the lesser of 25 percent of your compensation or $30,000. So you must subtract your $4,000 contribution from a ceiling of $10,000 (25 percent of $40,000).

Now that we have the fundamentals squared away, let's take a look at the various types of plans.

Remember, you have no control over many of these retirement programs. Your employer either has them in place—or doesn't. But you should know at least the basics about a future source of your bread and butter.

One for All and All for One

A *profit-sharing plan* is a type of defined-contribution plan. In the past, contributions were limited to profits—that is, your employer could contribute to the plan only if the company posted a profit.

But the 1986 Tax Reform Act changed all that.

Now, a company may contribute to one of these plans even if it has no profits. And it may vary its contributions from year to year.

A company may also base its contributions on a formula that takes a variety of factors into consideration, including your annual earnings. For example, your employer may limit contributions on your behalf to no more than 15 percent of your annual compensation.

Moreover, profit-sharing plans may distribute benefits to an employee before he or she leaves the company. For example, you could qualify for a distribution if you suffered a financial hardship—you lost your house and belongings in a fire, say.

An employer may deduct each year no more than 15 percent of the total compensation paid to all employees covered by the plan. Contributions on behalf of any one individual to all defined-contribution plans of the employer may not top the lesser of $30,000 or 25 percent of that person's annual compensation.

Money, Money

There are several other types of defined-contribution plans. Among them: employee thrift and savings plans, money purchase pension plans, stock bonus plans, and employee stock ownership plans.

Employee thrift and *savings plans* are usually set up as profit-sharing plans. Employees make after-tax contributions that are matched by the employer's contributions. Many employers frequently add a 401(k) plan to the traditional thrift and savings plan. The pretax nature of the employee contributions in a 401(k) plan provides a substantial advantage. In traditional thrift and savings plans, contributions are made on an *after-tax* basis. In some thrift and savings plans, however, pretax employee contributions have completely replaced after-tax contributions. In other plans, both pretax and after-tax employee contributions are allowed.

Money purchase plans are pension plans. So, for the most part, they distribute benefits only to an employee who has left the company or retired. The company sponsoring the plan must make contributions to it each year, even if the company posted no profits.

Contributions to a money purchase plan are based on a percentage of the compensation of all participating employees. The maximum deductible contribution that a company may make: 25 percent of the compensation of employees participating in all the company's defined-contribution plans.

Stock bonus plans are very much like profit-sharing plans. The chief difference: Employees have the right to receive their benefits in the form of company stock.

Employee stock ownership plans (ESOPs), by contrast, are plans that invest primarily in the stock of the company sponsoring the plan. They are set up as stock bonus plans, or a combination of a stock bonus plan and a money purchase plan.

What Now?

Just as important as understanding how money is put into a pension plan is knowing how to get it out. The rules differ for different types of plans. A profit-sharing plan, for instance, may make a distribution to an employee who has not yet left the company. But a pension plan—either a defined-benefit plan or a money purchase plan—usually may not.

Although the rules differ on when a plan may make a distribution, the regulations that say how the distribution will be taxed are very similar—except for lump-sum distributions.

Let's start with the big question: lump sum or annuity?

Out All at Once

If you take all the money out of your IRA in a single lump, you've got to pay the taxes on that withdrawal in a single lump too.

With other retirement plans you also pay tax all at one time. But you may use five-year forward averaging. This means that you may pay less tax.

The reason: Although you pay the tax in one year, you calculate it as though you received the distribution over five years. So, even though you pay the tax all at once—for the year in which you receive the distribution—you may pay it at lower marginal rates.

Note, however, that you may use five-year forward averaging only once. And you can't use it before reaching the age of fifty-nine and one-half, unless you reached age fifty by January 1, 1986. (See Chapter 36 for more on forward averaging.)

So if you get a lump-sum distribution from your pension plan before reaching that age—when changing jobs, for instance—roll the cash over into another qualified plan, including an IRA.

Why? Because if you don't, not only will you have to pay tax, but also you may owe the IRS a hefty penalty for early withdrawal. (There are, however, a number of exceptions to the rules, so check with an accountant or financial planner.)

Over Time

An alternative to the lump-sum distribution is an *annuity*, a payout of the money in your employer-sponsored pension plan that is spread over a number of years.

You may receive several kinds of annuities from an employer-sponsored plan. Most married people prefer to receive a *joint and survivor annuity*. Under this type of annuity, the plan distributes benefits until both the retired employee and the employee's spouse die.

Another form of annuity—the *life annuity*—guarantees payments until the retired employee dies. But benefits do not continue after the employee's death, even if the employee has a surviving spouse.

Some plans provide for annuity benefits that continue for a certain number of years—even after an employee dies. For example, you might be able to choose a benefit that will be paid for ten years after you retire (even if you do not live that long) or until you die.

In addition, plans often provide for an annuity to be paid over an employee's life expectancy. How does this type of arrangement work? When you retire, your life expectancy is determined from an actuarial table. Then payments are spread out over that length of time. Plans may also pay benefits over the joint life expectancy of an employee and his or her spouse.

The type of annuity you should select depends on a number of factors: your marital status; whether, if you're unmarried, you have a beneficiary to whom you want to leave a portion of your retirement benefits; and your health when you retire.

Whatever your retirement benefits are, they won't be tax free. Remember, some of the money you and your employer have contributed to your plan and all of the earnings that have accumulated over the years have never been subject to tax. Sooner or later, Uncle Sam wants his cut. In this case, he is getting it later.

If you made contributions to the plan, then, to figure the taxes on your retirement annuity, you must first calculate what's known as the *exclusion ratio.*

It's simple. Add up all the nondeductible contributions you made to the plan over the years. Then divide that figure by the total value of your interest in the plan (for example, your account balance in a defined-contribution plan).

What you get is the exclusion ratio. If you'd rather not do the calculation yourself, your plan administrator can probably tell you what your exclusion ratio is.

Now, multiply the amount of your annuity payment by the exclusion ratio. That's how much of your payment is tax free. You'll have to ante up to the IRS on the rest.

Should you live beyond your life expectancy—congratulations. But be aware that Uncle Sam will take note of the fact that you have now recovered all your nondeductible contributions from your retirement plan. From this time on, your entire annuity will be subject to tax.

Details, Details

Here's another new wrinkle in the tax law you should know about: a 15 percent tax on so-called *excess distributions*.

Distributions from qualified retirement plans, tax-sheltered annuities, and IRAs in excess of $150,000 or, if greater, $112,500 (indexed for inflation) are subject to a new 15 percent excise tax. The tax applies to the excess of the distribution over the ceiling.

So, in most cases, distributions that top $150,000 in any particular year will be subject to the tax. There are, however, several types of distributions exempt from this rule including:

- Distributions made when the participant in the plan dies
- Distributions made under a qualified domestic relations order, as long as the distribution is included in the income of the recipient
- Distributions that come from after-tax employee contributions
- Distributions rolled over into an IRA or other qualified plan

To determine whether you've received an excess distribution, all distributions you receive in one calendar year are added together.

For qualified lump-sum distributions, where you elect special forward averaging, the ceiling is raised to five times the normal limit. So, in most cases, the tax will apply to this lump sum if it tops $750,000. The excess distribution tax is applied separately to this lump sum.

You should know that the law provides a special grandfather provision for benefits you accumulated before August 1, 1986. Those benefits must exceed $562,500, and you must have elected to be covered by the grandfather provision on your 1987 or 1988 tax return. If you meet these two criteria, the portion of retirement benefits that you accrued before August 1, 1986, is exempt from the excise tax.

Note, though: The grandfathered amounts are included when it comes to determining whether you've made an excess distribution and, if the election has been made, the usual ceiling is reduced to $112,500, an amount that is indexed for inflation.

So the grandfather rule may not save you tax.

What Form of Distribution Is Right for You?

Of course, it depends on your circumstances whether it's best for you to choose a lump-sum distribution or some form of annuity payments. And note: Many plans do not even allow lump-sum distributions.

But consider the case of an employee—we'll call him David—who participates in both a pension plan and a profit-sharing plan. David's pension plan will provide him with ample retirement income. So he might want to receive benefits from the profit-sharing plan in a lump sum.

Then he could use the amount to, say, buy a vacation house for his retirement. If, on the other hand, his benefits from the pension plan are limited, he might want to receive distributions from both plans in the form of annuities.

What If You Wait Too Long?

Two types of rules govern payouts from pension plans—plan rules and tax rules. Different company plans have different withdrawal rules. First, though, let's look at the tax regulations.

Under current law, you must begin taking distributions from an employer-sponsored plan by April 1 following the year when you reach age seventy and one-half, even if you have not yet retired.

What if you don't begin withdrawing benefits from your employer-sponsored pension plan when the tax rules specify? The penalties are stiff: a 50 percent nondeductible tax on the excess of required distributions over actual distributions.

What If You Can't Wait?

Even if your plan allows you access to cash from the plan, you may get hit with a 10 percent penalty tax on amounts you withdraw before age fifty-nine and one-half.

The first point to check is what your plan rules allow. Your employer's plan itself may prohibit, or severely restrict, your access to your retirement money.

If your plan rules don't present any problems, the IRS allows you early access to your retirement funds without penalty under these circumstances:

- You use a distribution to pay for deductible medical expenses—that is, expenses that are more than 7.5 percent of your adjusted gross income.
- You begin receiving benefits in the form of an annuity. The annuity may be spread out over your life, the joint lives of you and your beneficiary (your spouse, say), your life expectancy, or the joint life expectancies of you and your beneficiary.
- You receive benefits as an annuity or as a lump sum when you retire at or after age fifty-five but before age fifty-nine and one-half.
- You receive distributions after you become disabled, or your beneficiary receives distributions after your death.

On the Installment Plan

Many employer-sponsored plans—because of IRS restrictions—don't allow employees to borrow from the plan. Others do, but only under certain circumstances.

Here is the lowdown.

Uncle Sam requires that you repay loans within five years. If you don't, the money you borrow is treated as a distribution. An exception to this rule: You use the money to buy a principal residence for yourself. Also, your loan payments must be in equal installments and be made at least quarterly—or, again, the money you borrow is considered a distribution.

May you deduct interest on loans from pension plans?

Interest on these loans is subject to the same restrictions as any other type of interest. (See Chapter 16 for details.) But if the loan is from a 401(k) plan and is secured by your contributions, you may not take an interest deduction.

The law also imposes a ceiling on loans from a plan. If your borrowings exceed the ceiling, the IRS treats the loan as a distribution. The ceiling: $10,000, or, if greater, one-half of the employee's interest in the plan, but never more than $50,000.

To figure out whether a loan meets the rules, you must add a new loan to the outstanding balance of all other loans you have taken from the plan. Also, the ceiling is adjusted for other loans you took from the plan during the preceding year. And this rule holds true even if you paid off the loans.

Knowledge Is Power

Until recently, pension plans were required to provide benefits automatically—in the form of an annuity—to both a married employee and his or her surviving spouse. But employees could opt out of this benefit without the consent of a spouse.

Also, pension plans had a limited obligation to pay survivor benefits to the widow or widower of an employee who died before retiring.

In order to address what many people felt were obvious inequities in the pension system, Congress adopted the Retirement Equity Act of 1984.

The act mandates that an employer still must offer automatic postretirement survivor benefits to an employee's spouse. In addition, the company must make available automatic preretirement survivor benefits to the spouse of any employee who dies with vested benefits in the plan.

And it prohibits employees from opting out of these benefits unless they secure their spouses' approval—in writing. In addition, the act reduces the age at which employers must allow employees to participate in company-sponsored pension programs.

It also permits new parents to take extended maternity and paternity leaves without losing out on future retirement income, and it provides for the distribution of pension benefits to divorced spouses.

Here's a rundown of some of the key provisions of the Retirement Equity Act.

Survivor Benefits

If you die before retiring, your vested interest in the plan must be paid to your spouse in the form of an annuity in the year when you would have reached the earliest retirement age under the plan had you survived. These rules do not apply to profit-sharing and stock bonus plans if these plans provide that your vested interest will be payable to your spouse when you die.

The law further dictates that survivor benefits be paid in the form of an annuity—a payment made yearly, quarterly, monthly, or at some other regular interval for a specified period of time, usually a person's lifetime.

Also, as we've seen, you may opt out of survivor benefits only by providing your employer with a notarized waiver that has been signed by both you and your spouse. Under the old rules, an employee could nix survivor benefits without the knowledge or consent of his or her spouse.

Eligibility Rules

In the past, employers could bar employees under the age of twenty-five from participating in company pension plans. The Equity Act imposed tough new restrictions on this practice. It cuts from twenty-five to twenty-one the minimum age at which workers must be included in any pension program.

Also, it reduces from twenty-two to eighteen the age at which employers must begin counting employees' years of service for vesting purposes. (*Vesting* is an employee's right—based on length of service—to receive benefits from a retirement plan, even if the employee leaves the company.)

Here is an illustration. Say a woman signs on with a company when she is eighteen years old. Under the company's retirement plan, employees are fully vested after six years of service. She resigns six years later to take a job with a competitor. She is six months shy of her twenty-fifth birthday.

Under the old rules, she would get nothing when she left—unless her employer was more generous than the law required. Under the Equity Act, she is entitled to the benefits accrued in her behalf (to the extent that she is vested), since her employer enrolled her in the pension program at age twenty-one.

Break-in-Service Rules

The Retirement Equity Act also changed the rules governing employer-sponsored retirement and savings plans for employees who leave a plan and then return months or years later.

Suppose, for example, a twenty-year-old man goes to work as a salesman for a chain of retail clothing stores. While employed there, he participates in the company's defined-benefit pension plan. And, under this plan, benefits become vested after employees have completed ten years of service.

He works three years, then resigns and works somewhere else for four years. Later, he returns to his former employer as an executive. He stays in his new job for seven years.

It comes time to compute his years of service for vesting purposes. Does the company have to give him credit for those first three years he worked?

Under the old law, the answer was no—the young man's "break-in-service" period was longer than the time he was previously employed with his company.

But under the new law, the answer is yes. The act says that if an employee leaves a job and returns, he or she must receive credit for that earlier period, unless the break in service is at least five years or the number of years included in the employee's previous service period, whichever is greater.

New parents are accorded an even sweeter deal. The law allows them to take a full year of maternity or paternity leave without it counting as a break in service. That time can then be added to the years allowed other workers, for a total of six years or more—in effect, until the child is old enough for school.

Divorce Rules

Finally, the law includes provisions for people who get divorced and are entitled to their ex-spouses' pension benefits. The courts have the authority to distribute a portion of a person's pension to a former spouse as part of a divorce settlement.

But the court orders must meet certain standards. They must specify the name and address of the worker and the ex-spouse. They must state how much the pension plan must pay (as either a percentage of the benefit or a dollar amount). And they must note when the payments have to start and how long they must continue.

Also, a divorced spouse can begin collecting a share of the working employee's pension at the early retirement age, even if the employee hasn't retired.

Say a man is fifty-five years old (the early retirement age under his employer's plan), but he doesn't want to retire. His divorced spouse, however, wants to receive her portion of his pension immediately. If the court orders payments, the company must honor her request.

Keep It Simple

Call them SEPs for short. What they—simplified employee pension plans—amount to is an employer contribution to your IRA. Instead of maintaining its own pension plan, a company using SEPs makes deposits to its employees' IRAs.

These plans also are a useful alternative to Keoghs as retirement plans for self-employed people and partners in small businesses. (See the next chapter for information on Keoghs.) In fact, SEPs have an advantage if you're self-employed and forget to open a Keogh by December 31. You don't have to open your SEP until your tax return is due.

SEPs were created in 1978 and have become quite popular for their simplicity. They're easy to adopt—you just use an IRS form. Here's how SEPs work.

An employer—or a self-employed person—establishes the SEP by setting up an IRA in its name and the name of each employee. Then the company contributes directly to these IRAs.

As an employee, if your adjusted gross income tops certain amounts, you may not set up a second, separate, deductible IRA, since you're considered an active participant in an employer-sponsored plan. (You may, however, make a nondeductible IRA contribution.)

The company deducts the amount it contributes on your behalf. And it does not report the amount as taxable income to you.

The maximum deductible contribution for a SEP is 15 percent of your compensation, up to $30,000. If you're self-employed, the maximum is the same as for a Keogh—15 percent of your self-employment income after the contribution—or 13.043 percent of your precontribution income.

You, the employee or self-employed individual, pay no taxes on the amount deposited for you. And—as with other plans—earnings on the money accumulate tax deferred until they are withdrawn.

Once the SEP money is deposited in the IRA, it is subject to the same restrictions as all IRA deposits. For example, if you withdraw funds before you reach age fifty-nine and one-half or become disabled, you're subject to a 10 percent penalty on the amount you take out. (See Chapter 32 for details.)

But IRAs set up through SEPs have an advantage over regular individual retirement accounts. As a rule, you may contribute more money to them. The only exception: if your self-employment earnings are very low. Since the maximum IRA deduction is the lesser of $2,000 or 100 percent of your earned income, you may be able to write off more with an IRA if you make very little from self-employment.

Yes, the law does allow you to make your own IRA contribution to an IRA established under the SEP plan. Also if your employer has twenty-five or fewer employees, a SEP may include a feature that works like a 401(k) plan. That is, you can make pretax contributions above the amount contributed by your employer. Your pretax contributions are subject to the same dollar limit that applies to 401(k) plans. But there still are limits to the amount of income you may shelter in this fashion. Also, your contribution plus your employer's to a SEP may not exceed the lesser of $30,000 or 25 percent of your annual salary.

Moving On

So far, we've talked primarily about pension plans for people who work for others. In the next chapter, we turn to plans designed for self-employed people—Keoghs.

35 *On Your Own*

Cashing In on Keogh Plans

*I*f you're self-employed or have some self-employment income—from moonlighting or consulting, say—Keogh plans are definitely worth considering.

These plans take their name from Eugene Keogh, the late congressman who sponsored the legislation creating them in 1962. The plans are also known as HR-10s—after the number of the House of Representatives tax bill that mandated them.

Congress created Keoghs for one simple reason. The lawmakers wanted to provide people who work for themselves with the same opportunity to save for retirement as people who enjoy the benefits of company pension plans. These days, the rules governing Keoghs are virtually identical to the rules governing corporate retirement plans.

Keogh plans are also similar to IRAs. As with an IRA, the amount of your contribution is tax deductible, and earnings accumulate tax deferred.

However, IRAs are designed for everyone who works and meets certain requirements. Keogh plans are specifically structured for businesspeople and professionals—doctors, lawyers, architects, writers, and so on—who work for themselves.

Moreover, Keoghs allow you to squirrel away far more each year than do IRAs. We advise anyone who earns money from self-employment to set up a Keogh—with one exception. If your self-employment income is quite limited, you might be better off with an IRA.

The reason: If you meet the rules, IRAs let you deduct 100 percent of your earned income up to $2,000. With Keoghs, as we'll explain in more

354

detail soon, you may deduct only 15 percent of income. So with only a little self-employment income, you may get to write off a greater amount with an IRA.

Like other retirement plans, Keoghs pack a one-two punch. You slash your tax bill while building your retirement nest egg at a much faster clip.

What else do you need to know about Keoghs? Read on.

Who Can Establish a Keogh?

Some people think Keogh plans are restricted to sole proprietors—people who file Schedule Cs with their personal income tax returns. But that is not the case.

Partnerships may establish Keoghs for their partners. And so may people who serve on corporate boards of directors and receive payment for their services. (They report these earnings as "miscellaneous income" on their tax returns.)

In short, any person who reports earnings from self-employment— no matter how small the income—may put away money in a Keogh.

Two for Two

Like employer-sponsored pension plans, Keoghs come in two varieties— *defined-contribution plans* and *defined-benefit plans.*

Their names reflect the difference between them. With a defined-contribution plan, you put away a certain amount—say, 15 percent of your income—every year.

With a defined-benefit plan, you contribute enough to the plan each year to fund a specified amount every year after retirement.

Let's take a look at each type of plan.

Defined-Contribution Plans

Defined-contribution plans are the most common kind of Keogh. This type of Keogh itself comes in two varieties:

- Profit-sharing plans
- Money purchase plans

With a *profit-sharing plan*, your annual contribution may vary from year to year. The cap on annual deductible contributions to a profit-sharing plan is 15 percent of your gross self-employment income—minus your contribution. So, in effect, you may contribute only 13.043 percent of your precontribution self-employment earnings.

With a *money purchase plan*, you pledge to contribute a fixed portion of your income. The maximum you may contribute each year is the lesser of $30,000 or 25 percent of your gross self-employment earnings—again, minus your contribution—which comes to 20 percent of your precontribution earnings.

You may also "pair," or combine, a money purchase plan with a profit-sharing plan. The advantage: You can increase the deduction limits over the amounts you could contribute to a profit-sharing plan alone. But you still have some flexibility in determining the level of contributions you want to commit to the combined plans.

Here's how pairing works.

Let's say you set up a money purchase plan to shelter from current taxation eight percent of your income before the contribution. You may contribute up to an additional twelve percent (for a total of 20 percent) to a profit-sharing plan.

And the amount you put into the profit-sharing plan is entirely up to you. This way, you may still protect from Uncle Sam's long reach as much as $30,000 or 25 percent of your income (20 percent precontribution income), whichever is less.

We recommend this paired strategy for people who want to set aside more than 13.043 percent of their earnings in a retirement plan but don't want to tie themselves to contributing a hefty percentage of their income year after year.

Defined-Benefit Plans

Defined-benefit plans are more complicated. The amount you contribute each year is based on the amount you intend to collect when you retire.

An actuary will determine how much you must put away annually to fund the level of benefits your plan specifies. The limit on how much you can deduct is based on the amount of your annual benefit at normal retirement age under the plan, usually age sixty-five. The deductible contribution cannot fund a benefit greater than $90,000 per year or 100 percent of your average earnings for the three consecutive years in which your earnings are the highest—whichever is less. (The $90,000 limit is phased in over your first ten years of participation in the plan.)

Say you give up your full-time position with a big oil company to start your own small management consulting business. You report self-employment income of $40,000 in 1987, $50,000 in 1988, and $60,000 in 1989. If you set up a defined-benefit Keogh in 1990, how much may you put away?

The answer: You may put away enough to fund a benefit of $50,000 a year, your average earnings for those three years. But note: You may not deduct, in any one year, more than your earned income for that year.

How much must you deposit to fund this benefit? The answer varies according to your age, life expectancy, and the assumed rate of return on your Keogh's assets. A person who is fifty-five years of age will obviously have to make larger contributions than a person twenty-five years old to fund the same $50,000 annual benefit. The reason: The older person is funding the benefit over a shorter period of time.

There is one drawback to defined-benefit plans: The $90,000 limit on benefits is reduced if you retire before your Social Security retirement age, which ranges from age sixty-five to sixty-seven, depending on the year you were born.

Who should set up a defined-benefit plan?

These types of Keoghs are best for people who are fifty or older and have substantial income they would like to shelter from taxes.

Money Talks

Keogh money—like IRA dollars—may be used to purchase certificates of deposit, stocks, bonds, mutual funds, money-market shares, or almost any other investment vehicle. You may establish a Keogh plan with a bank, insurance company, or any other financial institution.

The IRA restriction on collectibles applies to any retirement plans, including Keoghs, that allow people to direct the investment of their assets. The law even mentions "alcoholic beverages" as one of the prohibited items, since some investors have put money into rare wines. Also, the law doesn't allow you to invest Keogh dollars in U.S. gold and silver coins.

What happens if you have a Keogh plan and you invest Keogh funds in art, antiques, or other collectibles? The amount you've invested is treated as a distribution from the fund and becomes taxable income. In addition, if you haven't reached age fifty-nine and one-half, Uncle Sam socks you with a 10 percent penalty.

Cashing Out

Uncle Sam generally won't allow you to withdraw money penalty free from your Keogh plan until you reach age fifty-nine and one-half or become disabled. However, if you die before you reach age fifty-nine and one-half, the money deposited in your Keogh goes to the beneficiaries you named in the plan. And there is no penalty for them no matter what age they are when they withdraw funds.

Even if you choose never to retire, you must begin withdrawing money from your Keogh plan once you reach age seventy and one-half.

But here's a planning point worth considering: You may continue to make tax-deferred contributions to your Keogh after you reach age seventy and one-half, as long as you still report self-employment income. So you may deposit money at the same time you withdraw it. This strategy makes sense if you already have plenty of money to support your retirement and you want to earn tax-deferred savings. It doesn't make sense, however, if your tax-deferred savings are subject to the excess distribution tax that we discussed in Chapter 34.

The money you withdraw from a Keogh plan is taxed as ordinary income in the year you receive it—unless you roll it over into another account or you withdraw the money in a lump sum and qualify for five-year forward averaging. You may take payments in the form of an annuity— periodic payments for the rest of your life, the joint lives of you and your beneficiary, your life expectancy, or the joint life expectancy of you and your beneficiary. (See Chapter 36 for more on forward averaging.)

The rules governing withdrawals from Keoghs are the same as for company-sponsored pension plans. (See Chapter 34 for this information.)

Trust Yourself

It used to be that only a bank or other qualified financial institution—a brokerage house, for example—could serve as the trustee of a Keogh plan.

But now you may name yourself as trustee. This rule allows you—as trustee—to handle your Keogh's assets and hold legal title to them.

Tip: You may pay the cost of setting up a Keogh plan out of your own pocket, or you may subtract these amounts directly from your Keogh.

We advocate the former—and for good reason. The costs of setting up a Keogh plan—as well as any trustee or actuarial fees paid outside the Keogh—are treated as business expenses on your Schedule C.

But you get no such deduction if you pay fees from dollars contributed to your Keogh. What's more, you reduce the amount in your Keogh when you cover expenses in this way.

Master Plan

Most people establish Keoghs through master or prototype plans. These are offered by banks, brokerage houses, mutual funds, and many other financial institutions. You may also set up a "personalized" plan drawn up especially for you by an attorney. The advantage of such a plan: flexibility.

Master or prototype plans may not have the design features you need. For example, such a plan may not let you defer distributions past retirement age.

Also, a prototype plan offered by a bank, for example, may limit you to investing your Keogh dollars in products offered by that bank. (You may, however, set up as many of these plans as you like as long as you don't go over the yearly limits.)

You are under no such restrictions with a personalized plan. For it, you set up a checking account—John Doe, Keogh—and then purchase any investments you choose.

Caution: The cost of setting up a prototype plan is minimal. But a personalized Keogh can cost you upwards of $500 or more in attorney fees.

Team Effort

What happens if you have your own business?

If you set up a Keogh for yourself and make contributions to it, you must extend this benefit to your employees. Moreover, you usually may not recover the cost of contributions you make for employees from your employees' pay. You must make the entire contribution yourself.

And, you may not set aside more for yourself—on a percentage basis—than you do for your employees. In other words, if you contribute 15 percent of your income to a Keogh, you must contribute an amount on their behalf equal to 15 percent of their income. But you may take into account Social Security contributions you make for your employees. This is known as "integrating" the plan with Social Security.

Tip: Certain categories of employees can be excluded. This area is tricky, though, so you should get professional help. Moreover, although contributions for employees are deductible, they can add up. Our advice: Weigh the cost of contributions on behalf of employees against the benefits you receive. You may find you are better off not setting up a Keogh.

Cash in Hand

You can transfer stock or other property—rather than cash—to your Keogh plan. But there are complex tax rules you must follow. And you may get hit with a penalty. The bottom line: It's almost always better to contribute cash.

Hands Off

A great temptation to owners of Keogh plans is to dip into their funds to help defray the costs of a trip to Europe, say, or a child's education.

But you may not borrow from your own Keogh plan without unpleasant tax consequences. This rule applies if you're a sole proprietor or a partner with more than a 10 percent stake in the partnership.

What happens if you disregard this restriction? You must either pay back the loan immediately or pay an excise tax equal to the full amount of the loan.

Also, loans are considered a distribution from the plan if they exceed a certain percentage of your interest in the plan. This rule applies whether or not you are a sole proprietor or more-than-10-percent partner.

If you're wondering how the IRS discovers your borrowing, keep in mind that Keogh plans are not like ordinary bank or investment accounts. They are set up under special rules. And one of these regulations requires that you file an annual return (a series 5500 form) with the IRS each year. All loans must be reported on this return.

Enough Already

Take care when you compute the amount of your contributions to a Keogh plan. If you make contributions over the allowable amount, you are subject to a special excise tax—10 percent of the excess contribution.

This One's for You

A Keogh is always a good idea—unless, as we've seen, the amount you have to pay for employees outweighs the plan's advantages for you. Our advice is to put away as much as you can each year in a Keogh plan.

But keep this restriction in mind: The law requires that you establish your Keogh account by December 31 of each year. You don't have to contribute to the plan at that time, but the plan must be in place. Otherwise, no Keogh for you until the following year.

You may, however, still set up a simplified employee pension (SEP) plan. These plans are similar to IRAs. The ceiling on contributions to a SEP is 15 percent of your compensation, up to $30,000. (See Chapter 34 for more information about SEPs.)

36 *An Offer You Can't Refuse*

Your Guide to Early Retirement Packages

*I*n the past few years, more and more companies—in quest of lower costs and more efficient operations—have encouraged employees to take early retirement.

The bait: an attractive package of incentives.

In 1986 alone, one out of three U.S. companies offered early retirement incentives to older employees. If you are faced with this choice, what should you do?

In this chapter, we provide you with the information you need to evaluate an early retirement offer—or simply to decide to retire at a younger than average age.

Begin at the Beginning

Typically, early retirement packages include some combination of cash, pension benefits, insurance, offers of assistance in finding a new job (outplacement counseling), and financial planning. Cash payments usually are based on your salary and years of service with the company.

When it comes to figuring additional pensions, many companies add extra years of service in determining the benefits you'll receive.

Let's say the pension benefit your company pays equals 1 percent of your average compensation during the three-year period when your compensation was highest, multiplied by your years of service with the company. So if you worked for twenty years, and the early retirement package gave you another five years, you'd end up with 25 percent of your average compensation, rather than 20 percent.

Another popular form of pension benefit in early retirement incentive packages is a so-called *Social Security supplement*. The plan pays you an extra amount equal to what you'd receive in Social Security benefits when you reach age sixty-two. This supplement stops when you actually begin to collect your Social Security benefits.

Many companies also offer free medical and group life insurance coverage for a year. After the year is up, you have the right to buy coverage at group rates.

Sounds good, doesn't it? Usually these packages *are* worthwhile, which explains why so many people take advantage of them. But don't act without thinking the offer through carefully.

Here's what to do if you are offered early retirement.

Step 1: Calculate the "marginal value" of continuing to work.

For most people, one of the primary reasons for working is income. So you should ask yourself a key question before deciding whether or not you can afford to leave your job early. The question? How much more will I earn working full time than not working at all?

We refer to the difference as the *marginal value* of continuing to work—the difference that working makes in your income. Obviously, you're going to earn more as a worker than as a retiree. But how much more?

Look at the following tables. They analyze how much extra income a hypothetical employee—let's call her Maggie—takes home by working full time.

	WORKING	RETIRED
Salary	$42,000	—
Social Security	(3,213)	$ 8,700
Pension plan income	—	11,340
Other plan income	—	8,737

	WORKING	RETIRED
Federal income tax	$(5,401)	$(1,677)
Commuting expenses	(1,000)	—
Other expenses (clothes, meals, dry cleaning, etc.)*	(2,100)	—
After-tax income	$30,286	$27,100
Marginal income	$3,186	
Marginal hourly income	$1.72	

*Expenses are estimated at 5 percent of salary.

So, by continuing to work Maggie brings home only $3,245 more in annual income than she'd get if she left her company.

And her hourly rate—based on a standard 1,850-hour work year—comes to only $1.72 an hour, less than the minimum wage.

Now Maggie should ask herself whether or not it's necessary to work full time year round to earn $3,186 after taxes. Perhaps she could earn this amount by working part time—at a job with less work-related expense and less stress.

She would gain the advantages of working—stimulation, a sense of achievement, and social interaction—without sacrificing her other interests.

Here's another example to consider.

	WORKING	RETIRED
Salary	$75,000	—
Social Security	(3,924)	$ 9,000
Investment income	10,000	10,000

	WORKING	RETIRED
Pension plan income	—	$20,250
Other plan income	—	15,600
Federal income tax	(17,651)	(7,739)
Commuting expenses	(1,000)	—
Other expenses (clothes, meals, dry cleaning, etc.)*	(3,750)	—
After-tax income	$58,675	$47,111
Marginal income	$11,564	
Marginal hourly income	$6.25	

Expenses are estimated at 5 percent of salary.

Try your own "marginal value of work" cost analysis. You may be surprised at the affordability of retiring early.

Step 2: Examine the pension benefits you'd receive.

Will your benefits be reduced because you are retiring earlier than the normal retirement age under your company's plan? Will the pension check that you receive fund your retirement adequately until you qualify for Social Security benefits? How generous are the overall early retirement benefits compared with the benefits you'd collect if you continued to work for your company?

If you hadn't planned to retire for many years, you might be looking at benefits that are considerably less than those you had anticipated. To make up for the difference, you might need to find another job.

Step 3: Analyze payout options and your tax situation.

Most companies offer you a choice of pension settlement: lump sum or annuity.

Annuities have some attractions, the best being convenience. The investment decisions in managing your funds remain the pension trustee's problem.

But if you think you can manage the money well, you might want to take the lump sum. If you do, you may take advantage of forward averaging to minimize the tax due. Or you can delay the tax liability by rolling the money over into an IRA. This way you won't pay tax until you begin withdrawing money from the IRA.

So, here's the question: If you choose to take the lump sum, how do you decide which option—forward averaging or IRA rollover—will bring you the best financial return?

We're going to help you answer this question with some examples illustrating four different options. Each assumes a taxable distribution of $100,000, a taxable rate of return of 9.0 percent, and an after-tax rate of 6.5 percent.

In each case, your options are to elect forward averaging or to roll the money into an IRA. We assume the distribution rolled over into the IRA grows at 9.0 percent and the money invested outside of the IRA grows at 6.5 percent. This difference in rate reflects the taxes you would have to pay on the non-IRA earnings.

So, here are the four options:

- You invest the lump-sum distribution for five years and then withdraw it, also in a lump sum.
- You invest the distribution for ten years before withdrawing it, still in a lump sum.
- You invest the distribution for five years and then withdraw it in the form of a monthly annuity for twenty years.
- You invest the distribution for ten years and withdraw it in the same twenty-year monthly annuity.

Now for our example.

Should you roll over the money into an IRA or use special forward averaging? Let's look at forward averaging first. We'll assume that you were least age fifty on January 1, 1986, and were therefore eligible for ten-year—rather than five-year—forward averaging.

	PERIOD OF INVESTMENT	
	5 Years	*10 Years*
Distribution	$100,000	$100,000
Minus tax (forward averaging)	(15,360)	(15,360)
Amount available to invest	84,640	84,640
Amount available at end of period (6.5 percent return)	115,960	158,880
Minus taxes	0	0
Net amount available at end of period	$115,960	$158,880

Now, let's take a look at what happens if you roll the money over into an IRA.

	PERIOD OF INVESTMENT	
	5 Years	*10 Years*
Distribution	$100,000	$100,000
Minus tax	0	0
Amount available to invest in IRA	100,000	100,000
Amount available at end of period (9 percent return)	153,862	236,736
Minus taxes due upon distribution from IRA (28 percent)	(43,081)	(66,286)
Net amount available at end of period	$110,781	$170,450

It's pretty clear from the example that the choice—to take your distribution currently or roll it over into an IRA—depends on how long you intend to invest the money before finally withdrawing it.

If you expect to invest it for five years, you do better by choosing forward averaging. However, if you are willing to leave your retirement funds invested for ten years, the IRA rollover gives you a better return.

Okay, but this comparison assumes that, whichever choice you make, at the end of the five- or ten-year investment period, you withdraw the money in a single lump sum. You do have another option: to withdraw it periodically.

So now let's see what happens to your investment if, instead of taking a lump-sum distribution after five or ten years, you withdraw the principal and interest evenly over twenty years.

Again, we'll look at special forward averaging first.

	PERIOD OF INVESTMENT	
	5 Years	10 Years
Distribution	$100,000	$100,000
Minus tax (forward averaging)	(15,360)	(15,360)
Amount available to invest	84,640	84,640
Amount available at end of period (6.5 percent return)	115,960	158,880
Monthly annuity paid out for 20 years if you begin payments at end of investment period	865	1,185
Minus tax	0	0
Net monthly annuity	$ 865	$ 1,185

On the other hand, what if you roll the money into an IRA?

	PERIOD OF INVESTMENT	
	5 Years	10 Years
Distribution	$100,000	$100,000
Minus tax	0	0
Amount available to invest in IRA	100,000	100,000
Amount available at end of period (9 percent return)	153,862	236,736
Monthly annuity paid out for 20 years if you begin payments at end of investment period	1,384	2,130
Minus taxes due (28 percent)	(388)	(596)
Net monthly annuity	$ 996	$ 1,534

Clearly, if you plan to withdraw your retirement funds over a twenty-year period, you are far better off rolling over the initial distribution you get from your employer into an IRA.

Another point: Some states don't allow forward averaging for state tax purposes. Check your state law. Chances are, if your state doesn't permit forward averaging, you may want to roll over your money into an IRA to avoid a hefty state tax bill.

Step 4: Check out your cash flow.
Fill in the retirement cash-flow work sheet in Appendix IX as if you had accepted the offer. And ask yourself the tough questions.

Is your house paid for? If not, can you afford the mortgage payments without working? What about your medical costs? You'll need to pay for insurance coverage if it's not part of the package.

Also, can you count on additional income from anticipated inheritances, say, to boost your retirement income?

Your answers, plus the cash-flow work sheet, will give you a realistic idea of whether or not you can afford to accept.

Step 5: Examine your options outside the company.
If you find you have to—or want to—work after your "retirement," consider your chances of reemployment. Here's where a company-provided outplacement counselor comes in. If your company doesn't offer this service, you might find it worthwhile to consult a specialist in the field on your own.

Step 6: Review your mix of investments.
Take a look at your asset allocation. Are your investments earning 4 to 6 percent more than the rate of inflation?

If not, reconsider your allocation.

Step 7: See a financial expert if the choices appear too complicated.
If you're in an upper-income bracket, it usually pays to have an accountant or financial planner go over the company's offer.

The Part-Time Option

As we've seen, retirement plans aren't the only way to get what you need for retirement. Another option is to work part time after you retire. You might even take on a second career.

One businessperson we know lectures on entrepreneurship at a local university. Another writes a column about real estate for a local newspaper.

Another idea: Start your own small business. A longtime collector of Civil War memorabilia, for instance, set up shop as an antiques dealer after he took early retirement. Still another fulfilled her fantasy to run her own restaurant. And many executives retire early to start their own consulting businesses.

One note of caution, however: Calculate not only what you gain by working part time but what you lose. If you have extra earned income, you may lose some of your Social Security benefits. Also, the income you earn is subject to Social Security and federal and state withholding taxes. (See Chapter 31 for more information on how earned income influences the level of your Social Security benefits.)

PART NINE

Your Estate Plan

37 *You Can't Take It with You*

Facing the Hard Choices on Who Gets What

*E*state planning is not solely a matter of saving dollars and minimizing taxes. The process of planning your estate inevitably raises some difficult emotional issues.

For starters, it forces you to face the unpleasant fact of your own mortality: You are trying to plan for a time when you won't be around to make decisions. Other people—particularly people you love—will be affected by the plans you make now, and they will be expected to exercise their own judgment once you're gone.

In the chapters that follow, we'll get down to the nuts and bolts of estate planning—estate taxes, wills, and trusts. First, though, we'll take a look at the most difficult step in the estate planning process: deciding who gets what and when.

You Decide

To whom you leave your money and property is obviously a very personal decision. Most people, of course, think of planning for spouses, significant others, children, and relatives first. Then might come a favorite charity, such as an alma mater or research foundation.

Remember, though, what you leave—and whom you leave it to—is dictated by your financial profile. Some people consider it their responsibility to leave a legacy. Others—with a "you-can't-take-it-with-you" attitude—try to spend all they have before they die.

Still, for most people, the toughest question they face is how much to leave the children. Let's take a look.

Oh, Those Kids

"How much should I leave the children?"

You might find it surprising, but only in common-law countries—Great Britain and its former colonies—do people agonize over this question.

In much of the rest of the world, custom or law dictates that parental assets be divided according to ironclad formulas that specify that your spouse and offspring divvy up everything. But in common-law countries, people have the almost unlimited right to decide who gets what and when.

So whether you have a considerable fortune or merely a tidy nest egg to distribute, you must determine for yourself whether large bequests will have a positive or negative effect on your offspring.

What's the right approach for you, when it comes to your estate and your children? We can't give you the answers, but we do offer some suggestions.

Take your children into your confidence.
When your children are mature enough to discuss such matters, let them know, in general terms, the size of your anticipated estate and talk over with them your plans for it. They should certainly know if you're leaving them less than they might expect—and why.

If they're old enough, you should give them the opportunity to make their druthers known: Are they interested in running the family business? Do they have a preference about how their inheritances or trusts might be structured?

Teach responsible attitudes toward money.
If your children are young, put them on an allowance and give them opportunities to earn extra money on their own.

How children handle their allowances gives you a good idea of how they are likely to cope with an inheritance. Will they spend their money responsibly? Will they rest on your financial laurels, or will their ambitions force them to seek out extra income on their own?

Another way to teach children—particularly high school and college age youngsters—how to handle money responsibly: Let them set up their own checking accounts.

Tie up money as long as you think necessary.
In most states, eighteen or twenty-one is the legal coming of age. But most financial planners agree: Even a twenty-one-year-old is not mature enough to handle the responsibilities of a sudden windfall. Evaluate when your children might be capable of meeting this challenge, and withhold all bequests until that time.

Many parents are upping the age—to thirty, say—at which children can collect their money. Others are designing innovative trusts that pay out nothing until the child completes college or shows proof of earned income—and even then the trust shells out only enough to match the child's salary. (We cover trusts in Chapter 40.)

Concentrate on the first generation.
Limit your major gift giving to your own children. Let them worry about your grandchildren's inheritances. Only they know what will be good for their youngsters decades from now.

The Time Is Now

A word to the wise: The best time to start your estate planning is now. Remember, the longer you wait to begin, the better the chance that your heirs will be left to shoulder your responsibilities.

38 *All in the Family— For Now*

How to Slash Your Estate Tax Liability

As has often been said, two things in life are certain—death and taxes. Estate planning is the art of ensuring that one doesn't cause the other.

In this chapter, we show you how estates are taxed. We also suggest strategies to help you minimize taxes on your estate.

You may already know that some estates—those with a total value of $600,000 or less—escape federal estate tax altogether. But people often seriously underestimate the size of their estates and may end up with an unanticipated estate tax bill.

If you are a professional or an executive in a top position, for instance, there is a good chance that the value of your estate already tops $600,000 or will soon. Even if you don't have substantial personal wealth, "hidden" assets, such as life insurance and pension or profit-sharing benefits, may cause your taxable estate to exceed the $600,000 threshold.

Let's begin with the basics.

Add It Up, Add It All Up

Uncle Sam imposes an entirely separate tax—known as the federal estate tax—when you die. In most cases, your taxable estate—the amount that is subject to tax—is less than its gross value. That's why one of the first—and most important—elements in estate planning is calculating this taxable amount. Fortunately, the task isn't difficult. Here's how to get a rough estimate.

Take a look at your net worth work sheet in Appendix II. If you filled it out while you were reading Chapter 2, you're already ahead of the game.

Now, tally up your cash and the market value of your assets—for this purpose, you should use the face value of your life insurance.

Make sure you do not overlook "hidden" assets. For example, count the dollars—the inherent value or spread in your unexercised stock options, say—accumulating in your fringe benefit and compensation packages. Also count any other company benefits payable at your death.

Don't forget, also, to include your half of jointly held property. And add in the value of personal property, such as cars, furniture, antiques, jewelry, and collectibles.

Next, subtract your liabilities, estimated funeral and burial expenses ($3,000 to $5,000 is typical), and estimated costs of administering your estate (2 to 5 percent of the gross value of the estate is average).

Also, subtract your charitable bequests and, finally, bequests to your spouse—the marital deduction. The remaining amount is your taxable estate—that is, the amount subject to federal estate taxes.

Oh, Bliss

Now you know how to compute your taxable estate. In a moment, we'll go on to figure the tax. First, though, there are two critical tax breaks you need to know about. They are the unlimited marital deduction and the unified credit.

We start with the unlimited marital deduction.

This helpful provision in the tax code allows you to leave your entire estate—no matter what its size—to your spouse tax free.

Let's say that you're sixty years old. Your wife is forty, and you have no children. A wealthy man, you die and leave your entire estate—$3 million—to your wife.

She may enjoy her fortune free of taxes—thanks to the marital deduction. But this deduction doesn't mean that Uncle Sam won't collect eventually. The IRS gets what's coming to it—but only after your wife dies.

Of course, if your wife decides to remarry, the marital deduction applies to the estate she leaves as well. That means she can pass along, tax free, everything that you left her, plus any of her own assets, to her new husband, should she die first.

Theoretically, that chain of events could repeat itself indefinitely, but the IRS is patient. Sooner or later your estate, and whatever has been added to it, will pass into the hands of someone other than a surviving spouse—children, or a deserving niece or nephew, perhaps. When it does, the marital deduction no longer applies. The estate tax comes due. Shortly, we'll show you how to make maximum use of the marital deduction.

Now, however, let's look at the unified tax credit.

This credit applies to everyone, not just to married couples. And it amounts to an exemption from taxation of estates of $600,000 or less. Here's how it works.

Let's say you die in 1989. A childless widower, you leave your estate worth exactly $600,000 to your younger sister. As required by law, your executor—in this case, also your sister—files an estate tax return (Form 706) with the IRS within nine months of your death.

A separate tax schedule—which we show on the next page—applies to estates. (The same schedule applies to gifts. As you can see, the estate tax, like the income tax, is progressive—that is, the tax rates increase with the size of the estate.)

Your sister looks at the schedule and computes an estate tax of $192,800. The next step: She subtracts the amount of the unified credit— set by law at $192,800—from the tax due. The remainder: zero. Your estate of $600,000 owes no federal taxes.

What happens if you pass along an estate valued at more than $600,000? The tax on an estate mounts quickly. If, instead of just $600,000, you had left your sister $700,000, the estate would have owed Uncle Sam $37,000, or 37 percent of the $100,000 in excess of $600,000.

ESTATE AND GIFT TAXES, 1990

If Your Taxable Estate is Between		You Owe	Plus	On Amount Over
$ —	$ 10,000	$ —	18%	$ —
10,000	20,000	1,800	20	10,000
20,000	40,000	3,800	22	20,000
40,000	60,000	8,200	24	40,000
60,000	80,000	13,000	26	60,000
80,000	100,000	18,200	28	80,000
100,000	150,000	23,800	30	100,000
150,000	250,000	38,800	32	150,000
250,000	500,000	70,800	34	250,000
500,000	750,000	155,800	37	500,000
750,000	1,000,000	248,300	39	750,000
1,000,000	1,250,000	345,800	41	1,000,000
1,250,000	1,500,000	448,300	43	1,250,000
1,500,000	2,000,000	555,800	45	1,500,000
2,000,000	2,500,000	780,800	49	2,000,000
2,500,000		1,025,800	50	2,500,000

Estate Tax Planning Strategies

While there may be some very generous tax provisions in the IRS code, you still must take the time to plan your estate carefully if you want to minimize taxes. Here are four estate planning strategies you should consider.

Maximize use of the unified credit.

While the law allows you to leave all your holdings to your spouse without incurring any tax, doing so isn't always a good idea.

Consider this example. The founder of a small chain of retail clothing stores, you die in 1990 and leave an estate valued at $1.2 million to your husband.

Under the marital deduction rule, the estate owes no tax. But when he dies several years later, he leaves the estate to your two children.

Now the estate (assuming no growth) totals $1.2 million, and only $600,000 is sheltered from tax by the unified credit. The tax on the unprotected $600,000 is $235,000.

A better idea: Instead of leaving your full estate of $1.2 million to your husband, divide your estate into two equal $600,000 shares. The marital share goes to your husband, and the unified credit shelter share—or bypass share—goes to your two children *after* your husband's death.

You place this bypass share in a trust—known, naturally enough, as a *bypass*, or *credit shelter*, *trust*. And the trust provides that income may be distributed either to your husband or to your children during your husband's lifetime. When he dies, the principal passes to the children.

Now you haven't wasted the tax benefit of the unified credit—and you've saved $235,000 in estate taxes. Here's how.

Half your estate went to your husband. That portion isn't taxed because of the marital deduction. The remaining $600,000 is in trust for your husband and children—and that sum escapes taxation thanks to the unified credit. When your husband dies, his estate totals only $600,000, an amount that, again, the unified credit saves from Uncle Sam's long reach.

Try a QTIP trust.

When Congress adopted the 1981 Economic Recovery Tax Act, it introduced an important concept called *qualified terminable interest property*.

Also known as a *life interest*, this provision allows you to leave income to your spouse while directing who will receive your property after the death of your spouse. And it lets you defer estate tax until your spouse dies.

Here's an example. You specify in your will that your husband annually receive all income from an office building you own. When he dies, your will says, the building goes to your daughter.

So your husband gets income from the building each year—but for his lifetime only. Your daughter inherits the building after he's gone. Since the property qualifies for the estate tax marital deduction, taxes aren't due until your husband dies.

Obviously, taking advantage of the QTIP can pay dividends. Using this provision of the tax law makes particularly good sense when you have been married previously.

In your will, you can grant your second spouse a life estate in your property. But the QTIP lets you make certain that your estate won't be shifted away from the ultimate beneficiaries of your choice—your children.

Incidentally, the QTIP trust may look quite similar to a bypass trust— that is, the income goes to the spouse and the remainder to the children at the spouse's death. In fact, the provisions may be identical. The key difference that allows the QTIP trust to qualify for the marital deduction: a written election filed with the estate tax return.

Use gifts to your family to reduce the size of your estate.

Uncle Sam allows you to give up to $10,000 tax free each year to each of your children—or to any other person, for that matter.

If your spouse joins in the giving, the amount the two of you may annually bestow rises to $20,000 per recipient. This means a couple with two children may make tax-free gifts to their children of up to $40,000 a year, a couple with four children, $80,000 a year, and so forth.

And gift giving makes for good tax planning, if you can afford it. The reason: By disposing of your assets while you're living, you save a considerable amount of estate tax.

Here's an example.

You add up your taxable estate, and the total comes to a handsome $2.4 million. You know you should distribute a portion of this estate before you die. Otherwise, you face an enormous estate tax bill.

So, beginning in 1989, you and your spouse make annual $20,000 gifts to each of your three children. At the end of ten years, you've given away $600,000, tax free.

The estate tax saved: $286,000. And this savings assumes that the $600,000 would not have grown in value and that you would have spent, rather than saved, any earnings on the principal amount.

With your gift strategy you've accomplished two key objectives: You've divided your wealth among your family members—and you've saved a considerable amount in estate taxes.

Should you give someone more than the annual tax-free amount? Yes, if you're wealthy enough to be financially secure *and* you want your family to have substantial gifts during your lifetime. Gifts that top the $10,000 annual exclusion use up your lifetime unified credit. So you can make gifts of up to $600,000 ($1,200,000 for a married couple) more than the annual exclusion before paying any gift tax.

Keep in mind that the original value of gifts over the annual tax-free amount will be taken into account when determining your estate tax. However, all post-gift appreciation and income will be excluded from your estate.

Give gifts to charity.
Charitable contributions you make during your lifetime are not counted as part of your estate—and for good reason. The property no longer belongs to you.

But gifts you make at the time of your death—that is, testamentary bequests in your will—are deductible for estate tax purposes. So be as generous as you wish—with one caveat. Charitable gifts are terrific for estate tax savings, but you must always consider your own security and the uncertainty of the future. Don't give away what you may need later on. (See Chapter 40 for information on setting up charitable trusts.)

Three Typical Estate Plans

If you're married, you must be particularly careful in adding up your assets. Here's why. Let's say you and your spouse own a house with a hefty mortgage, a car, and some other personal property. And you have a small amount of savings.

You do not make any estate plan, since your combined net worth—you think—falls well below the $600,000 unified credit deduction ceiling.

But what about your combined life insurance coverage? Or your pension and profit-sharing plans? When you add in these additional assets, you may find that your estate comes to well over $600,000. And your lack of planning can result in totally unnecessary estate taxes.

That said, let's look at three possible estate planning scenarios for married couples.

Small Combined Estates ($600,000 or Less)

With the unified credit, your combined estates escape federal income taxes entirely. So you should structure your assets to avoid state and local taxes and provide for any children.

To achieve this end, you and your spouse might write wills leaving your entire estate to the surviving spouse—or to any children if only one spouse is living.

Medium-Sized Estates (About $600,000 to $1.2 Million)

Medium-sized estates are often the hardest to plan.

The reason: Equalization tactics that make good tax sense often aren't very practical. For example, to avoid estate taxes altogether, each spouse should have no more than $600,000 in assets while he or she is living. And when one spouse dies, the survivor should not be left with more than $600,000.

But it is sometimes difficult—and often unwise—to make this happen. For one thing, the spouse who is "richer" rarely has enough in liquid assets to transfer funds to the "poorer" spouse.

Also, while $600,000 is a lot of money, a widow or widower might be much more comfortable with access to still more—particularly if the survivor is still young.

So what should you do if your estate falls within the medium-sized category? Here's one idea. First, within the bounds of common sense, transfer enough liquid assets to bring the "poorer" spouse's wealth up to

$600,000. Remember, though, you're giving up control over these assets.

Then, to ensure maximum flexibility after the first spouse dies, each spouse should leave his or her entire estate to the other spouse. But each should also have the ability under the other spouse's will to "disclaim assets"—that is, choose not to inherit them—so that these assets pass to a bypass trust. That trust may permit the survivor to receive income, and even principal if needed.

Now the surviving spouse has two choices: to disclaim assets to the bypass trust to remove them from the survivor's taxable estate; or to take all the assets. Even if the survivor chooses the second option, he or she can reduce the estate tax by spending the money or by making tax-free gifts to family, friends, or charity.

Large Estates (More Than $1.2 Million)

If your estate is approximately $2.5 million or more, consider starting an annual gift program for your children, grandchildren, or anyone else who is dependent on you for financial support. This strategy is good tax planning and also permits you to share your wealth with loved ones during your lifetime.

If your estate comes to between $1.2 million and $2.5 million, you may want to limit your gift giving to meet specific needs—a down payment on a house, for instance—rather than embarking on a regular gift-giving program.

If you're uncomfortable making outright gifts to your children, consider a Crummey trust. This trust—which we cover in detail in Chapter 40—limits your children's access to the trust assets; but gifts to it still qualify for the $10,000 annual exclusion.

As long as your marriage is reasonably harmonious, both your wills should contain credit shelter trusts with the balance going to the surviving spouse, either outright, in a "regular" marital trust, or in a QTIP trust.

Another point: Estates of more than $1.2 million should also include a provision in the estate documents to allow the executor to equalize the estates. Of course, if you live in a community property state, you will probably find that state law does the "equalizing" for you.

Making the estates equal in size is helpful when both spouses die within six months of each other. It can save up to $117,000 in estate taxes.

Roll Up Your Sleeves

One final word to the wise: It takes time to master the basics of estate taxes, but it's time well spent. With only a modest amount of planning, you can significantly reduce your estate tax liability.

39 *Where There's a Will, There's a Way*

Your Guide to Wills

Let's go straight to the heart of the matter. Six out of ten Americans do not have wills. If you do not have a will, make one. If you do have a will, review it.

This advice may sound old hat. But, as you will see in this chapter, not making a will—or not reviewing an existing will—can distort or destroy the best intentions.

Do It!

What happens if you die intestate—without a will?

For starters, a court in your state—not you—selects someone to administer your estate. In most cases, that person is your surviving spouse.

"That's just fine," you say. But wait a minute.

Suppose you are survived by children from two marriages. Can you count on your surviving spouse to treat the children from both marriages fairly? Not always.

Or say your spouse dies before you, and you are survived by four children. In many states, each child is given an equal say when it comes to administering a parent's estate. That arrangement can lead to family squabbles over who gets what.

Also, the courts may require your administrator to post a bond of $1,000 or more and charge that expense to your estate.

Not leaving a will can have particularly dire consequences if there is no qualified and competent relative or other person prescribed by law to administer your estate.

In this situation, many states require that the court appoint a public agency to take charge. And this agency—often known as the public administrator—manages your estate as one of hundreds, or even thousands, in its charge.

Granted, your estate must be distributed under the dictates of state law. But the laws in all states provide only for the transfer of assets to legally specified relatives. So no portion of your estate can go to special friends—or to your favorite charities. And if you die without those relatives, the state takes all your possessions.

Finally, let's say you are survived only by a minor child. A court appoints a legal guardian, and you have no say in who takes care of your youngster—or how.

Get It in Writing

Now that you're convinced that a will is vital, you need to know what it should contain. Wills come in only two varieties: *witnessed wills* and handwritten or—as they are called in legalese—*holographic wills*. Witnessed wills are valid in all fifty states. But only eighteen states—Arkansas, California, Iowa, Kentucky, Louisiana, Mississippi, Montana, Nevada, North Carolina, North Dakota, Pennsylvania, South Dakota, Tennessee, Texas, Utah, Virginia, West Virginia, and Wyoming—recognize holographic wills.

Remember, however, that state laws vary and frequently change. Also, even those states recognizing a holographic will usually require that it be dated, written, and signed in your handwriting only—that is, it must contain no printed or typed material.

A witnessed will, on the other hand, may be typed or handwritten. But it is valid only if it is signed by witnesses. In other words, you could type up or write out a will, sign it, and have it witnessed by two people—neither of whom have to be notaries—and be reasonably certain that you have a will that will stand up in court.

Most states require two or more people to witness the signing of a will. But—as always—there are exceptions to the rule. Connecticut, Georgia, Maine, New Hampshire, South Carolina, and Vermont require three witnesses.

In some states, a new and very convenient type of witnessed will known as a *statutory will* is available. It comes on a printed form with written instructions explaining how to fill in the blanks. You can find these wills at your local bar association or even stationery stores.

Statutory wills can serve you well if you have a modest estate and no complicated bequests. But, for most people, our advice is to play it safe. Have your lawyer prepare your will. That way, there should be no question of its validity.

Where Do I Begin?

Before you sit down with your attorney, it's a good idea to familiarize yourself with the standard ingredients of wills. Let's run through them.

The opening paragraph of the will identifies you—the so-called *testator*—by name. It gives your place of residence and states that you are knowingly making your will and revoking all prior wills.

Next appears a statement that directs your *executor*—the person you appoint to manage your estate and see that your assets are distributed according to your wishes—to pay promptly your burial expenses and all debts and taxes. These are the first claims against your estate.

A word of warning: You should understand how your will allocates debts, expenses, and taxes in your estate. Unless you specify otherwise in your will, each gift may bear a *pro rata* portion of those charges—even the gift of your fishing rod to cousin Ralph.

So if you want these expenses handled differently, you must say so in your will. Specify from what pool of assets you want your debts, expenses, and taxes paid.

Specifically Speaking

Of course, the primary purpose of a will is to indicate how you want your assets divided after your death. So the bulk of your will is devoted to this topic.

Many people want to leave a relative or friend a particular heirloom or some other personal property—say, one hundred shares of stock in the family business. Others want to leave something to charity—a collection of first editions to the local library, for instance, or a parcel of land to their alma mater. These gifts are known as *specific bequests* and are listed in your will first.

When you make specific bequests, you should include any items with sentimental value—a trophy, perhaps, or your college degrees. If you don't make your wishes crystal clear, these items usually end up in a grab bag, with your executor deciding who gets what.

Here's a suggestion on how to handle bequests of items of little or purely sentimental value. Bequeath all these items to one trusted person— your spouse, perhaps—along with nonbinding instructions in a separate letter listing the individuals you want to receive the items. Then leave it up to that same trusted person to distribute the gifts according to your wishes.

You don't want a long list of these gifts in your will, because each time you change the list, you must alter your will. And that can get expensive. If you use the method we suggest, you can revise the nonbinding instructions as often as you like without altering the will itself.

You should know, however, that nonbinding instructions are not part of your will. So the person you ask to carry out your instructions is not legally bound to do so. The only way to make absolutely certain that an item goes to a particular person is to include that bequest in your will.

Generally Speaking

The second type of bequest, a *general bequest*, is, as its name suggests— general, not specific.

Say you want to leave $10,000 to your old friend Sue Smith, and you state as much in your will—"I leave to my friend Sue Smith $10,000." This may sound like a specific bequest. But it's not.

A specific bequest would state, "I leave to my friend Sue Smith the $10,000 on deposit in Account Number 333-333-333 at the XYZ National Bank."

A general bequest, on the other hand, does not specify the source of funds from which the gift is drawn.

Leftovers

Another term you should know: residual estate. Your *residual estate* is what remains of your assets after you subtract your specific and general bequests.

Say you instruct your executor to make four general gifts—$1,000 to each of your nephews, for example. You want your remaining assets divided equally among your surviving spouse and your three children. These remaining assets are known as your residual estate.

Who has the first claim on your estate? Recipients of specific and general bequests—not recipients of your residual estate.

Caution: As a rule, specific legacies are paid before general legacies. So make sure there is enough left over in your estate for your beneficiaries after your specific and general bequests and after all debts, expenses, and taxes are paid.

Another question to ask when you list specific legacies in your will: What happens if you suffer financial reverses and neglect to change your will? Will the part of your estate that goes to your primary heirs—your residual estate—be smaller than you intended?

If the answer is yes, reconsider your specific and general bequests. You may want to eliminate some of them.

With a Little Help from My Friends

When it comes to making wills, parents of minor children have an additional responsibility. They must name a guardian for their children.

And take note: The courts won't honor your choice if you are survived by a spouse who is the natural parent, even if you are divorced and have full custody. If you die, your child goes to your former spouse. However, if your spouse dies before you do, you can ensure your children have the guardian of your—not the court's—choice by naming someone in your will.

Naming a guardian for your children is also a sound precaution should both parents die in the same accident. But be sure to discuss the matter with potential guardians before you make a final selection. You want someone willing and able to do the job.

Many people name their parents as guardians for their children. If your mother and father are elderly, however, a better choice might be a brother, sister, or close friend.

If you can't decide on a guardian for your children, you may designate someone in your will—your father or mother, say—to name a guardian.

Tip: State that the guardian you name doesn't have to file a bond, which many states require. These bonds can cost $1,000 or more.

Naming an Executor

You named someone to care for your children. Now you must name someone to take care of your money. The same person can hold both jobs. The decision is yours—but exercise care when you make this choice.

An executor is responsible for managing your estate until your assets are distributed. He or she files your estate tax return, even makes investment decisions. So, ideally, he or she should be somewhat knowledgeable about taxes and investments.

You should also know that executors are entitled to fees. These commissions are fixed by the laws of each state. Some states allow the courts to determine them. Others base them on the size or complexity of your estate. Typically, the fees run from 1 to 3 percent of the gross estate.

If you name two people to act as coexecutors, the fees may double. So find out from your attorney the rules in your state before you name multiple executors.

But fees—or the lack of them—should not dictate whom you choose as executor. You want the person or persons who will do the best job. Most people choose their spouse. The next choice: a trusted relative, friend, or business associate.

If you have a simple estate—a home and cash in the bank, for example—settling your estate should take less than a year, and there will probably be few problems. So even an unsophisticated family member or friend can probably manage with the help of your attorney or accountant.

But if you anticipate family squabbles or you think your spouse or friend will need assistance in handling the estate, consider naming your attorney or another trusted adviser as coexecutor.

And if your circumstances warrant—your estate is sizable and complicated—name a professional, such as a bank or trust company officer, to act as executor. You may add a family member or friend as coexecutor if that will make you rest easier. After all, sometimes two heads are better than one.

When you draw up your will, you usually list a first, second, and third choice for executor. The third choice for most people is an institution, such as a bank or trust company. This third option is a precaution in case your first two choices predecease you.

Last Wishes

Finally, include in your will any special instructions. For example, you may want to make sure your executor keeps certain investments for your heirs, carries on your business, or liquidates it.

If your will gives no hint of your intentions, your executors will do what they think best. And remember, they are bound by state laws, which may not allow them the flexibility to handle your property as you would have liked.

You may also want to specify in a letter of instructions the type of funeral you want. The more specific you are, the less burdened your family will be with tough decisions at a difficult time. Moreover, you will ensure that you get what you want.

One last point: Many people today do not want to be kept alive by "extraordinary measures"—life-support machines and so forth. If you're one of them, consider making a so-called *living will* that states your opposition to such heroic measures. In many states, these wills are not legally binding. But at the very least, you will have made your wishes known to family and friends.

Say What You Mean and Mean What You Say

Your attorney will draft your will. But it is up to you to make sure that the document expresses your desires precisely. You want your will to be clear enough so that your heirs—or any court, for that matter—can determine your intent.

Maybe you've heard the story about the man who left his favorite niece an annual income for "as long as she remained above the ground." When she died, her husband put her remains in a mausoleum—above the ground—and collected the money for the rest of his life.

Need we say more on this subject?

Name Names

Make it easy for your attorney. He or she needs to know your full legal name, date of birth, Social Security number, address, and telephone number. So bring along this information when you first visit your lawyer.

And provide this same identifying information for your spouse, children, and all other people mentioned in your will. Also include full legal names and addresses for any charities you mention.

In addition, your attorney will want your marital history. Are you married now? Were you ever divorced? If so, what are the names of your former spouses? Does your divorce decree require that you make certain gifts in your will to your former spouse? To your children? Your attorney will want to see to it that these former marriage partners exercise no claim on your estate—unless you so desire.

Another important point: A will remains valid unless revoked. If your circumstances change, so should your will. The law assumes that your last will expresses your wishes, even if that will is fifty years old.

Missing Links

You know what a will includes. Now you need to know what it doesn't contain.

You may find it odd, but you may not dispose of certain assets by will. Benefits from your insurance policies, for instance, are typically paid to a named beneficiary. They do not pass through your will.

But Uncle Sam still gets his cut. The proceeds of life insurance policies are added to your gross estate for tax purposes unless you do not "own" the policies. When do you not own a policy? When you don't have the right to change beneficiaries, borrow the cash value of the policy, or exercise other ownership rights in the policy.

You also may not will property—such as houses and bank accounts—held in joint tenancy. For example, if you and your spouse own your home as joint tenants, the survivor takes title when one spouse dies, regardless of what your will says.

But—and here's the kicker—the value of this property is still added to your gross estate for tax purposes. (See the previous chapter for more information about estate taxes.)

Finally, pension benefits that go to a surviving spouse or another named beneficiary also pass outside your will. So do U.S. savings bonds that name a beneficiary in the event of your death.

Keepsake

A will that is impossible to find is as useless as no will at all. So keep yours where it can easily be found by your executor. Do not put it where it can be stolen, destroyed, or lost.

Our advice: Keep a copy in your safe-deposit box, but ask your attorney or accountant to keep the original of your will in his or her safe. Or, if you name a bank or trust company as executor, ask an officer of that institution to hold on to your will. Also, keep a copy of your will in your home—in a filing cabinet, perhaps, or desk drawer. And let your primary beneficiaries know where it is.

40 *Trust Me*

Your Guide to Trusts

When it comes to estate planning, people sometimes shy away from learning about trusts. But these handy devices are not as complicated as they seem.

And knowing how to make use of trusts is vital if you want to save your heirs time, trouble, and—frequently—taxes.

Trusts serve three important functions:

- They provide a vehicle to manage your assets.
- They can exempt all or part of your estate from probate—the court process that ensures the orderly distribution of your assets.
- They can eliminate or reduce estate taxes.

Trusts fall into two broad categories—inter vivos and testamentary. Let's take a look at each.

Inter Vivos Trusts

An inter vivos—or living—trust goes into effect while the grantor of the trust is still alive. Inter vivos trusts themselves come in two varieties: revocable and irrevocable.

Revocable Trusts
A revocable trust allows you, the grantor, to control—for as long as you live—the assets that you place in trust. In other words, you may put money

or property into the trust and withdraw your assets at any time—hence the term *revocable*.

Because you have full use of the property in the trust—as well as the income from it—the trust does not affect your income or estate taxes. You pay income tax on the earnings of the trust while you are living, and your estate pays estate tax on the assets in the trust when you die.

But a revocable trust can still be useful. Why? Revocable trusts can provide for the orderly management and distribution of your assets if you become incapacitated or incompetent. For this reason, many wealthy people use these trusts to protect their assets.

The trust makes it easier for family members to intervene. By setting up a trust, you've said, in effect, "If I no longer can handle my own affairs, here's what I want done." You've designated someone you have faith in to oversee your affairs. So there's no doubt about your wishes.

Revocable trusts have another plus: As we've seen, you have full control over your assets in them while you live—you can withdraw principal at will, and you pay tax on any earnings. But when you die, these trust assets aren't subject to probate.

And avoiding probate can pay off—especially if you have a large and complicated estate. It means that the assets of the trust go directly to your heirs—named as beneficiaries of the trust—as you wanted. The disposition of your property is not tied up in red tape. You also escape probate and administration fees and expenses, which can run into thousands of dollars.

Revocable trusts do have their drawbacks. Among them: They can be a nuisance to set up and operate, since you have to register your assets in the name of the trust.

Another minus: administering the trust. For smaller and less complicated estates, probate is probably simpler and less time consuming and costly than creating and administering a trust.

Irrevocable Trusts

With the second type of inter vivos trust, called an irrevocable trust, you relinquish all control over your assets once you place them in the trust. The good news about an irrevocable trust: Not only do you eliminate probate, your estate can avoid paying federal estate taxes on the trust's assets.

Be warned, though. Irrevocable trusts have some serious disadvantages. First, you give up control over all or a big chunk of your assets. Doing so may leave you with insufficient resources for the rest of your own life. Also, the assets you transfer to irrevocable trusts constitute a gift in the eyes of Uncle Sam, so you may have to pay gift taxes on them.

If you have a large estate, though, irrevocable trusts let you reduce its size—thus slashing your estate tax liability.

Testamentary Trusts

Now to testamentary trusts. Unlike inter vivos trusts, you create testamentary trusts in your will. They don't take effect until you die.

After your death, the trust becomes one of the beneficiaries of your will. In turn, the beneficiaries of the trust can be anyone or any institution you want—your spouse, children, or favorite charity.

The most appealing feature of a testamentary trust: You may rest assured that after you die your assets will be managed in the manner you want.

By spelling out beneficiaries and conditions when you create the trust, you protect your heirs from the machinations of unscrupulous individuals or from their own inability to manage large sums of money properly. Of course, you also tie their hands, allowing them less prerogative to manage the assets intelligently in the face of changes or conditions that you didn't anticipate in your will.

One of the most common types of testamentary trusts is the unified credit or bypass trust (discussed in Chapter 38). The purpose of this type of trust: to avoid estate tax at the death of the second spouse.

Generation-Skipping Transfers

In the good old days, many estate plans of the very wealthy contained testamentary trusts that accomplished so-called *generation-skipping transfers*. At your death, you could place assets in a trust that paid income to your children. The assets themselves passed to your grandchildren on your children's death.

The advantage: Your estate was taxed once when you died and a second time—if any assets remained—when your grandchildren died, but you skipped the round of taxation that would have occurred when your children died.

Alas, the ability to transfer huge fortunes through generation-skipping transfers has diminished. The rules have become much harsher. A special generation-skipping tax—with rates equal to the maximum estate tax rate— applies to transfers to grandchildren, whether the gifts are direct or from a trust.

One major exception: You can make a total of $1 million in generation-skipping transfers to your grandchildren before the gifts will be subject to the tax. If you already have an estate plan that contains generation-skipping trusts, you may have to update the plan so that it complies with the current law.

The Best Offense

Now that you're familiar with the basic types of trusts, let's look more closely at some specific trusts and how you can use them to protect your assets for your heirs.

Qualified Terminable Interest Property Trust

As we saw in Chapter 38, Qualified Terminable Interest Property Trusts (QTIPs) are based on a concept known as the *qualified terminable interest* or *life interest*.

This provision in the tax code lets you specify in your will who will receive your property after your spouse dies. And it allows you to put off any estate taxes until that time.

Irrevocable Life Insurance Trusts

With irrevocable life insurance trusts, you escape taxation in both estates— yours and your surviving spouse's.

Here's how these trusts work: When you die, the trust receives the proceeds from your life insurance policy. Irrevocable life insurance trusts are appropriate if

- You and your spouse have an estate, including life insurance, of more than $1.2 million
- You have a significant amount of life insurance
- You and your spouse face heavy federal estate taxes at the second death

The money in the trust can be used in several ways.

Let's say you set up an irrevocable life insurance trust. You designate that your wife receive income from the trust until her death. At that time, the assets in the trust pass to your two children.

You die cash poor but leave to your spouse a 500-acre dairy farm valued at $1 million. Proceeds from your $500,000 life insurance policy go to your insurance trust, and this amount is not included in your taxable estate. How will your spouse pay estate taxes on the farm?

The trust purchases from your estate a portion of the family farm. The farm remains "in the family," but money is raised to pay estate taxes.

Life insurance trusts may also be used to provide income and limited principal to the surviving spouse and to provide income and principal to the children.

You must be sure that your trust is carefully drafted so you, the grantor, avoid gift tax and estate tax consequences. Transfers of life insurance within three years of death are includable in the transferor's estate.

If your trust is to be used to pay estate taxes, it pays to buy a "second-to-die" insurance policy. These policies, which often carry a lower premium than traditional policies, pay off at the second death—when the proceeds are needed for estate taxes. Or you may insure the younger—or healthier—spouse.

Keep in mind that the trust should not have to pay estate taxes. Instead, authorize the trustee to use the insurance proceeds to buy assets from or lend cash to your probate estate.

Most life insurance trusts are types of Crummey trusts, which we discuss next.

Crummey Trust

The Crummey trust's unfortunate name comes from the plaintiff in a well-known tax court case. Crummey trusts are a boon for people with enough assets to be able to make lifetime family gifts. If you're lucky enough to fall into this category, you should look into setting up a Crummey trust.

The trust lets you reduce your estate by making gifts. But here's its advantage over making the gifts outright: The trust protects your assets if you're concerned about the ability of the recipients—minor children, say—to handle money.

To fund a Crummey trust, you transfer to it up to $10,000 each year. Or, if you're married, you and your spouse together may transfer up to $20,000 a year.

As you saw in Chapter 38, the law allows you to give up to $10,000 a year—$20,000 for husband and wife—with no gift tax consequences. But in order to qualify for this tax break, a gift must be a "present interest"— that is, the recipient of your gift must be able to use it immediately.

How is this possible if the money is going into a trust? Here's how: The beneficiary must be allowed to withdraw the gift from the trust— usually for a period of 60 days—and must be notified of this right.

Usually, when your recipients know that further gifts depend on their allowing past gifts to remain in the trust, they'll quickly understand that exercising this immediate withdrawal right may not be in their best interest.

You must include this withdrawal notice provision in irrevocable life insurance trusts, as well, to avoid gift tax problems. But you can also use the same hint of future gifts to persuade beneficiaries to exercise patience—in this case to be sure that enough cash remains in the trust while you're living to pay the premiums.

Minor's Trusts

Minor's trusts have long been a popular technique for saving on income, gift, and estate taxes. The reason: Earnings from the assets are taxed at the trust's or child's usually lower rate. The initial gift is a present interest eligible for the annual gift tax exclusion—$10,000 from one parent, $20,000 from both.

Income may be either distributed or accumulated for your child.

However, any remaining principal and accumulated income must be distributed to your child no later than his or her twenty-first birthday.

Another important point: Don't forget the rules governing the taxation of children. Income over $1,000 of children under the age of fourteen is taxed at their parents' rates. Income of children fourteen or older is taxed at their rates.

(For more on minor's trusts, see Chapter 27. For more on how children are taxed, see Chapters 25 and 26.)

Charitable Trusts

Charitable trusts take two forms: charitable remainder trusts and charitable lead trusts. Both types can produce income and estate tax savings.

Charitable remainder trusts make sense for those who want to have their charitable cake and eat it too. You donate money or property to the trust. Income from these assets goes for a fixed period to any beneficiary you designate—including you—in the form of an annuity. At the end of that period, the balance of the trust goes to charity.

A *charitable lead trust* is just the opposite. The charity gets the annuity, and the balance at the end of the term passes to your family or some other beneficiary.

Warning: Charitable trusts are extraordinarily complicated. If you want to set one up, seek help from a skilled attorney.

Trust One Another

No one expects you to become a trust expert. But trusts are excellent devices for controlling wealth and directing your income. So knowing the basics—and putting your knowledge to work—can make life simpler for both you and your heirs.

Epilogue

We have not offered you a get-rich-quick manual. There is no way to plan to get rich quick. That's like planning to hit the jackpot in Las Vegas or Atlantic City. Luck is a wonderful thing—but don't bet your future on it.

Our approach is sensible and realistic. It doesn't focus on how much money you have, but on how wisely you use it. It doesn't emphasize what you don't have and can't get, but suggests ways of making the most of what is available to you.

We started off by helping you get organized. Then we showed you how to build a rational, systematic framework for personal financial planning by learning about yourself.

You first asked yourself the tough questions about your stage of life, life-style, tolerance for risk, responsibilities, and financial resources. Then you set goals and objectives. Finally, you were ready to select the financial strategies that would get you where you want to go.

Along the way, you learned the importance of being realistic about yourself—and the trade-offs you are, or are not, prepared to make in your financial life. And you probably discovered another essential part of the financial planning process: talking about finances and planning your finances with your spouse, your children, even your parents. We view constructive family dialogue on financial issues as one key element of fiscal health.

Remember this: The time you invest in personal financial planning is worthwhile. Just taking the uncertainty and guesswork out of your financial life is an important goal and well worth the time required. And getting comfortable with where you are headed financially is vital.

Financial planning is not a separate part of your life, isolated from your dreams and goals. Indeed, your finances are an integral part of everything else you hope to do and want to achieve.

So resolve to take the lessons of this book to heart. Begin at the beginning, by learning more about yourself. Then decide where you're headed. Plot your course—and bon voyage.

Appendices

A P P E N D I X · I

Your Guide to Record Keeping

---

*T*he difference between having your financial affairs neat and well maintained on the one hand or in a state of disaster on the other is usually a matter of simple organization. There's no genius required and just a small amount of work.

And think of the benefits: no more hours spent searching for that one canceled check, anxiety over those misplaced stock certificates, or days gathering material so you can prepare your tax return.

Organization is worth the minimal effort it requires. Besides, the real work comes in setting up a system. Once that's done, you'll save all sorts of time in the day-to-day management of your financial affairs.

Create your own system, use a friend's—or use ours. Here are some practical organizing tips that we've found helpful.

Facts on File

If you don't yet have them, get a desk and a file cabinet. Keep in the desk material that you use almost daily—stationery, office supplies, bills to be paid, documents to be filed, and a record of cash receipts. Use the file cabinet to store materials and documents you use less frequently.

406

Use folder systems in both the desk and the file cabinet. It makes filing and finding records that much easier.

Folders to keep in your desk:

- Bills to be paid
- Documents to be filed, such as insurance policies
- Cash receipts journal (which we'll come to later)
- Stock transactions
- Record of children's financial affairs (or a separate folder for each child), including gifts received and income from trusts
- Tax planning and financial planning articles you've clipped

Folders to keep in your file cabinet:

- Household bills paid (by year)
- Canceled checks and bank statements (by year)
- Tax returns (by year)
- Personal financial statements
- Home and home improvement records
- Investment account statements, including IRAs and Keoghs
- 401(k) plan documents
- Prospectuses and quarterly reports
- Bank passbooks and certificates
- Partnership investments
- Copies of wills or trusts
- Record of company benefits
- Employment contract
- Life insurance policies
- Disability insurance policy
- Health insurance policy
- Auto insurance policy
- Homeowner's insurance policy
- Umbrella insurance policy

Also, get yourself a loose-leaf binder—or borrow one from one of your children. It can help keep in one place all your records of a semi-permanent nature.

For example:

- Professional advisers' names and addresses
- Contents of your safe-deposit box
- List of credit cards and telephone numbers
- Your financial plan, including your goals and objectives
- Current ideas or thoughts on personal financial planning strategies
- Spending plan
- Asset-allocation strategy

You should also keep a record of cash receipts, or a cash receipts journal. You probably already have a cash disbursements journal—your checkbook. So you have a record of what you pay out.

But, if you are like most people, you probably do not have an orderly way of recording the cash you receive. Your journal can be as complicated as you like, or as simple—date, payer, amount, total deposited, date deposited.

Why would you want to keep a record of receipts?

A record allows you to look back at any time and "remember" who paid you what and when. At the end of the year, you can use the journal to double-check, for example, that you received all your dividend checks from a particular mutual fund or all interest payments on a certificate of deposit.

You could, if you wanted, also add a series of columns for the types of receipts you anticipate during the year—dividends, interest, rent, and so on.

Weed out your documents periodically. There is no need to keep everything forever—even if you have plenty of space. Don't keep buying more file cabinets. Instead, throw some records away. How long should you keep items? Here's a table to help you out.

HOW LONG SHOULD YOU KEEP YOUR RECORDS?

Short term (1 to 3 years)	Household bills
	Expired insurance policies
Medium term (4 to 6 years)	Tax returns and supporting data
	Bank statements

	Canceled checks and check registers (except checks for major purchases)
	Cash receipts journals
	Paid loan documents
Long term (indefinitely)	Checks and receipts for major purchases
	Brokerage statements
	Home purchase and home improvements documents
	Business or income property documents
	Wills and trusts
	Gift tax returns
	Papers dealing with an inheritance
	Nondeductible IRA contribution documents

Also, rent and use a safe-deposit box. It's the best place to store valuables, including stocks and bonds, infrequently used jewelry, and a list and photos of expensive possessions, such as antiques or works of art. Use the safe-deposit box, as well, to store copies of wills and trusts, partnership agreements, and other legal documents.

Sound simple, don't they, these organizing suggestions? They are, and so much easier than searching for lost records in piles of old bills, tax forms, receipts, and recipes. Resolve to get organized. Then do it.

A P P E N D I X · I I

Your Net Worth Work Sheet

Date:

                                             FAIR MARKET VALUE

Cash and Cash Equivalents

Your checking account(s) $_____

Savings account(s)   _____

Cash management account(s)   _____

Money-market account(s)   _____

Credit union account(s)   _____

Certificate(s) of deposit   _____

Stocks and Bonds

Stocks

Bonds   _____

Mutual funds   _____

Unit trusts   _____

Fixed-income securities   _____

Options   _____

Futures   _____

Commodities   _____

Real-Estate Investments

Value of your home   _____

Value of your vacation home   _____

Rental property   _____

Real-estate partnerships   _____

Other   _____

ASSETS	FAIR MARKET VALUE

Other Investments

Partnerships:
  Oil and gas $ _____

  Other   _____

Ownership interests in businesses   _____

Collectibles

Gold and silver   _____

Art   _____

Antiques   _____

Other (stamps, etc.)   _____

Retirement Assets

IRA   _____

Keogh   _____

401(k)   _____

Company pension plan   _____

Profit sharing   _____

Savings plan   _____

Insurance

Cash value of life insurance   _____

Surrender value of annuities   _____

Personal Property

Automobiles   _____

Boats   _____

Campers   _____

Plane   _____

Jewelry   _____

Household furnishings   _____

Other   _____

Total $ _____

LIABILITIES	VALUE OR BALANCE
Home mortgage	$
Vacation home mortgage	
Other real-estate debts	
Automobile loans	
Tuition loans	
Other installment loans	
Credit cards:	
Bank	
Retail stores	
Airline	
Oil companies	
Other	
Credit lines:	
Overdraft line	
Home equity line	
Unsecured credit line	
Income taxes	
Property taxes	
Margin loans from brokers	
Miscellaneous debt	
Total	$

Net Worth

Assets	$
Less liabilities	
Net worth	$

Your Cash-Flow Work Sheet

INCOME	MONTH	YEAR
Your salary	$_____	$_____
Commissions	_____	_____
Bonus	_____	_____
Your mate's salary	_____	_____
Commissions	_____	_____
Bonus	_____	_____
Income from business	_____	_____
Dividends	_____	_____
Interest	_____	_____
Rent paid to you	_____	_____
Income from trusts	_____	_____
Gifts to you	_____	_____
Alimony received	_____	_____
Pensions	_____	_____
Social Security	_____	_____
Other retirement income	_____	_____
Tax refunds	_____	_____
Other	_____	_____
Total	$_____	$_____

EXPENDITURES	MONTH	YEAR
Home		
Mortgage or rent	$_____	$_____
Electricity	_____	_____

413

EXPENDITURES	MONTH	YEAR
Gas	$ _____	$ _____
Water and sewer	_____	_____
Telephone	_____	_____
Property taxes	_____	_____
Homeowner's insurance	_____	_____
Household help	_____	_____
Furniture	_____	_____
Other household items	_____	_____
Home maintenance	_____	_____
Other maintenance costs (appliances, etc.)	_____	_____
Other	_____	_____

Family

Food and grocery items	_____	_____
Clothing	_____	_____
Laundry and dry cleaning	_____	_____
Toiletries and drugs	_____	_____
Child care	_____	_____
Children's camp expenses	_____	_____
Birthday, holiday, and other gifts	_____	_____
Education expenses	_____	_____
Medical expenses	_____	_____
Medical insurance	_____	_____
Dental expenses	_____	_____
Dental insurance	_____	_____
Life insurance	_____	_____
Other insurance expenses	_____	_____
Other	_____	_____

Transportation

Gasoline	_____	_____
Auto insurance	_____	_____
Auto maintenance	_____	_____

EXPENDITURES	MONTH	YEAR
Other auto expenses	$_____	$_____
Other travel expenses	_____	_____
Other	_____	_____
	_____	_____
	_____	_____
	_____	_____

Leisure

Magazines, books	_____	_____
Movies and theater	_____	_____
Cable television	_____	_____
Vacations	_____	_____
Restaurant meals	_____	_____
Club memberships	_____	_____
Other	_____	_____
	_____	_____
	_____	_____
	_____	_____

Income Taxes

Federal, withheld	_____	_____
Federal, estimated	_____	_____
State, withheld	_____	_____
State, estimated	_____	_____
Other	_____	_____

Other

Installment loans	_____	_____
Payroll savings	_____	_____
IRA contributions	_____	_____
Keogh contributions	_____	_____
401(k) contributions	_____	_____
Investment expenses	_____	_____

EXPENDITURES	MONTH	YEAR
Accountant's fees	$_____	$_____
Attorney's fees	_____	_____
Charitable contributions	_____	_____
Political contributions	_____	_____
Other	_____	_____
	_____	_____
	_____	_____
	_____	_____
Total	$_____	$_____
Total income	$_____	$_____
Total expenses	$_____	$_____
Surplus or shortfall	$_____	$_____

A P P E N D I X · I V

Compound Interest of $1 Principal

The amount to which $1 will accumulate at the end of the specified number of years

YEARS	4%	5%	6%	7%	8%	9%	10%	11%	12%	13%	14%	15%
1	1.04	1.05	1.06	1.07	1.08	1.09	1.10	1.11	1.12	1.13	1.14	1.15
2	1.08	1.10	1.12	1.14	1.17	1.19	1.21	1.23	1.25	1.28	1.30	1.32
3	1.12	1.16	1.19	1.23	1.26	1.30	1.33	1.37	1.40	1.44	1.48	1.52
4	1.17	1.21	1.26	1.31	1.36	1.41	1.46	1.52	1.57	1.63	1.69	1.75
5	1.22	1.27	1.33	1.40	1.47	1.54	1.61	1.68	1.76	1.84	1.93	2.01
6	1.26	1.34	1.42	1.50	1.59	1.68	1.77	1.87	1.97	2.08	2.20	2.31
7	1.32	1.40	1.50	1.61	1.71	1.83	1.95	2.08	2.21	2.35	2.50	2.66
8	1.37	1.48	1.59	1.72	1.85	1.99	2.14	2.30	2.48	2.66	2.85	3.06
9	1.42	1.55	1.69	1.84	2.00	2.17	2.36	2.56	2.77	3.00	3.25	3.52
10	1.48	1.63	1.79	1.97	2.16	2.37	2.59	2.84	3.11	3.39	3.71	4.05
11	1.54	1.71	1.90	2.10	2.33	2.58	2.85	3.15	3.48	3.84	4.23	4.65
12	1.60	1.80	2.01	2.25	2.52	2.81	3.14	3.50	3.90	4.33	4.82	5.35
13	1.66	1.89	2.13	2.41	2.72	3.07	3.45	3.88	4.36	4.90	5.49	6.15
14	1.73	1.98	2.26	2.58	2.94	3.34	3.80	4.31	4.89	5.53	6.26	7.08
15	1.80	2.08	2.40	2.76	3.17	3.64	4.18	4.78	5.47	6.25	7.14	8.14
16	1.87	2.18	2.54	2.95	3.43	3.97	4.60	5.31	6.13	7.07	8.14	9.36
17	1.95	2.29	2.69	3.16	3.70	4.33	5.05	5.89	6.87	7.99	9.28	10.76
18	2.03	2.41	2.85	3.38	4.00	4.72	5.56	6.54	7.69	9.02	10.58	12.38
19	2.11	2.53	3.03	3.62	4.32	5.14	6.12	7.26	8.61	10.20	12.06	14.23
20	2.19	2.65	3.21	3.87	4.66	5.60	6.73	8.06	9.65	11.52	13.74	16.37

A P P E N D I X · V

Compound Interest of $1 Per Year

**The amount to which $1 per year payable at the end of each year
will accumulate at the end of the specific number of years**

YEARS	4%	5%	6%	7%	8%	9%	10%	11%	12%	13%	14%	15%
1	1.00	1.00	1.00	1.00	1.00	1.00	1.00	1.00	1.00	1.00	1.00	1.00
2	2.04	2.05	2.06	2.07	2.08	2.09	2.10	2.11	2.12	2.13	2.14	2.15
3	3.12	3.15	3.18	3.21	3.25	3.28	3.31	3.34	3.37	3.41	3.44	3.47
4	4.25	4.31	4.37	4.44	4.51	4.57	4.64	4.71	4.78	4.85	4.92	4.99
5	5.42	5.53	5.64	5.75	5.87	5.98	6.11	6.23	6.35	6.48	6.61	6.74
6	6.63	6.80	6.98	7.15	7.34	7.52	7.72	7.91	8.12	8.32	8.54	8.75
7	7.90	8.14	8.39	8.65	8.92	9.20	9.49	9.78	10.09	10.40	10.73	11.07
8	9.21	9.55	9.90	10.26	10.64	11.03	11.44	11.86	12.30	12.76	13.23	13.73
9	10.58	11.03	11.49	11.98	12.49	13.02	13.58	14.16	14.78	15.42	16.09	16.79
10	12.01	12.58	13.18	13.82	14.49	15.19	15.94	16.72	17.55	18.42	19.34	20.30
11	13.49	14.21	14.97	15.78	16.65	17.56	18.53	19.56	20.65	21.81	23.04	24.35
12	15.03	15.92	16.87	17.89	18.98	20.14	21.38	22.71	24.13	25.65	27.27	29.00
13	16.63	17.71	18.88	20.14	21.50	22.95	24.52	26.21	28.03	29.98	32.09	34.35
14	18.29	19.60	21.02	22.55	24.21	26.02	27.98	30.09	32.39	34.88	37.58	40.50
15	20.02	21.58	23.28	25.13	27.15	29.36	31.77	34.40	37.28	40.42	43.84	47.58
16	21.82	23.66	25.67	27.89	30.32	33.00	35.95	39.19	42.75	46.67	50.98	55.72
17	23.70	25.84	28.21	30.84	33.75	36.97	40.54	44.50	48.88	53.74	59.12	65.08
18	25.64	28.13	30.91	34.00	37.45	41.30	45.60	50.40	55.75	61.72	68.39	75.84
19	27.67	30.54	33.76	37.38	41.45	46.02	51.16	56.94	63.44	70.75	78.97	88.21
20	29.78	33.07	36.79	41.00	45.76	51.16	57.27	64.20	72.05	80.95	91.02	102.44

Your Life Insurance Needs Work Sheet

I. Cash Needs

A. Estimated final and administration expenses
(This includes medical and funeral costs, probate and
administration and executor fees, etc. Assume 5% of
your gross estate, which includes total assets, life insurance proceeds, and retirement plan death benefits.) $_____

B. Education fund
(Current college cost per child times number
of children)   _____

C. Payoff of debts, including mortgage (Optional)   _____

Total $_____

II. Annual Income Needs

A. Annual income requirement
(Annual income required to maintain your current standard of living—50% to 80% of your total present before-
tax income) $_____

B. Social Security benefits (Annual survivor payments for
your spouse and children)
This is an extremely complicated calculation. However,
for purposes of this estimate, use the following average
amounts:

1989 INCOME	BENEFIT PER SURVIVOR	MAXIMUM FAMILY BENEFIT
$19,000	$5,928	$14,616
37,000	8,388	19,584
48,000 +	8,940	20,892

(_____)

C. Spouse's annual income $(_____)

D. Other income (_____)

E. Net income required
(II.A less II.B less II.C less II.D) $_____

F. Principal needed to provide income
(Lump sum that if invested at 4% over inflation would
provide the average annual income required [II.E times
factor from following table]) $_____

NUMBER OF YEARS INCOME REQUIRED	FACTOR
1	0.961
2	1.886
3	2.775
4	3.630
5	4.452
6	5.242
7	6.002
8	6.733
9	7.435
10	8.111
11	8.760
12	9.385
13	9.986
14	10.563
15	11.118
16	11.652
17	12.166
18	12.659
19	13.134
20	13.590

III. Available Assets

A. Current available assets (For example, cash,
stocks, bonds, real estate) $_____
B. Current life insurance proceeds _____

C. Lump-sum death benefits from retirement plans $_____

Total $_____

IV. Insurance Needed

  A. Cash needs (from I) $_____

  B. Principal needed to provide income (from II)   _____

  C. Minus available assets (from III)   _____

  Total $_____

A P P E N D I X · V I I

Your College Funding Work Sheet

PERSONAL DATA

1. Child's age   _____
2. Number of years until college   _____
3. Estimated number of years in college   _____
4. Estimated annual inflation rate between now and end of college   _____%
5. Estimated annual college costs in today's dollars   _____
6. Estimated after-tax rate of return   _____

AMOUNT NEEDED

7. Number of years for inflation adjustment (Add Line 2 to ½ of Line 3)   _____
8. Inflation adjustment factor (use Appendix IV) _____yrs. (Line 7) at_____% (Line 4)   _____
9. Annual college costs (Line 8 × Line 5)   _____
10. Total college costs (Line 9 × Line 3)   _____

FUTURE VALUE OF COLLEGE FUNDS

11. College funds currently invested   _____
12. Future value factor for funds currently invested (use Appendix IV) _____yrs. (Line 7) at _____% (Line 6)   _____
13. Future value of college funds (Line 11 × Line 12)   _____

422

REQUIRED ANNUAL SAVINGS

14. Shortage (surplus) in college funds
    (Line 10 minus Line 13)   _____

15. Factor for computing annual savings
    (use Appendix V)
    ____yrs. (Line 7) at____% (Line 6)   _____

16. Annual savings for college costs
    (Line 14 divided by Line 15)   _____

SOURCE: *Adapted from a work sheet by LINC.*

A P P E N D I X · V I I I

Sample College Funding Work Sheet

PERSONAL DATA

1. Child's age   _12_
2. Number of years until college   _6_
3. Estimated number of years in college   _6_
4. Estimated annual inflation rate between now and
   end of college   _5%_
5. Estimated annual college costs in today's dollars   _$12,000_
6. Estimated after-tax rate of return   _8%_

AMOUNT NEEDED

7. Number of years for inflation adjustment
   (Add Line 2 to ½ of Line 3)   _9_
8. Inflation adjustment factor
   _9_ yrs. (Line 7) at _5_% (Line 4)   _1.55_
9. Annual college costs (Line 8 × Line 5)   _$18,600_
10. Total college costs (Line 9 × Line 3)   _$111,600_

FUTURE VALUE OF COLLEGE FUNDS

11. College funds currently invested   _$16,000_
12. Future value factor for funds currently invested
    _9_ yrs. (Line 7) at _8_% (Line 6)   _2.00_
13. Future value of college funds (Line 11 × Line 12)   _$32,000_

REQUIRED ANNUAL SAVINGS

14. Shortage (surplus) in college funds
    (Line 10 minus Line 13)   _$79,600_
15. Factor for computing annual savings
    _9_ yrs. (Line 7) at _8_% (Line 6)   _12.49_
16. Annual savings for college costs
    (Line 14 divided by Line 15)   _$6,373_

A P P E N D I X · I X

Your Retirement Cash-Flow Work Sheet

INCOME   YEAR

Your pension $_____
Social Security   _____
IRA   _____

Your spouse's pension   _____
Social Security   _____
IRA   _____

Income from business   _____
Dividends   _____
Interest   _____
Rent paid to you   _____
Income from trusts   _____
Gifts to you   _____
Alimony received   _____
Tax refunds   _____
Other   _____
                                       _____

Total $_____

EXPENDITURES	YEAR

Home

Mortgage or rent	$ _____
Electricity	_____
Gas	_____
Water and sewer	_____
Telephone	_____
Property taxes	_____
Homeowner's insurance	_____
Household help	_____
Furniture	_____
Other household items	_____
Home maintenance	_____
Other maintenance costs (appliances, etc.)	_____
Other	_____

Family

Food and grocery items	_____
Clothing	_____
Laundry and dry cleaning	_____
Toiletries and drugs	_____
Birthday, holiday, and other gifts	_____
Medical expenses	_____
Medical insurance	_____
Dental expenses	_____
Dental insurance	_____
Life insurance	_____
Other insurance expenses	_____
Other	_____

EXPENDITURES   YEAR

Transportation
Gasoline $_____
Auto insurance   _____
Auto maintenance   _____
Other auto expenses   _____
Other travel expenses   _____
Other   _____
                                _____
                                _____

Leisure
Magazines, books   _____
Movies and theater   _____
Cable television   _____
Vacations   _____
Restaurant meals   _____
Club memberships   _____
Educational expenses   _____
Other   _____
                                _____
                                _____

Taxes
Federal, withheld   _____
Federal, estimated   _____
State, withheld   _____
State, estimated   _____
Other   _____
                                _____
                                _____

EXPENDITURES	YEAR

Other

Installment loans	$_____
Investment expenses	_____
Accountant's fees	_____
Attorney's fees	_____
Charitable contributions	_____
Political contributions	_____
Other	_____
	_____
Total	$_____
Total income	$_____
Total expenses	$_____
Surplus or shortfall	$_____

A P P E N D I X · X

Social Security Form SSA-7004PC (Request for Earnings and Benefit Estimate Statement)

You may request a statement of earnings from the Social Security Administration by submitting Form SSA-7004PC, available from any Social Security Administration office. Or you may send a copy of this appendix, with the appropriate information filled in, to:

> Social Security Administration
> Wilkes-Barre Data Operations Center
> P.O. Box 20
> Wilkes-Barre, Pennsylvania 18703

YOUR SOCIAL SECURITY EARNINGS RECORD

▶ For a *free* statement of earnings credited to your Social Security record, complete this form. Use form for only *one* person.

▶ All covered wages and self-employment income are reported under your *name* and Social Security *number*. So show your name and number *exactly* as on your card. If you ever used another name or number, show this too.

▶ The name and address blocks *must* be completed in order to receive a statement of your earnings.

▶ If you have a separate question about Social Security, or want to discuss your statement when you get it, the people at any Social Security office will be glad to help you.

SOCIAL SECURITY ADMINISTRATION

Request for Earnings and Benefit Estimate Statement

Social Security is a program that touches the lives of nearly all Americans. Although many people think of it as only a retirement program, it is actually a package of protection that provides for you and your family when you retire, become severely disabled, or die. Social Security is a base you can build on, now and in the future, with savings, other insurance, and investments.

To help you plan for your own financial future, I am pleased to offer you a free statement which shows your Social Security earnings history, tells you how much you have paid in Social Security taxes, estimates your future Social Security benefits, and provides some general information about how the program works.

To receive your statement, please fill out the form on the reverse, and mail it to us. You should receive your statement in 6 weeks or less.

SOCIAL SECURITY ADMINISTRATION

Request for Earnings and Benefit Estimate Statement

To receive a free statement of your earnings covered by Social Security and your estimated future benefits, all you need to do is fill out this form. Please print or type your answers. When you have completed the form, fold it and mail it to us.

1. Name shown on your Social Security card:

First ⬜⬜⬜⬜⬜⬜

Middle Initial ⬜

Last ⬜⬜⬜⬜⬜⬜

2. Your Social Security number as shown on your card:

⬜⬜⬜ - ⬜⬜ - ⬜⬜⬜⬜

3. Your date of birth:

Month ⬜⬜ Day ⬜⬜ Year ⬜⬜

4. Other Social Security numbers you may have used:

⬜⬜⬜ - ⬜⬜ - ⬜⬜⬜⬜

⬜⬜⬜ - ⬜⬜ - ⬜⬜⬜⬜

5. Your Sex: ⬜ Male ⬜ Female

6. Other names you have used (including a maiden name):

7. Show your actual earnings for last year and your estimated earnings for this year. Include only wages and/or net self-employment income subject to Social Security tax.

A. Last year's actual earnings:

$ ⬜⬜⬜ , ⬜⬜⬜ . 0 0
  Dollars only

B. This year's estimated earnings:

$ ⬜⬜⬜ , ⬜⬜⬜ . 0 0
  Dollars only

8. Show the age at which you plan to retire: ⬜⬜

9. Below, show an amount which you think best represents your future average yearly earnings between now and when you plan to retire. The amount should be a yearly average, not your total future lifetime earnings. Only show earnings subject to Social Security tax.

Most people should enter the same amount as this year's estimated earnings (the amount shown in 7B). The reason for this is that we will show your retirement benefit estimate in today's dollars, but adjusted to account for average wage growth in the national economy.

However, if you expect to earn significantly more or less in the future than what you currently earn because of promotions, a job change, part-time work, or an absence from the work force, enter the amount in today's dollars that will most closely reflect your future average yearly earnings. Do not add in cost-of-living, performance, or scheduled pay increases or bonuses.

Your future average yearly earnings:

$ ⬜⬜⬜ , ⬜⬜⬜ . 0 0
  Dollars only

10. Address where you want us to send the statement:

Name

Street Address (Include Apt. No., P.O. Box, or Rural Route)

City   State   Zip Code

I am asking for information about my own Social Security record or the record of a person I am authorized to represent. I understand that if I deliberately request information under false pretenses I may be guilty of a federal crime and could be fined and/or imprisoned. I authorize you to send the statement of my earnings and benefit estimates to me or my representative through a contractor.

▶ Please sign your name (Do not print)

Date   (Area Code) Daytime Telephone No. ⬜⬜⬜⬜⬜ SP

ABOUT THE PRIVACY ACT
Social Security is allowed to collect the facts on this form under Section 205 of the Social Security Act. We need them to quickly identify your record and prepare the earnings statement you asked us for. Giving us these facts is voluntary. However, without them we may not be able to give you an earnings and benefit estimate statement. Neither the Social Security Administration nor its contractor will use the information for any other purpose.

Form SSA-7004-PC-OP1 (6/88) DESTROY PRIOR EDITIONS

A P P E N D I X · X I

Social Security Retirement Benefits Table

AVERAGE INDEXED MONTHLY EARNINGS	WORKER AGE 65	SPOUSE AGE 65	TOTAL AGE 65 BENEFIT	WORKER AGE 62	SPOUSE AGE 62	TOTAL AGE 62 BENEFIT	WORKER 65 & SPOUSE 62
$4,000	$1,144	$572	$1,716	$915	$429	$1,344	$1,573
3,975	1,140	570	1,710	912	427	1,339	1,567
3,950	1,136	568	1,704	908	426	1,334	1,562
3,925	1,132	566	1,698	905	424	1,329	1,556
3,900	1,129	564	1,693	903	423	1,326	1,552
3,875	1,125	562	1,687	900	421	1,321	1,546
3,850	1,121	560	1,681	896	420	1,316	1,541
3,825	1,117	558	1,675	893	418	1,311	1,535
3,800	1,114	557	1,671	891	417	1,308	1,531
3,775	1,110	555	1,665	888	416	1,304	1,526
3,750	1,106	553	1,659	884	414	1,298	1,520
3,725	1,102	551	1,653	881	413	1,294	1,515
3,700	1,099	549	1,648	879	411	1,290	1,510
3,675	1,095	547	1,642	876	410	1,286	1,505
3,650	1,091	545	1,636	872	408	1,280	1,499
3,625	1,087	543	1,630	869	407	1,276	1,494
3,600	1,084	542	1,626	867	406	1,273	1,490
3,575	1,080	540	1,620	864	405	1,269	1,485
3,550	1,076	538	1,614	860	403	1,263	1,479
3,525	1,072	536	1,608	857	402	1,259	1,474
3,500	1,069	534	1,603	855	400	1,255	1,469
3,475	1,065	532	1,597	852	399	1,251	1,464
3,450	1,061	530	1,591	848	397	1,245	1,458
3,425	1,057	528	1,585	845	396	1,241	1,453
3,400	1,054	527	1,581	843	395	1,238	1,449
3,375	1,050	525	1,575	840	393	1,233	1,443
3,350	1,046	523	1,569	836	392	1,228	1,438

AVERAGE INDEXED MONTHLY EARNINGS	WORKER AGE 65	SPOUSE AGE 65	TOTAL AGE 65 BENEFIT	WORKER AGE 62	SPOUSE AGE 62	TOTAL AGE 62 BENEFIT	WORKER 65 & SPOUSE 62
$3,325	1,042	$521	$1,563	$833	$390	$1,223	$1,432
3,300	1,039	519	1,558	831	389	1,220	1,428
3,275	1,035	517	1,552	828	387	1,215	1,422
3,250	1,031	515	1,546	824	386	1,210	1,417
3,225	1,027	513	1,540	821	384	1,205	1,411
3,200	1,024	512	1,536	819	384	1,203	1,408
3,175	1,020	510	1,530	816	382	1,198	1,402
3,150	1,016	508	1,524	812	381	1,193	1,397
3,125	1,012	506	1,518	809	379	1,188	1,391
3,100	1,009	504	1,513	807	378	1,185	1,387
3,075	1,005	502	1,507	804	376	1,180	1,381
3,050	1,001	500	1,501	800	375	1,175	1,376
3,025	997	498	1,495	797	373	1,170	1,370
3,000	994	497	1,491	795	372	1,167	1,366
2,975	990	495	1,485	792	371	1,163	1,361
2,950	986	493	1,479	788	369	1,157	1,355
2,925	982	491	1,473	785	368	1,153	1,350
2,900	979	489	1,468	783	366	1,149	1,345
2,875	975	487	1,462	780	365	1,145	1,340
2,850	971	485	1,456	776	363	1,139	1,334
2,825	967	483	1,450	773	362	1,135	1,329
2,800	964	482	1,446	771	361	1,132	1,325
2,775	960	480	1,440	768	360	1,128	1,320
2,750	956	478	1,434	764	358	1,122	1,314
2,725	952	476	1,428	761	357	1,118	1,309
2,700	949	474	1,423	759	355	1,114	1,304
2,675	945	472	1,417	756	354	1,110	1,299
2,650	941	470	1,411	752	352	1,104	1,293
2,625	937	468	1,405	749	351	1,100	1,288
2,600	934	467	1,401	747	350	1,097	1,284
2,575	930	465	1,395	744	348	1,092	1,278
2,550	926	463	1,389	740	347	1,087	1,273

AVERAGE INDEXED MONTHLY EARNINGS	WORKER AGE 65	SPOUSE AGE 65	TOTAL AGE 65 BENEFIT	WORKER AGE 62	SPOUSE AGE 62	TOTAL AGE 62 BENEFIT	WORKER 65 & SPOUSE 62
$2,525	$922	$461	$1,383	$737	$345	$1,082	$1,267
2,500	919	459	1,378	735	344	1,079	1,263
2,475	915	457	1,372	732	342	1,074	1,257
2,450	911	455	1,366	728	341	1,069	1,252
2,425	907	453	1,360	725	339	1,064	1,246
2,400	904	452	1,356	723	339	1,062	1,243
2,375	900	450	1,350	720	337	1,057	1,237
2,350	896	448	1,344	716	336	1,052	1,232
2,325	892	446	1,338	713	334	1,047	1,226
2,300	889	444	1,333	711	333	1,044	1,222
2,275	885	442	1,327	708	331	1,039	1,216
2,250	881	440	1,321	704	330	1,034	1,211
2,225	877	438	1,315	701	328	1,029	1,205
2,200	874	437	1,311	699	327	1,026	1,201
2,175	870	435	1,305	696	326	1,022	1,196
2,150	866	433	1,299	692	324	1,016	1,190
2,125	862	431	1,293	689	323	1,012	1,185
2,100	859	429	1,288	687	321	1,008	1,180
2,075	855	427	1,282	684	320	1,004	1,175
2,050	851	425	1,276	680	318	998	1,169
2,025	844	422	1,266	675	316	991	1,160
2,000	836	418	1,254	668	313	981	1,149
1,975	828	414	1,242	662	310	972	1,138
1,950	820	410	1,230	656	307	963	1,127
1,925	812	406	1,218	649	304	953	1,116
1,900	804	402	1,206	643	301	944	1,105
1,875	796	398	1,194	636	298	934	1,094
1,850	788	394	1,182	630	295	925	1,083
1,825	780	390	1,170	624	292	916	1,072
1,800	772	386	1,158	617	289	906	1,061
1,775	764	382	1,146	611	286	897	1,050
1,750	756	378	1,134	604	283	887	1,039

AVERAGE INDEXED MONTHLY EARNINGS	WORKER AGE 65	SPOUSE AGE 65	TOTAL AGE 65 BENEFIT	WORKER AGE 62	SPOUSE AGE 62	TOTAL AGE 62 BENEFIT	WORKER 65 & SPOUSE 62
$1,725	$748	$374	$1,122	$598	$280	$878	$1,028
1,700	740	370	1,110	592	277	869	1,017
1,675	732	366	1,098	585	274	859	1,006
1,650	724	362	1,086	579	271	850	995
1,625	716	358	1,074	572	268	840	984
1,600	708	354	1,062	566	265	831	973
1,575	700	350	1,050	560	262	822	962
1,550	692	346	1,038	553	259	812	951
1,525	684	342	1,026	547	256	803	940
1,500	676	338	1,014	540	253	793	929
1,475	668	334	1,002	534	250	784	918
1,450	660	330	990	528	247	775	907
1,425	652	326	978	521	244	765	896
1,400	644	322	966	515	241	756	885
1,375	636	318	954	508	238	746	874
1,350	628	314	942	502	235	737	863
1,325	620	310	930	496	232	728	852
1,300	612	306	918	489	229	718	841
1,275	604	302	906	483	226	709	830
1,250	596	298	894	476	223	699	819
1,225	588	294	882	470	220	690	808
1,200	580	290	870	464	217	681	797
1,175	572	286	858	457	214	671	786
1,150	564	282	846	451	211	662	775
1,125	556	278	834	444	208	652	764
1,100	548	274	822	438	205	643	753
1,075	540	270	810	432	202	634	742
1,050	532	266	798	425	199	624	731
1,025	524	262	786	419	196	615	720
1,000	516	258	774	412	193	605	709

AVERAGE INDEXED MONTHLY EARNINGS	WORKER AGE 65	SPOUSE AGE 65	TOTAL AGE 65 BENEFIT	WORKER AGE 62	SPOUSE AGE 62	TOTAL AGE 62 BENEFIT	WORKER 65 & SPOUSE 62
$975	$508	$254	$762	$406	$190	$596	$ 698
950	500	250	750	400	187	587	687
925	492	246	738	393	184	577	676
900	484	242	726	387	181	568	665
875	476	238	714	380	178	558	654
850	468	234	702	374	175	549	643
825	460	230	690	368	172	540	632
800	452	226	678	361	169	530	621
775	444	222	666	355	166	521	610
750	436	218	654	348	163	511	599
725	428	214	642	342	160	502	588
700	420	210	630	336	157	493	577
675	412	206	618	329	154	483	566
650	404	202	606	323	151	474	555

Index

About the Authors

Price Waterhouse is a leading worldwide professional organization of tax advisers, accountants and auditors, and management consultants. Through a global network of firms practicing in 400 offices in ninety-nine countries and territories, Price Waterhouse professionals provide a wide range of advisory services to individuals, businesses, nonprofit organizations, and government entities.

Price Waterhouse has long been a leader in personal financial planning services. The U.S. firm's Personal Financial Services group has provided financial planning assistance to thousands of executives in corporate-sponsored programs. This group also conducts seminars on a variety of financial planning subjects for corporate executives. In addition, Price Waterhouse prepares computer-assisted financial planning reports and is the nation's largest provider of personal financial plans for middle-income individuals.

Stanley H. Breitbard is a CPA and a partner of Price Waterhouse. He is the firm's national director of Personal Financial Services. He is also immediate past chairman of the American Institute of Certified Public Accountants personal financial planning executive committee. A popular speaker on financial planning subjects and author of numerous articles, Mr. Breitbard earned his B.A. and M.B.A. from the University of California, Berkeley.

Donna Sammons Carpenter is a former senior writer at *Inc.* magazine and a best-selling author. Ms. Carpenter has written seven other books, all on business topics, and her articles have appeared in a variety of national magazines and newspapers. A recipient of the Unity Award for investigative reporting, she has garnered more than fifty awards for reporting, business writing, and interviews. Ms. Carpenter received her education at the University of Kentucky and Marshall University.